Trollope, Anne Karen,
Cloud messenger : love
and loss in the Indian H
2016.
33305239947
gi   11/07
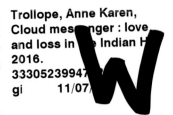

Cloud Messenger

Love and Loss in the Indian Himalayas

by Karen Trollope-Kumar

 FriesenPress

Suite 300 - 990 Fort St
Victoria, BC, V8V 3K2
Canada

www.friesenpress.com

Copyright © 2016 by Karen Trollope-Kumar
First Edition — 2016

All rights reserved.

No part of this publication may be reproduced in any form, or by
any means, electronic or mechanical, including photocopying,
recording, or any information browsing, storage, or retrieval
system, without permission in writing from FriesenPress.

ISBN
978-1-4602-8769-9 (Hardcover)
978-1-4602-8770-5 (Paperback)
978-1-4602-8771-2 (eBook)

1. Biography & Autobiography, Cultural Heritage

Distributed to the trade by The Ingram Book Company

The Journey

Garhwal

Uttarkashi

Guptkashi

Tehri

Anjanisain

Mussoorie

Rudrapragag

Dehradun

Adi Badri

Gairsain

Baijnath

Ganga River

Rishikesh

Kausani

Hardwar

Kumaon

Nainital

Haldwani

Uttarakhand

India

Kumaon

Garhwal

Foreword

Karen Trollope from Canada and Pradeep Kumar from India met in Lucknow in 1981. Their immediate mutual attraction led to a four-year courtship, mostly conducted in letters back and forth between Canada and India. They were married in a Hindu ceremony in 1985, and worked in the Himalayas for most of the period between 1985 and 1996.

This is a fascinating record of Karen Trollope Kumar's discovery of India, and of the day-to-day life and culture of the families she encountered who lived in villages perched on the steep hillsides of the Himalayan foothills. She explored the culture and behaviour of the Garhwali hill people, observing their struggles for existence, which were made harder by deforestation, erosion, and the depletion of water and food supplies. As a physician, she examined ways to strike a health-enhancing balance between traditional beliefs and customs that determined how babies entered the world of the Himalayas, and modern Western medical and obstetrical practice that improved survival chances for both babies and their mothers.

She became fluent in Hindi, the language spoken in most of India today, and had to adjust to a whole new way of life with unfamiliar values, customs, and behaviour. Her account of all this is self-effacing, but it involved much hardship, and was emotionally stressful. Meanwhile, she was producing a family of her own: a beautiful little girl, Sonia, then a handsome boy, Raman.

Political and ethnic tensions were part of the backdrop to the Kumar family's existence. Corruption and violence culminated in murder and threats to their lives. Nature was violent, too—an earthquake in 1991 caused much death and destruction. Karen and Pradeep were heavily involved in both immediate aftercare and longer-term reconstruction.

This is a wise book with profound thoughts about spirituality, values, relationships, cultures, traditions, and customs; and about love that transcends cultural boundaries. Here, find subtle, gentle humour, and lyrical descriptions of mountain scenery, alpine forests and meadows, and long treks over hills and through valleys with exotic birdsong as background music. There is so much to enjoy, so much to learn, so much to make you think in this book, that one should own it and reread it often.

John Last, OC, MD
Ottawa, Canada

Cloud Messenger

CHAPTER ONE:

The Call To Adventure

"Expect the unexpected," I had been told when I left Canada for two months of medical studies in India.

Clutching that idea like a talisman, I made the dizzying plunge into the chaos, contradiction, and charm of India. I arrived in the middle of a September night, just after a late monsoon rain. As I stepped off the plane in Delhi, I was enveloped by a warm blanket of humid air, redolent with the smell of flowers, diesel oil, and rain-soaked earth. I paused for a moment on the tarmac, inhaling deeply. Thunder grumbled in the distance, and a few fat drops of rain spattered against my cheeks.

"*Chelo! Chelo!*" barked a man behind me. Passengers were pouring out of the plane, anxious to reach the terminal before the rain began. Surrounded by a flood of people, I was swept from the aircraft to the terminal building. Inside the entry hall, the momentum of the group was suddenly checked, slowed by the barriers of bureaucracy. The smoothly flowing river of humanity broke into turbulent eddies at the immigration desks, where bored officers stamped passports with maddening deliberation. Beyond these formidable obstacles, thin streams of passengers trickled toward the arrivals hall.

The hall was packed with jostling people who all seemed to be talking at once. With a sudden shock, I realized that I couldn't understand a word of the conversations whirling around my head. My initial fascination with the surroundings suddenly dissolved, and my heart began to pound.

I struggled through the crowds to a line of ancient luggage carousels. I spotted the correct one, and squeezed into a spot where I could see the bags emerging onto the belt. After retrieving my luggage, I made my way to the transit lounge to wait for my connecting flight to Lucknow, in the state of Uttar Pradesh.

Several hours later, I boarded a small propeller plane for the last leg of my journey. As the plane began to taxi down the runway, a bolt of lightning streaked across the sky, followed by a terrific crack of thunder. The full fury of the storm hit us a few minutes after takeoff. The plane began to buck wildly, tossing the passengers against each other. Feeling a cold knot of fear coiling in my belly, I stared fixedly out of the window at the slanting sheets of rain. The woman sitting beside me clutched my arm, and we exchanged looks of mutual horror. After a terrifying two-hour flight, we began our descent. When we finally bumped down onto the runway, I heaved a heartfelt sigh of relief. As we disembarked, my fellow passengers smiled and nodded at me. A bond had sprung up among us, the survivors of a terrifying experience.

When I stepped out of the aircraft into the driving rain, the woman who'd been sitting next to me unfurled a large umbrella and pulled me under it. Arm in arm, we hurried across the tarmac into the terminal building.

After I'd collected my luggage, I was relieved to see a bespectacled young man holding a sign with my name printed on it. He introduced himself as a medical student from King George Medical College, where I would be studying. I followed him out of the building to the parking lot, and he helped me pack my luggage into the trunk of a large white car.

The driver pulled out onto the main road leading to Lucknow. A bewildering array of vehicles surrounded us—scooters carrying two, three, or even four people; carts pulled by buffalo; brightly decorated trucks with "Horn Please" painted on the back. One of these trucks suddenly pulled out to overtake another vehicle, and came roaring directly toward us. The driver of our car swerved to let the truck pass. I briefly closed my eyes, trying to stay calm.

As we approached Lucknow, the road narrowed into a congested city street. I gazed out the window, transfixed by the sights around me. Two plump, sari-clad women were sitting in a bicycle rickshaw pulled by an elderly man whose grizzled head was bent over the handlebars, his lean legs straining on the pedals.

Seeing my look of concern, the young man beside me said earnestly, "It is a pity, is it not, that such an old man should be working so hard? But that is our India. There is so much of poverty here."

"Yes, I can see that," I replied thoughtfully, watching the rickshaw driver as he maneuvered through the crush of vehicles and pedestrians. He narrowly missed a vendor carrying a tray of coconut chunks who was wending his way through the crush of vehicles. The coconut vendor shouted angrily, jumping sideways to avoid a collision. The driver of our car braked sharply, and we stopped just inches away from the vendor. Recovering quickly, he pushed his tray toward us and offered us his wares. Moments later, a swarm of grimy children wearing torn rags pressed up against the car window, hands outstretched. I averted my gaze, not knowing how to react. The driver waved them all away and drove on to the medical school.

King George Medical College was a welcome oasis of calm, separated from the noisy marketplace by a pair of massive gates. On campus, elegant buildings surrounded by sweeping lawns created an atmosphere of space and light. White-coated medical students clutching books and stethoscopes walked among the buildings, chatting and laughing, or looking serious and intense. The driver drew up in front of the women's hostel, and a young woman stepped out to greet me. She was slim and pretty, with a sweet smile. For the first time since I'd arrived in India, I felt the knot of anxiety within me loosen a little.

"*Namaste*," she said. "I am Saroj, and I can show you your room."

Over the next few days, this lovely young woman became my guide and companion. Saroj was twenty-six—my age—and already in her final year of an obstetrics residency. She made arrangements for my meals in the mess hall, and showed me how to eat with my fingers and use a folded *roti* to scoop up food. She gave me a tour of the campus, and even provided a synopsis of the current political situation in India: Prime Minister Indira Gandhi was opposing a movement by radical elements of the Sikh community to establish a separate state.

The next morning, I went to meet Dr. B K Srivastava, head of the department of social and preventive medicine. This department was housed in a concrete building whose outer walls were cracked and stained, its cement stairs crumbling at the edges. It was a marked contrast from the lovely buildings elsewhere on campus. Dr. Srivastava was a large, imposing man in his forties, who greeted me formally and asked me questions about medical training in Canada. He then handed me a densely typed sheet that outlined the next few weeks of activities for students studying social and preventive medicine. I would be attending lectures and going on field trips to the rural site where the SPM department held regular clinics.

As I walked back to the women's hostel, I could hardly contain my excitement. I'd been longing to study tropical medicine ever since I entered medical school. *Perhaps this period of study will shape my future career*, I mused.

That evening, I talked with Saroj about my enthusiasm for social and preventive medicine, and shared my dream of a career in international health.

"It may be an exciting career, but what about your personal life?" Saroj said doubtfully. "Getting married and having a family—surely that is the best goal in life."

I rolled my eyes. "Oh no, I am not planning to marry at all. For me, my career is much more important than family life."

Saroj raised an eyebrow, but tactfully changed the subject. She invited me to join her on a shopping trip to Hazratganj, the main market of Lucknow on the following Sunday.

"Two of my other friends will be going as well," she said. "We'll really enjoy together."

On Sunday afternoon, Saroj and her friends came to pick me up. Two men on bicycle rickshaws were waiting for us outside the women's hostel. I climbed onto the narrow seat, feeling uncomfortable at being transported by human power. Gripping the frame of the rickshaw, I was swept into a world of sounds and sights that both fascinated and frightened me. Throngs of people filled the streets, spilling out of shops and merging into the pulsing crowds. Women wearing brilliantly coloured saris and bangles dazzled my senses. Sounds throbbed in my ears: the shouts of shopkeepers, the cries of children, the chatter of women. A legless beggar sitting on a rough wooden cart propelled himself toward me, extending an imploring hand. An elephant walked ponderously ahead of us, surrounded by traffic that swirled like a river around a huge gray boulder.

After we'd finished our shopping, Saroj and her friends took me to see a Bollywood movie. Although I couldn't understand a word of the dialogue, it hardly mattered. The sensory experience was overwhelming, with its improbable plot, its melodramatic scenes, and its lively music and dance. By the time I reached my room that evening, my head was spinning. I thought back to the advice I'd received before leaving Canada: "Expect the unexpected." After that day's events, I felt I was becoming quite proficient at doing just that.

But nothing could prepare me for the events of October 8, 1981, just a week after my arrival in India. It was the festival day of *Dussehra,* and the medical school was closed. Feeling lonely, I wandered into the pediatric hospital, hoping to be able to join ward rounds. A young man wearing a white coat was standing at a circular stone table in the central hall of the building. He looked up from the chart he was reviewing and our eyes met. That moment is sealed in my memory: the pivotal point in my life. I see him as he was that day, his deep brown eyes lit with sudden surprise, his fine-boned hands holding the chart, his stance of alertness and presence. Neither of us said anything for several long moments. Between us flowed a mysterious connection, an experience as old as humankind yet as fresh and surprising as the first day of spring.

"I'm a visiting medical student from Canada," I said hesitantly. "I am interested in pediatrics and I wondered if . . ." My voice trailed off.

"Yes. . . . Yes, of course. Please come with me and I can show you our department," he stammered.

He led me out of the main lobby, up a flight of stairs, and into the pediatric wards. As we walked, I learned that my guide's name was Pradeep Kumar, and that he was the chief pediatric resident for the hospital. His English was halting and accented, so I had to concentrate closely on his words. My memories of that walk through the wards are all sensory—the harsh smell of phenol disinfectant, the anxious eyes of a mother holding an emaciated baby, the feeble cry of a young child. The condition of the wards was distressing. Beds were crammed into poorly lit, cavernous rooms, and parents of the children seemed to be camped out on the narrow spaces between the beds.

Horrified, I said, "But surely conditions could be better than this?"

"There are many nice, very nice children's hospitals in Lucknow," said Pradeep. "But they are expensive and so they are only for the rich people. This hospital is for the poors."

He saw my shocked face and said, "That is the terrible thing about India. Rich and poor, they have such different lives."

We walked through two similar wards, and then we peeped through the glass of the isolation ward. "Here, we have patients with infectious diseases," said Pradeep, "like diphtheria, meningitis, tuberculosis. We have to keep them apart from the other children."

"Diphtheria?" I said with surprise. "I think it's been wiped out completely in Canada. And as for TB, well, I've seen one or two adults with it, but never a child."

"No TB?" replied Pradeep, a note of disbelief in his voice. "It's very common here in India. Every day I am seeing many children with TB."

He glanced at his watch and said, "I must go to our outdoor department—I have my duty now. Will you like to see the patients with me?"

"Yes, I'd love to," I said, following him along the hall and down a flight of stairs. Long before we reached the outpatient department, I could hear the high-pitched wail of babies and the murmuring of mothers, punctuated by an angry quarrel between two women.

Pradeep pushed open a swinging door and we walked through a large waiting room filled with children and their mothers. There was no examination room. Pradeep simply sat down at a sturdy wooden table at one end of the waiting room. On this table sat a jar of thermometers, a stethoscope, a flashlight, and a prescription pad. I pulled up a battered metal chair next to him and watched

the proceedings with curiosity. Though I couldn't understand
Hindi, I was surprised by how much I could grasp simply from the
body language and facial expressions of the parents and children.
The pace of the clinic was rapid, and after two hours, Pradeep had
seen nearly thirty children.

After examining each child, Pradeep would tell me a bit about
the diagnosis and his treatment approach. His calm and competent demeanor impressed me, and he was clearly at ease with his
patients. As the clinic came to an end, he said rather tentatively,
"Today is the festival of *Dussehra*. And in the evening there will be
some ceremonies in the city. Will you like to see that?"

I agreed quickly. I was curious to see the festivities, but I was
even more interested in getting to know this young man better.
Promising to be ready in a couple of hours, I left the hospital to
walk back to the women's hostel where I was staying.

That evening, Pradeep picked me up promptly at six o'clock,
as promised. Gone was the calm, professional young doctor I'd
met that morning. He was now wearing trendy sunglasses, black
bellbottoms and a flashy shirt. His wavy black hair was carefully
combed into a fashionable style, and he was riding a shiny scooter.
He looks like he just stepped out of a Bollywood movie, I thought,
trying to suppress a giggle. Later, I would learn that that he'd borrowed the clothes and sunglasses from one friend, the scooter
from another, and money from a third.

I was wearing a sari, purchased a few days earlier with Saroj's
help. I climbed cautiously onto the scooter, sitting sideways as I'd
seen other women do. My perch felt precarious, as I had to grasp
the folds of the sari with one hand, while hanging onto a bar at
the back of the seat with the other. We roared through the streets
of Lucknow, leaving the medical college district behind us and
heading north of the city.

After a heart-stopping ride of about twenty minutes, I heard a
muted rumble like distant thunder.

"What's that noise?" I shouted to Pradeep over the roar of the scooter.

"Just wait—you'll see!" replied Pradeep. At the top of a slight rise in the road, he stopped the scooter. Below, we could see a vast river of humanity flowing through the streets, surging forward with immense power. The sight was awe-inspiring, yet frightening as well. I'd never seen so many people crowded into such a small area.

"Look—that's where everyone is going!" said Pradeep, pointing ahead. From our vantage point, I could see an imposing tomb in the Moghul style facing an enormous open ground teeming with more people.

"That is the tomb of a *nawab* of Lucknow. His name was Saadat Ali Khan and he died a couple of hundred years back. And this whole area used to be called Victoria Park in British days," Pradeep said, adeptly weaving the scooter through the crowds.

An enormous straw effigy of the demon god Ravana had been erected in the centre of the park. A man stepped forward holding a burning brand and set it alight. The crowd roared with delight as orange flames tore through the dry straw. Pradeep explained that the destruction of Ravana by the hero-god Rama and his troops marks the beginning of the celebration of *Diwali*, a joyous occasion when Hindu families gather to share meals and greet friends and family.

To escape from the press of the crowds, Pradeep and I climbed the stone steps of the tomb. Now we could see over the vast throngs of people to the sinuous curve of the Gomti River in the distance. We settled down on a step to talk.

"So, have you always wanted to become a doctor?" I asked.

"No, I never wanted to," he replied, with an emphatic shake of his head.

"Really? What did you want to do?"

"I wanted to study Hindi literature. And write poetry, as well. Also, I wanted to study Western philosophy. Bertrand Russell, Albert Camus, Schopenhauer, Nietzsche, all of those people. I am always reading their works."

"Why didn't you take an arts degree, then?" I asked, looking at him with heightened interest.

"That was just not possible," Pradeep said. "A family like mine—we were not rich at all, so I had to find a way to stand in my society. I studied very hard, for weeks and weeks, and then I appeared in the pre-medical test and I was selected for KGMC. My father couldn't believe it, because I was always so careless about my studies."

"You're almost finished now. You'll be a pediatrician in a year. Then what are you going to do?" I asked.

He was silent for a few minutes. Then he burst out, "Here in India, families with a son in medical school want him to start private practice and get rich. I hate that! I don't want to live in some dull town of Uttar Pradesh, sitting in a clinic forever."

"Well, what do you want?" I asked, intensely curious.

"I want to live in Himalayas, serving the poors," he replied with determination.

"Really? Why the Himalayas? Why not Lucknow? There are many poor people right here."

"The Himalayas, they are such beautiful mountains, so mysterious. I can't explain you properly why I love them so much. When I was a small boy, I went with my family to the city of Hardwar for holidays. I kept looking at the hills, wondering what was beyond them. And then last year, I traveled to the Valley of Flowers in Garhwal region of Himalayas. You can't imagine—it was like another world. And that is when I decided that I will live somewhere in those hills."

"The Valley of Flowers, that sounds magical," I murmured.

Pradeep nodded, a faraway look in his eyes. Then he asked, "What about you? Where do you want to live in future?"

"Well, I have kind of a similar idea. I've always wanted to work in some remote part of the world—maybe Africa. You know, in a place where people really need doctors. I never wanted to be an ordinary family doctor in Canada."

"I think that's a very good idea," he replied with enthusiasm.

"So what motivates you, what makes you different?" I asked.

"I will try to explain you," replied Pradeep. He began to tell me about his lifelong fascination with a search for spiritual meaning, struggling to find words to express complex philosophical ideas. I lost the thread of his argument and asked him to explain it again.

He sighed in exasperation, "English language! It is so difficult. And it is not beautiful, like my language. Hindi is language of poetry and love."

"But English can be beautiful, when spoken well," I said, defending my mother tongue.

"English is language of colonizers of my people," Pradeep said with sudden vehemence. "Why I should learn it?"

I tried not to giggle. "Well, it's useful when you want to talk to an English-speaking girl."

Pradeep stared at me for a moment, and then relaxed into a smile. "I never wanted to speak English until today. People in India would say to me, 'God is playing a joke on you.'"

I smiled back at him, enjoying the idea that God might like to tease his human creations.

"So do you believe in God?" I asked.

To my surprise, Pradeep's face darkened. "No! Absolutely not. I hate God."

"What do you mean?"

"God, gods, goddesses—it's all rubbish and it holds people back. We Indians are never going to move forward unless and until we get rid of all that."

I raised my eyebrows. "Do you see an alternative?"

Pradeep replied firmly, "Marxism. That's the only way I see." He reached into his shirt pocket and pulled out a pack of cigarettes. Lighting one, he lapsed into a thoughtful silence.

I gazed at the crowd milling below us. The park was ringed by dozens of small tents and stalls, dazzling with colour and bustling with activity. There were carts piled high with firecrackers, shops displaying silken saris, stalls heaped with garlands, balloons and toys. Vendors shouted, women haggled, children laughed. It was a chaotic scene, crackling with energy and argument.

I noticed something else, too, something more difficult to define. A woman stood before a display of gaudy sculpted figures of Laxmi, the goddess worshipped in this festival season. She selected one with great care, and wrapped it in a length of old sari cloth. At the next stall, she chose incense sticks and garlands, each movement careful and deliberate. A temple bell clanged. I suddenly realized that a hidden rhythm flowed below the outward chaos. Religious devotion created this, bringing a subtle order to the life unfolding before me.

"Pradeep," I said, finally, "I don't know your country very well, but somehow I just don't think that Marxism would be a good fit."

He nodded abstractedly, lost in thought. I studied him surreptitiously, trying to analyze why I found him so attractive. He had a slight, slim build, and was only a little taller than I was. Though he was good looking, it was not his physical appearance alone that appealed to me. Suddenly, I realized what it was. *He's an unusual person with a passion for life, someone who wouldn't hesitate to take a risk. Someone who would live every minute fully.*

He stubbed out his cigarette and pulled another out of the pack. He struck a match and lit the cigarette, then inhaled deeply. This small act was filled with a kind of crackling energy that seemed to course through his body.

We talked about our families. I learned that he had a younger brother who was completing a graduate degree in mathematics and a sister who was still living at home, in the city of Ghaziabad outside Delhi. His large extended family lived in cities and towns all around the state of Uttar Pradesh. I described my parents and my three brothers, a small nuclear family. We'd emigrated from South Africa years ago, where most of our relatives still lived.

So began our whirlwind romance. The very next evening Pradeep turned up at my hostel with two of his friends. At the Clark's Avadh Restaurant, we ate a meal served on large steel plates called *thalis*: *dal*, rice, potato with cauliflower, and a mixed vegetable. I found the flavours intriguing but too spicy. Tears streamed down my face as I worked my way through the meal.

Pradeep looked concerned. "Add *dahi* to the food, that will help," he said, pushing the bowl of yoghurt over to me. After we finished eating, we sat on the lawn outside the hotel until long after dark, chatting about everything from medicine to music. Pradeep's friend Mahesh had an open, cheerful face, always ready with a joke. By contrast, Wasim Khan had an intense, melancholic personality. Tall and angular, he had a habit of tapping his foot restlessly, suppressing a barely contained energy. He shared Pradeep's interest in philosophy and poetry, and was passionately fond of music, particularly the haunting Urdu *ghazals* with their themes of pain and loss.

I was supposed to be studying social and preventive medicine at the college, but I was so preoccupied with matters of the heart that I learned very little during my stay. After my medical elective was over, I had three weeks of vacation. Pradeep had been telling me about his travels in the Himalayan foothills, and he invited me on a trip to explore this special part of India.

We set off by overnight train to Haldwani, the railhead at the base of the Kumaon Himalayas. The Kumaon region of the foothills is bordered on the west by the Garhwal Himalayas, and to the north lies Tibet.

"We'll catch a bus from this place," said Pradeep, as we scrambled down from the train and hurried out of the station.

The looming bulk of the Himalayan foothills lay ahead, shrouded in deep purple shadow. Shafts of early-morning sunlight glanced off the eastern flanks of the hills, illuminating the tawny grass that covered the higher reaches of the slopes. Below this lay a dense blanket of forest, which swathed the hills like a cape. As the sun rose and the purple shadows lifted, the lower slopes of the hills became visible. Here, the rich green of the forest gave way to dull brown land denuded of trees.

"Look how barren that land looks," I said. "There's been a lot of deforestation."

"It's a terrible problem in these hills," replied Pradeep. "Women in those villages have to walk so far to get wood and water. It's a great burden for them."

We walked to the dusty bus stand in Haldwani. There, at an outdoor stand called a *dhaba,* we fortified ourselves with cups of hot tea and sweet *jelebis,* deep-fried before our eyes by a man sitting behind an enormous *kadai* bubbling with hot oil. We then climbed aboard an ancient bus, crowded with village folk. Our destination was Kausani, a little hill village where Gandhi had had a small *ashram.*

The bus wound slowly upward along narrow roads that clung to the hillside. In the valley below, I could see a village, each stone house topped by a heavy slate roof. In a terraced field beyond the village, a bull plodded steadily, pulling a man standing on a wooden plough.

"They're getting the fields ready for the winter crop," Pradeep said.

As we drew closer to the village, we could hear dogs barking and the faint shouts of children. A small stone temple was tucked into a fold of the hills, a triangular red pennant fluttering from its roof.

The bus rounded a hairpin curve, lurching to a side. Pradeep reached over to steady me, his arm lightly curving around my shoulders. I leaned against him, enjoying his gentle touch. As we continued our journey toward Kausani, I suddenly became aware of a strange feeling that the landscape was familiar, and that I had come home. I had never been anywhere remotely resembling this place, yet I had this overwhelming sense of belonging. Perhaps this was because I was falling in love with my companion. But, no. It was more than that; a visceral feeling of recognition of the land.

Lost in thought, I hardly noticed that we were approaching the straggling outskirts of Kausani. When the bus came to a shuddering stop in the centre of town, Pradeep and I shouldered our backpacks and threaded our way through the crowds milling about the bus stand.

Pradeep pointed to a low, whitewashed building on a hill above the town.

"That's the Gandhi ashram. From there, we will be seeing whole range of Himalayas," he said enthusiastically. We began to climb the winding road toward the ashram, a faint breeze ruffling our hair. As we walked, I tried to describe my strange experience on the bus to Pradeep. He nodded and said, "Yes, I can explain you. We Indians would say that you feel at home here because you are from this place. Most likely you were born in these hills in one of your past lives."

"Do you really believe that?" I asked incredulously.

"Of course I do. You and I must have met many, many times before. And that is why you came from Canada and found me."

I stared at him. *Can he really be serious?* I wondered. Studying his face, I noticed that his expression was earnest and intent, without a trace of mischief. Completely bemused, I said nothing, and we walked the rest of the way up the hill in silence.

We reached the Gandhi ashram, a modest structure surrounded by low outbuildings. But beyond the ashram—what
splendour! A grand sweep of Himalayan mountains stretched
across the horizon, sunlight glancing off the snow-capped peaks.
I felt the beauty of that scene like a great wave, flooding my being
with joy.

After standing in awe-struck silence for several minutes,
Pradeep and I wandered over to the lip of the hill, where we sat on
a low stone wall. We soon fell into an earnest conversation about
our hopes and dreams for our lives that stretched before us, filled
with endless possibility.

"This valley, the Garur valley," said Pradeep, sweeping an arm
to encompass the land below. "I am thinking that I will come and
live here and serve these people. They are poor, and they suffer.
They are really suffering from so many illnesses."

I gazed down at the lush valley, with the shining ribbon of
water curving along its floor. Fields of yellow mustard lined the
river, and I could see dozens of miniscule figures of women bent
over their work on the land. I considered Pradeep's idea to settle
in this valley. *This guy is even more of a dreamer than I am! But I
somehow think that he'll actually do it.*

The sun was setting, bathing the valley in a golden glow. As the
last rays of light slowly faded, a cold breeze sprang up. I shivered.

"Now we must find somewhere to stay," said Pradeep. "The
Gandhi ashram is just there and they take guests." His voice
trailed away.

I could imagine the accommodations. I'd get a narrow bed in a
women's dorm.

"Let's not stay there. I don't think Mahatma Gandhi would
really approve of the two of us," I said, giving his hand a squeeze.

Beyond the ashram was a small hotel, a low-slung cement
building that was still under construction—the outer wall at the far

end had iron rods sticking out of the cement. But it looked clean enough, and its location overlooking the valley was spectacular.

"I am going in to ask for a room, " Pradeep said. "Hide behind this tree. If the hotel people see you, they'll charge us three times the price."

Feeling foolish, I stepped behind a towering pine. Our being together was probably completely inappropriate, I thought. On my trip to India I'd been hoping to understand as much as I could, to cross the boundaries of culture and religion. However, those hopes had never included a wild love affair with a young Indian doctor.

Pradeep emerged from the hotel reception, room key in hand. Feeling awkward, I picked up my backpack and followed him. The room was very small, the bed occupying most of the available space. The only decoration was a calendar on the cement wall facing the bed featuring a brilliantly coloured image of Ganesh, the elephant-headed deity. I remembered Pradeep telling me that people prayed to Ganesh when they started any kind of new venture.

Well, Ganesh, I hear that you are the god of new beginnings. So here I am embarking on this mad relationship with Pradeep. This fits your mandate, I think. Give me your blessings.

We put our backpacks down and sat stiffly beside each other on the edge of the bed—there was nowhere else to sit.

"Pradeep, I hope that you don't think . . ." I began hesitantly. "Well, what I mean is, in your culture, you know, I'm just not sure . . ." But my stumbling attempt to reflect upon sexuality in this cross-cultural context faded away as Pradeep turned to kiss me. Our hesitancy dissolved, and we were swept away by a tide of passion as elemental as the ocean.

That magical visit to Kausani was the last trip we took together during my stay in India. My two-month adventure was ending. On the train journey from Lucknow back to Delhi, I opened my

journal and took out a long envelope, the official letter from the
dean of Dalhousie University, sanctioning my request to study
in India and requesting that I write a report about what had I
learned. An interesting assignment, indeed!

Pradeep accompanied me back to Delhi. On our last evening
together, our imminent separation weighed heavily on our minds.

I said, "I keep thinking about those *ghazals* that you used to
sing, with Wasim. Weren't they about the loss of a loved one, and
the pain of separating from the beloved?"

"Yes. Like this one." Pradeep began to sing a haunting melody.

"Phool kitabon mein milen. . . . What does it mean?" I whispered, not wanting to break the spell of the music.

"It means, 'Now we will be separated. And perhaps we shall
only meet in dreams. Our love will be like a flower pressed
between the pages of a book.'"

That image of a tiny flower fluttering from the pages of a
book stayed with me through the long flight back to Canada.
Would our love really become like that dried flower—a sweet but
faded memory?

CHAPTER TWO:

Taking The Plunge

Pradeep's first letter arrived within two weeks of my return to Canada, introducing the first delicate thread of connection. At that time, email was unavailable and phone was unreliable. Pradeep and I became masters of the art of letter-writing, although our style of writing could hardly have been more different. One memorable letter from Pradeep began:

"I sit here on the banks of the river Gomti, and gaze at the sky. A monsoon cloud floats above me. My heavy heart lifts. For this is the Cloud Messenger, and I will request him to carry the message of my love to you across the oceans to Canada."

The same letter included a translation from Sanskrit of a poem by Kalidasa, one of India's most beloved poets. Kalidasa lived in the fourth century AD and was celebrated in the court of the great ruler Chandragupta. "*Meghdoot*"—the Cloud Messenger—is Kalidasa's love poem, a literary treasure of India.

The story goes that Kubera, treasurer of the gods, has a group of divine attendants called the Yakshas. One of them had recently married and is so smitten with love that he neglects his duties. Kubera becomes angry and banishes him to a forest far away from his wife, who lives on a remote mountaintop in the Himalayas. The dejected Yaksha longs to communicate with her.

One day during the monsoon, the Yaksha sees a rain cloud floating by. Calling out to the cloud, he begs it to carry a message of love to his wife. He describes in captivating detail the route that the cloud must take to reach her far away in the Himalayas. The Yaksha then expresses his love, pouring out his devotion with extraordinary poetic beauty.

As I read the poem, I imagined Pradeep sitting by the river, gazing into the sky and contemplating the Cloud Messenger. He would often include a pressed flower, a drawing, or a poem, and his letters were invariably crafted with love. He rarely mentioned his daily life, his medical career, or his future plans. While touched by the romantic tone of his letters, I found myself trying to puzzle out his life between the lines. What had happened after I left India? What was happening in his medical career? What did he think about the future (if any) of our relationship?

My own letters were detailed accounts of my daily life, with anecdotes about patients, tales of outdoor adventures, and musings about our future. Though Western culture has its own body of love poetry, I somehow could not imagine expressing myself in this way.

How profoundly communication is shaped by culture! India's is pervaded by romantic imagery that springs from a rich heritage of mythology and religious tradition. The great epics of Hinduism— the *Mahabharata* and the *Ramayana*—are filled with tales of love and loss, death and rebirth. In Indian films, stories of love play out against dense backgrounds of traditional values. The films almost invariably have happy endings in which love triumphs against all odds. In the Muslim tradition, there are also poetic and romantic visions of life. Lucknow, the city where Pradeep was living, was the ancient seat of the *nawabs*, the Muslim princes who ruled before and during the British Raj. In their culture, elegant poetry and exquisite manners were prized. Practical accounts of daily affairs would hardly be considered fit subjects for letters or for conversation.

Over the next four years, Pradeep and I continued to write two or three times a week, amassing enormous volumes of correspondence. One summer, Pradeep came for a six-week visit to Canada, a golden time of re-connection and joy. I had a job as camp doctor in the Muskoka area of Ontario, and we stayed in a little cottage by the side of a lake. My medical duties were light, and our days flowed along with a delightful rhythm. We wandered through the woods, paddled a canoe along the lake, and joined campfires with the children in the evenings.

Our cottage had a screened verandah facing the lake, enclosed on either side by a dense curtain of trees. This special spot was a paradise for two young lovers, peaceful and private.

One evening we were sitting on the verandah watching the rippled surface of the lake turn gold and pink as the sun dipped below the horizon. We'd been talking about our future, a subject of endless discussion. Pradeep told me that he was certain we were destined to be together for life, and that evening he offered a vision of what that might look like. He wanted me to join him in India where we could live and work in the Himalayan foothills. The idea was breathtaking in its sheer audacity.

Could I actually do something as wild as that? I gazed at the darkening surface of the water, noticing the shadow made by a rocky cliff that jutted out over the lake on the south side. Marrying Pradeep and moving to the Himalayan foothills would be like diving off that high rock into unknown waters. Questions buzzed through my brain like angry hornets: *What if? What if?*

The haunting cry of a loon echoed across the lake, and I shivered at the eerie sound. *Life is full of unknown dangers. I mustn't make a foolish decision. I couldn't possibly take a risk like that,* I thought.

I sat quietly, saying nothing. As the days went by, Pradeep's invitation stayed with me, tantalizing yet disturbing. He would be returning to India in a few days, and our impending separation weighed heavily on my mind.

I must give him some sort of answer, I thought. *I just have to explain why I can't accept his invitation.*

On the last evening of his visit to Canada, I said quietly, "Pradeep, I keep on thinking about what you asked me. You know, about moving to India, marrying you, living in the Himalayas."

We sat in silence for some time as I struggled to formulate my thoughts.

"Well, I just don't see how it could ever work. We are from such different cultures. We'd face so many problems, so many obstacles."

At this, Pradeep turned to me, his eyes shining. "But, wouldn't that be the fun of it all? Sorting things out? If we love each other, we can do that!"

"Pradeep, life is not a Bollywood movie! Things really can go wrong. What if we began to have disagreements, fights? What if we begin to hate each other?"

Pradeep looked horrified. "I can never hate you, no matter what happens. And I know that we are meant to be together forever, not just in this life but in many more lives to come."

"I don't even believe in reincarnation. How can you be so certain that we'll be happy together? What if we marry, and then a few years later we decide to divorce?"

At this, Pradeep looked genuinely shocked. "Of course not! We will never divorce. Nobody in my whole extended family has divorced. Married means married."

"Well, we have a different view in Canada. We believe that if you are not happy with your partner, you should divorce."

"But that is so wrong! You must trust to life."

He reached out his hand. I saw tears glistening in his eyes, but he didn't try to dissuade me. We simply sat quietly together until darkness closed around us. That night, I lay awake for hours, reviewing his invitation again and again. The rational side of my brain marshaled its arguments, and I thought, *I was right to refuse him. The idea is impractical and dangerous.* But then a question floated up from a deeper level of my brain. *And yet? And yet?*

We drove to the airport the next day, talking very little. After he'd checked in his luggage, we sat for a few precious minutes together. I said to him, "Pradeep, perhaps I will come and visit you in India next year. By then, we may both have other ideas about the future. But we can see."

We hugged each other goodbye, too full of emotion to speak. I watched him walk through the departure gates. He turned briefly to wave, and then he was gone. I remained standing there for several minutes, conscious of a great heaviness in my chest. Finally, I managed to leave the departure area and walk out of the airport to the parking lot. A sudden gust of wind blew my thin shirt against my chest, making me shiver. Summer was nearly over.

Two weeks after Pradeep's departure, I began a new life. I'd been offered my first full-time job as a family physician in Thunder Bay, Ontario. Those initial months of practice were both exciting and terrifying. I worked in a clinic, in the emergency department of the hospital, and as an assistant in the operating room. I delivered babies and cared for dying patients. To be a witness to these awe-inspiring moments was a privilege.

Every day when I returned from work, I'd eagerly open my mailbox to look for a letter from Pradeep. When I opened the slim blue envelopes, out would tumble stories—stories of our love, of the mountains, of ideas, of hopes. I treasured those letters, a fragile link to our imagined future together.

A year after I'd begun my work in Thunder Bay, I took a month's holiday and went to India, where Pradeep and I had a joyous reunion. On that visit, we traveled to the Garhwal region of the

Himalayan foothills. The sources of the Ganges River arise high in these mountains, each one a pilgrimage site for devout Hindus.

We travelled toward the little town of Devprayag, situated at the confluence of two tributaries of the Ganga. The road snaked upward into the hills before beginning to wind down to the town. When we reached the highest point, we got out to admire the view. We could see the temple that marked the spot where the rivers join, and the flight of stone steps leading down to the water where the faithful could bathe. Standing there, I suddenly remembered gazing at the cliff beside the lake in Canada, thinking that a move to India would be like plunging into unknown waters. I'd been too frightened to accept that challenge. Now here I was in India, standing on a cliff above this river. Looking down, I felt a chill of fear. *Am I mad to even consider this? Moving to India and marrying Pradeep would be an enormous leap of faith.*

"Look," said Pradeep, pointing upward. An eagle was soaring across the river, moving with an elegant sweep of its wings. I caught my breath at the beauty of the scene before me: the tumbling turquoise water, the plunging cliffs, the faraway temple, and this magnificent bird, now spiralling lazily upward on a draft of warm air. I thought of lines from a Mary Oliver poem:

> *Still what I want in my life is to be willing to be dazzled—to cast aside the weight of facts and maybe even to float a little above this difficult world.*

Over the next few days, I turned that line of poetry over in my mind, debating its meaning for my current dilemma. *Well, yes, I do want to be dazzled by life. And that's all very well. But do I really want to "cast aside the weight of facts"? That sounds a little irrational.*

Then another line of thought surfaced. *But on the other hand, must all our decisions be based on rationality? What would we humans be like if we made every decision like that? Surely there is a truth of the heart, which is beyond rationality. . . .*

At the end of my three-week visit, I accepted Pradeep's invitation to marry him and move to India. I had decided to take the plunge off that cliff.

Over the next few months, I began the process of severing my ties in Canada. A friend who'd been a classmate was looking for a family medicine opportunity, and she agreed to take over my medical practice in Thunder Bay. A few weeks before leaving, I threw a party where I gave away most of my possessions. Finally, the only remaining decision to be made was how to reach India on a one-way ticket without paying the outrageous prices charged by the regular airlines. In London, England, I bought a cut-rate one-way ticket at a travel shop that sold last-minute seats. I had to depart within hours, leaving no time to send a telegram ahead to notify anyone of my impending arrival. I arrived in New Delhi alone and unannounced, in September of 1985.

After collecting my luggage, I walked tentatively into the arrivals hall. It was three in the morning, and I was unsure what to do next. I fought back the fear of being lost in an unknown world, with no familiar landmarks to guide me. In the far corner of the arrivals hall I noticed an information booth for travellers. At this desk, a helpful clerk listened to my story.

"You want a hotel room? Have you come to India on a holiday? No? You have come to get married? But then where are your future husband and his family? Are they not here?" The clerk leaned toward me, visibly concerned.

Feeling that I should reassure him, I said that all I needed was a recommendation for a hotel. He looked at me doubtfully, and then pulled out a map of New Delhi.

"Go to the Centre Point Hotel," he said. "It is a good place for single ladies travelling alone because you can get there on the airport bus. You should not be taking taxis by yourself in the middle of the night."

I thanked him, and carefully tucked the map into my purse. Walking out of the airport, I was immediately enveloped by the warmth of the Indian night, the smell of diesel oil and flowers, the shouts of taxi drivers, and the happy cries of families reunited. Suddenly I heard a familiar voice by my side: the clerk from the information desk!

He said, "I have finished my night's duty. Now I will escort you to the Centre Point Hotel. You are coming to live in my country, and so I must take care of you."

Alarmed, I told him that I was quite capable of taking care of myself. But he was rapidly propelling my baggage cart in the direction of a waiting airport bus, and shouting at a coolie to load my bags on top of the vehicle. As the bus roared toward New Delhi, my newfound friend shouted questions into my ear.

"How did you meet your future husband? What did your parents say when you told them you wanted to marry an Indian? What did *his* parents say? What kind of marriage will you have? What kind of work does your husband do?"

Shouting answers back at him over the roar of the bus's engine, I began to feel amused. This was certainly a warm welcome onto the lap of Mother India! True to his word, my chaperone deposited me safely at the front desk of the Centre Point Hotel, and gave a brief synopsis of my life history and present predicament to the man at the front desk. Then, saluting me with a traditional Indian "*Namaste*," he disappeared into the night.

The next morning, I sent Pradeep a telegram to say that I'd arrived in India. He was staying with his parents in Ghaziabad, an industrial city about 20 kilometres outside Delhi. The telegram should have arrived within hours, and I knew he would come at once after receiving it. I spent the day resting and relaxing at the hotel, catching up on my journal and daydreaming about the future.

I thought about the hotel clerk's questions: What did your parents think about your decision to marry? What did his parents think? I remembered the shock and concern in my parents' eyes when I told them about our plans.

"Marry an Indian man and move to India? Are you out of your mind?" my father had said angrily.

"No, of course not!" I flared back. "I've known Pradeep for nearly four years. This is not just some idle daydream!"

My mother looked stricken. "Your plans could be very dangerous," she said, anxiously. "I don't think India would be a safe place to live. And Indian men might hold very old-fashioned attitudes toward women."

"Oh Mum, don't worry about that!" I said. "Pradeep is a wonderful man and our marriage is going to be an equal partnership."

"You'll lose the freedom and opportunities that you have in Canada," my father warned. "And what about your career as a doctor? You've just gotten nicely established in that practice in Thunder Bay—are you going to throw that all away?"

I tried to explain my longing for an unusual life, a life of exploration and discovery. But to my pragmatic father, these dreamy visions were insubstantial and foolish.

One day, my father said, "Well, I hope you and that Indian husband of yours are not planning to have children."

"Yes, we'd like to have a family," I responded. "Why not?"

"He is brown and you are white—your children might turn out to be striped!" my father snorted.

I tried to ignore this comment, though it stung. Behind his seemingly humorous words floated an amorphous shadow of old fears and prejudices; ancient taboos against bearing children with mixed blood. Both my parents had grown up in South Africa during the era of apartheid. They had never supported the policies of the government, and the blatant racism of that country had been one factor in their decision to emigrate. Both were well-educated and held liberal views, but my plans to marry an Indian man posed a tough challenge.

Pradeep's parents had also been unhappy about our proposed marriage. He is from a conservative Hindu family in which arranged marriages are the norm. Pradeep's parents had been searching for a suitable match for their older son, and the news of our relationship came as a shock. For Indian parents, the marriage of a son has many layers of significance. A good marriage to a suitable young woman brings honour to the parents, while a marriage that ends in divorce casts a shadow across the entire extended family. His parents expressed their concern that our marriage might not last, since I was unlikely to share their traditional family values.

Indian parents rely on their sons for support in their old age, and when they search for a daughter-in-law, they consider her potential as a future caregiver. As a Canadian woman who knew nothing of their language, culture, or family traditions, I must have seemed a risky prospect.

Pradeep and I spent many months talking over our decisions with our families, and both sets of parents eventually gave us their blessing, a tribute to their love. We began to make plans for the wedding ceremony, to be held in India.

Now the long years of waiting to be together were over at last. Pradeep reached the Centre Point Hotel that evening and we had a joyous reunion. Our wedding date was set for the eighteenth of October, and Pradeep's mother had taken on the task of the organizing. Because it would not be appropriate for me to come to Pradeep's home in Ghaziabad before the wedding, I spent the next three weeks in Delhi. I'd have time to acclimatize myself to India and to reconnect with Pradeep, whom I had not seen in over a year.

One of our favourite places was the Lodi Gardens, where ancient tombs from fifteenth-century Muslim rulers stood amidst acres of beautifully landscaped grounds. On our first afternoon together, we sat under the shade of a chestnut tree in the gardens and talked eagerly about the future. Pradeep's recent letters had been filled with enthusiastic descriptions of his new abode in Sivananda Ashram, just outside the little town of Rishikesh at the edge of the Himalayan foothills. I wanted to hear all about the place that he had chosen for our future home.

"You know that I'm medical officer in Sivananda Charitable Hospital," said Pradeep. "And I think you know something about the ashram already?"

I'd received many tattered brown envelopes covered with Indian stamps in my Thunder Bay mailbox. I'd pored over the printed material about Sivanand Ashram, learning that a charismatic young man named Swami Sivananda had founded the community in the early 1930s. Initially, Sivananda Ashram had just been a tiny spiritual community that had attracted a few swamis and spiritual aspirants. But Swami Sivananda had a great spiritual presence, and the ashram kept growing.

"How many people live there nowadays?" I asked.

"It's quite a big place. Must be more than hundred permanent residents, men and women."

"So are all the residents really serious spiritual seekers?" I asked.

"Most of them. But there are some few strange characters who don't have much interest in spirituality. I think they live there because they have nowhere else to go. Swami Sivananda used to say, 'Let those who need us stay.' Those who are truly on the path to God will find their own way."

"Tell me more about the hospital. What is it like?" I asked.

"Well, it's very plain and simple, but more and more patients are coming. People are lining up for hours to see us. You'll be surprised—all different types of people are coming. There are villagers from the mountains, people from the slums, swamis from the ashrams, even foreigners who come to Rishikesh as tourists. Every day is interesting."

"What about living in the ashram?" I asked. "Are you sure I would be welcome there, being a foreigner and a woman?"

"Oh yes," said Pradeep, confidently. "I've discussed it with Swami Krishnananda, the general secretary. Everyone will love you, I know it."

I wonder about that. I can't imagine how someone like me would fit into a Hindu spiritual community. Pradeep tends to be breezily self-confident about so many things.

As we wandered through the gardens, I asked, "How are the preparations for the wedding coming? I feel bad that your mother has to do all this work."

I knew that traditionally it would be the duty of the bride's family to organize the wedding celebration. My family had provided some money for the ceremony but that was all they could do.

"My mother's a great organizer and she loves this kind of thing," replied Pradeep. "And I have told her to make it really simple. We'll just cut out most of the ceremonies and make it short. She's not happy about that idea, though."

"Well, neither am I," I replied, indignantly. "If I'm going to be married in a traditional Hindu wedding, then I definitely want to go through all the proper ceremonies! I want to see you riding in on a white horse, and all that stuff."

Pradeep looked guilty. "The white horse?" he said. "I already told my mother that we won't have a horse or any such thing. It'll be really plain and simple."

"Forget it, Pradeep. No horse, no wedding." I said firmly.

When I met Pradeep the next day, he said, "My mother is thrilled. We are going to have every ceremony. And I have arranged for a white horse."

A day before the wedding, we traveled to the airport to pick up my brother, Len, arriving from Canada to represent my family. Because my father had recently undergone major surgery, neither parent could attend the ceremony. My brother's presence would be necessary in some key elements of the wedding. When we picked him up at the airport, he looked flustered. British Airways had lost his luggage, and he had no suitable clothes for the wedding.

"Do not worry!" said Anil, my future brother-in-law. "This is India. You will see that all problems can be solved."

Within hours of arriving in India, Len was measured for a suit by a tailor in Delhi, who assured him that it would be ready in time for the ceremony. I was delighted to see my brother, a familiar presence in this Indian environment that still seemed strange.

The evening before the wedding is a time for the women of the bride's family to gather and celebrate the coming event. The fact that I had no female relatives in India did not pose a problem. Women from Pradeep's large extended family flocked to the house where I was staying, gathering around me like brilliantly coloured birds. I couldn't understand Hindi and few of them spoke English, but with sign language and lots of laughter, we managed to communicate.

I found myself being taken firmly in hand—there was much to be done. A woman came to decorate my hands and feet with *mehindi,* the henna paste that is applied to the skin in intricate designs. As she worked, the women around me sang, one of them keeping time with a drum held between her knees. The *mehindi* took nearly two hours to apply, but the time passed easily in an atmosphere of warm camaraderie.

That night, sleep was elusive. The *mehindi* dried on my skin and couldn't be washed off until morning, and it was itchy. But there was much more on my mind than physical discomfort. The wedding the next day would be a leap of faith into the unknown. Worries buzzed like hornets in my mind.

Pradeep and I really don't know each other well. We've spent only a few weeks together, though we met four years ago.

Bridging the gulf of cultural differences between us would be a challenging task. Another huge challenge also loomed before me: to adapt to life in an ashram in a small Himalayan town.

As I lay sleepless that night, I reflected on the paths I had traveled to reach this significant crossroad. As a girl of eight, I remember gazing intently at an advertisement for the work of CARE, which featured a photo of an African girl about my own age. I wondered, Who is she? What is her life like? Could she ever be my friend? A burning desire seized me: to understand her life and be meaningful to her in some way. I wondered if perhaps I was meant to be a missionary in Africa. After all, I was born there, although I'd lived there only a few years.

But these ideas changed abruptly during early adolescence, when a minister in our church spoke about Christianity as the only true path to the Divine. A sudden, sharp revelation burst into my consciousness: No! This could not be true. The Divine must be revealed endlessly, to every group of people throughout human history, in ways that hold meaning for that particular society. My sense of disillusionment was acute and painful, and in my earnest need for truth, I distanced myself from the faith of my childhood.

As my dreams of becoming a missionary evaporated, a new idea began to germinate. I would study to be a doctor, and would go to Africa to work. I had no particular talent or inclination for the study of medicine, and medical school proved to be a gruelling ordeal. As a student, I was taught to use the tools of scientific reductionism to study the human body as an intricate machine. This concept challenged my intuitive sense of the body as far more than this, the ground for one's emotional and spiritual being. But I plugged away at my studies with determination, believing that the skills I was learning would ultimately prove useful.

Meeting Pradeep had changed the locale for my life's work from Africa to India, but that didn't matter. The idea of the quest—to seek understanding beyond the boundaries of culture and religion—was as alive as ever. Now, with a partner who shared many of the same goals, I felt that I was at last embarking on my life's voyage of discovery. With this comforting thought, I eventually dropped off to sleep.

It seemed only moments later that I felt my shoulder being gently touched. Pradeep's younger sister Nimmi had come to begin preparing me for the ceremony. I took a bath and washed off the dried *mehindi*, which left delicate ochre-coloured patterns on my hands and feet. The elegant red silk wedding sari was shaken free from its tissue paper and I began to get dressed. One of Pradeep's aunts helped me to tie the sari, each shimmering fold falling beautifully in place. Another aunt brought jewellery for me to wear. Most Indian brides are laden with gold jewellery at their wedding, a significant part of their dowry. I was grateful to be able to borrow this finery for my wedding day.

Two pretty twin girls of about ten years old, cousins of Pradeep, said a shy *Namaste* to me. They led me through the gathering throngs of guests to a secluded spot that offered a view of the courtyard outside the marriage hall. Before long, I could hear the sound of the *shehnai*, a traditional wind instrument played at the time of a wedding. Happy shouts and laughter mingled with the beating of drums signalled that the *barat* was arriving, the procession that accompanies the groom to the wedding. Watching eagerly, I was delighted to see Pradeep riding up to the hall on a white horse, accompanied by dozens of family members.

Pradeep and I sat on elegant red thrones on an elevated platform, surrounded by elaborate decorations made of marigold blossoms. When all the guests were gathered, the first ceremony began. Each of us placed a magnificent garland of flowers around the other's neck. As we did so, the guests called out their good wishes and showered us with rose petals.

Next came the central ceremony of the wedding. Pradeep and I were led to an inner room where we were seated cross-legged under a flower-bedecked wooden canopy. The *pundit* sat opposite us, and began to chant the ancient Sanskrit mantras that are layered with intricate meaning. He laid a fire in an iron cauldron, and poured some *ghee*[1] onto the pile of sticks. After the fire was lit, he continued to intone the mantras that were to prepare bride and groom for the most sacred ceremony of the marriage rituals, in which they would walk seven times around the fire, making seven vows to each other. At the moment when I had to take the first steps around the fire, I was briefly overcome by a wave of panic. I tried to focus on small details of my surroundings—the smell of the dried herbs being tossed into the fire, the sound of the pundit's voice, and the sight of Pradeep's hands tying the scarf that would bind us together as we walked. I got shakily to my feet, and took the symbolic first steps of a journey of a lifetime.

A grand wedding feast followed this ceremony, and I was introduced to literally hundreds of Pradeep's relatives. The idea of having such an enormous extended family was astonishing. My own family in Canada is very small, and I'd never imagined a gathering of this kind. I'd memorized one phrase in Hindi, *"Mujhe apse milkar behut kushi hui"*, which means, "I am very pleased to meet you," and I repeated this over and over to the smiling family members who came to greet me. The rest of the day's ceremonies passed in a blur of sounds and smells and colours.

After the ceremony, Pradeep and I returned to his parents' home in Ghaziabad, traveling in a flower-bedecked car. The house was filled to bursting with Pradeep's relatives, already sharing the first of many rounds of tea.

....

1   clarified butter, often used in Hindu ceremonies

Ammaji, Pradeep's grandmother, beckoned to me.[2] She led me into the back bedroom where she had a little shrine set up, the altar covered with images of the Hindu gods and goddesses. She worshipped here every morning, lighting incense and murmuring prayers.

"*Dekho* (Look!)" she said to me, softly. Beside the little statue of the potbellied elephant god Ganesha stood a small crucifix, with fresh flowers at its base. As I looked at that tiny image of Christ on the cross, I marvelled at the ways in which the Hindu religious tradition can absorb and adapt. As Ammaji welcomed me into the family, she added Jesus to her pantheon of gods.

Pradeep's mother took my arm and showed me where we would be spending our wedding night. The master bedroom of the little house had been prepared for us. The bed was covered with hundreds of scattered rose petals, arranged in an intricate design. On the bedside table were a pitcher of milk and a bowl of almonds, foods symbolic of sexuality and fertility. As evening fell, Mummyji and her sisters unrolled mattresses and bedding and spread them on the floor of the living room and second bedroom. At least twenty of Pradeep's relatives would be spending the night. Staying in a hotel is not only expensive but would be considered inappropriate for visiting family members. I watched the little house being transformed into a dormitory with a mixture of fascination and unease. So many people in such a small space. . . .

After Pradeep and I disappeared into our bridal chamber, I managed to forget about all the guests. How wonderful it was to spend that night in his arms! Flute music by James Galway created a beautiful background for our night of love. So many barriers had blocked our path, but now the long years of waiting were behind

....

2   the suffix "ji" is added to indicate a relationship of respect;—thus, Amma (grandmother) becomes Ammaji.

us. We had made the commitment to married life, and now at last we were beginning this great adventure together.

The next morning we woke to the sounds of Pradeep's family having their early morning cup of tea. Pradeep rolled out of bed and walked to the door, planning to get us some tea, as well. But he suddenly hesitated.

"This is awful," he said. "I am too shy to go out there."

Eventually, he opened the door. A gale of laughter swept through the room, and his male cousins dragged him off for some teasing. Moments later, a giggling group of women rushed into the bedroom and crowded around me. One of Pradeep's aunts elbowed me, knowingly, obviously wanting to know some details about the night before. I was quite relieved that I didn't know any Hindi.

Several days after the wedding, Pradeep and I were ready to leave for our new home. He had been living in Sivananda Ashram for two years, but his parents and his grandmother still could not understand his decision to live and work in such a place.

The night before we left, Ammaji drew Pradeep aside. Not understanding a word of their conversation, I focused on observing their body language. Ammaji was leaning toward Pradeep, her hand on his arm, speaking in a voice that was concerned and compelling. Pradeep's tone was soft and reassuring. But then Ammaji pulled back and shook her head vigorously, disbelief clearly evident in every line of her body.

"What was that all about?" I asked as soon as we were settled in bed.

"Ammaji is very worried about us. She asked why we are going to live in an ashram, when we could settle down in a town and start a private practice. I explained her that we don't want to live just like ordinary people. We want to serve the poors and explore the deepest meanings of life."

"So what did Ammaji think of that?"

"She thought it was a very foolish idea," Pradeep replied. "She said poverty is something that you escape from, not something that you embrace."

Ammaji's views on poverty were shaped by experiences that were very different from ours. She had grown up in pre-independence India, and was married by the age of sixteen. Her husband worked as a village bookkeeper, bringing home a modest wage. He contracted tuberculosis in his twenties, and his desperate search for treatment consumed much of the meagre family resources. He became more and more ill. When he died at the age of thirty, Ammaji faced the grim reality of life as a widow with a young family to support. The years that followed were filled with struggle. She found a home with relatives, but the spectre of poverty haunted her for many years. She had given birth to five children, but only one survived to adulthood, Pradeep's father. The others died of childhood illnesses, compounded by malnutrition.

No wonder Ammaji's views on poverty were very different from our idealistic and seemingly naive ideas. Our choice to live in an ashram and explore our spiritual lives was also incomprehensible to her. She said, "Life in an ashram is not appropriate for a boy from your caste. You must do something suitable to your *dharma*."

"*Dharma*" can be roughly translated as "duty." The concept is embedded in Hindu ideas about caste and the proper way to live. Each caste has traditional roles and obligations, and it is expected that a dutiful child will follow the path laid out by his or her ancestors. In modern India, the caste system still shapes people's ideas about their future occupation and their prospective partners, though this is changing as the winds of modernization blow through the country. Pradeep's family members are of the Bania caste, whose traditional occupations involved trading, selling, and money lending. Many of Pradeep's vast family network are still involved in business, though the younger generation has also taken up professional occupations in fields such as medicine, engineering, and computer science. As a group, Banias tend to be conservative and family-oriented. Relationships are of great importance, and in Pradeep's extended family, almost all marriages are still arranged with partners from within the Bania caste. Our marriage was a notable exception.

Though Ammaji did not agree with our choices, she was always a loving presence in our lives. She would cook and mend and knit for us, and I know that she prayed for us every day. Perhaps it was those prayers that sustained us as we began to take our first steps on that mysterious journey of creating our own family.

CHAPTER THREE:

On The Pilgrim's Path

After the wedding, Pradeep and I decided to take a journey to Gaumukh, one of the sources of the Ganges River.[3] We would travel by car to the small town of Gangotri, high in the Himalayan foothills, and then walk for two days to reach Gaumukh. My brother, Len, accompanied us on this grand adventure. We travelled by train to the town of Hardwar, where Pradeep rented a vehicle and a driver. On a brilliant morning in late October, we began our journey, driving first to Rishikesh, the little town that would soon become our home.

From there, the road followed the course of the river, snaking upward into the Himalayan foothills. The scenery became more dramatic with each passing kilometre as rolling hills grew into massive mountains. On the other bank of the river we occasionally caught a glimpse of the old footpath used for centuries by pilgrims walking to the source of the Ganga. Now with the advent of roads, these paths have fallen into disuse. How different the scenery

....

3   The Ganges River is called the Ganga by Indians, and I will use this name throughout the rest of the narrative.

must have been for those pilgrims long ago! From Rishikesh to
Gangotri, the hills were once covered in dense Himalayan forest,
home to tigers, leopards, elephants, and bears. These animals
could be very dangerous to pilgrims, who slept at night in flimsy
shelters or in the open.

Uncontrolled lumbering operations during the British era
along with increasing population pressure on the land have
resulted in serious deforestation across the Himalayan foothills.
Without forest cover, the hills have become progressively drier.
On some denuded hillsides, the only vegetation we saw was
cactus, stark evidence of the desiccation of the land.

Another consequence of deforestation became all too apparent
as we continued our journey into the hills. Without trees to bind
and stabilize the soil, landslides were common. This year, unex-
pectedly late monsoon rains added to the problem, and we confronted terrifying washouts in the roads. One slip on the rock and
mud of an unstable landslide and the car would have catapulted
into the valley far below. The journey suddenly turned from a
carefree jaunt to a true pilgrimage, fraught with hazard.

We stopped for a late lunch at a wayside *dhaba*, the small
eating places that are ubiquitous throughout Garhwal. We ordered
rice and *dal*, a lentil soup that is the staple protein for much of
India. The *dal* was too spicy for both Len and me, so we contented
ourselves with rice and hot fresh *rotis*, the round flatbread eaten
throughout North India.

As our car wound upward into the mountains, we began to
catch glimpses of the glistening peaks of the high Himalayas. The
road had become very narrow and rough. As we rounded a curve,
we saw an army officer jump out of his Jeep and run toward us,
waving his arms.

"Don't go on! Turn back!" he said. "A big landslide just happened. . . . Road is gone."

"Is there no other way to Gangotri?" asked Pradeep.

"No, this is the only road. You must turn around and go back," replied the officer. With that, he stepped into his Jeep and drove off.

"Oh, how disappointing!" I exclaimed. "We've come so far, and we can't get to Gangotri after all."

Pradeep said slowly, "I think I must have a look at that landslide. Maybe it's not quite so bad."

"Impossible" is a word that is simply not in Pradeep's vocabulary. We continued cautiously along the road for another couple of kilometres until we reached the landslide. A massive portion of the hill above the road had broken loose and slid down, obliterating the road completely. Occasional rocks and boulders continued to tumble down the slope.

"Let me have a closer look," said Pradeep, leaping out of the car. We watched him trot toward the landslide, shaking our heads in disbelief.

A few minutes later, he was back.

"We'll get to Gangotri!" he said happily. "A bus is stuck on the other side of the landslide. It's turning around right now. All we have to do is walk over the landslide and catch that bus to Gangotri."

"You've got to be kidding," I gasped. But Pradeep had already started to unload backpacks from our taxi, while carrying on a rapid conversation in Hindi with our driver. He pulled out a roll of bills and paid him.

Strapping on our backpacks, we approached the landslide cautiously. We could see that a number of other travelers had already crossed on foot and a rough path had been created over the enormous pile of rocks and soil.

Pradeep shouldered his backpack and stepped carefully onto the narrow path across the shifting soil. When he reached the other side, he called out to us encouragingly, "I'll keep an eye open for falling rocks."

When I was crossing the landslide, my foot slipped a little and I nearly lost my balance. During the few moments that it took to regain my footing, a shower of small rocks came hurtling down from the cliff above. Fortunately, I was able to move ahead quickly and join Pradeep on the other side. For several hair-raising minutes, Pradeep and I watched as Len crossed the landslide. Breathing a collective sigh of relief, we joined the group of about a dozen other travelers who'd made the same precarious passage. We passed our backpacks up to a man on the roof of the bus, and he strapped them onto the luggage rack. Half an hour later, we set off.

The road to Gangotri had been badly damaged by washouts and was strewn with boulders that had tumbled down from the steep slope above the road. The ride was terrifying. Every time we came to a particularly dangerous spot on the road, the passengers would begin to chant "Hare Rama! Hare Rama!"—the Hindi equivalent of "Hail, O Lord Rama!" Whether it was due to these fervent prayers or sheer good luck, we reached the little hamlet of Gangotri safely, just as it was getting dark.

My brother whispered, "Now I know where to find God. He may not spend much time in Toronto, but he's certainly on the job here!" The bus driver helped us retrieve our backpacks from the roof and pointed out the tourist bungalow. Breathing prayers of gratitude for our deliverance, we trudged along the muddy path to the rest house.

A good sleep had a remarkably restorative effect on all of us. By nine o'clock the next morning, we'd left Gangotri behind and begun our trek to Gaumukh. We came to a small bridge over the rushing turquoise torrent that was the Bhagirathi River, which flows down through the mountains to meet the Alaknanda River, another tributary that forms the Ganga. Below, we gazed down at huge white boulders that had been moulded by the tumbling water into fantastic shapes. Beyond the bridge, we could see the pilgrim trail following the course of the river upstream toward the magnificent mountains that marked our destination. With the morning sun on our faces, we began to walk the trail.

"We are now in *dev bhoomi*—land of the gods," exclaimed Pradeep. "Can you see why we people gave that name to these mountains? Such beauty!"

"I read somewhere that pilgrims have been walking this trail for more than two thousand years," I said. "And this is just one trail. There are so many more."

In high season, the pilgrim trail is crowded with Hindu devotees from every walk of life, some on foot, others riding ponies, others being carried by porters. But by late October, very few pilgrims remain. We met two families from Rajasthan on the trail, the men wearing brightly coloured cotton turbans and the women adorned with heavy silver jewellery. The only other people we saw were two stout men riding on ponies.

Ahead of us loomed a dense forest of magnificent deodar trees, some of them with trunks more than three metres in diameter. As we entered the forest, the shadows of these great trees embraced us. We fell silent, drawn into this mysterious realm where sombre tones of olive green blended with the muted darkness of the tree trunks. Our pace slowed, as if it were sacrilege to rush through this hushed place of beauty. These timeless moments are like doorways to the soul, I thought. In these moments, we break through the confines of the ordinary world and glimpse the eternal.

Pradeep slipped his hand into mine and we walked together like two children, lost in this world of wonder. Ahead, a slanting shaft of sunlight illuminated an open glade, where dense layers of evergreen needles carpeted the forest floor.

"Can you imagine a more sacred spot?" Pradeep whispered to me. "So many saints and sages have meditated in these forests, for hundreds of years."

"I can feel their silent presence," I murmured.

The forest gradually began to recede, as if the great trees were slowly stepping back from their meeting with us. Sunlight began to stream through the branches and a light breeze ruffled our hair. As we emerged from the forest, a splendid valley spread out before us, with the thin turquoise stream of the Bhagirathi River winding through. Once again, I had an uncanny experience of feeling at home in those mountains, just as I had on my first visit three years earlier. It was a feeling of belonging; almost a sense of recognition.

The trail ascended gradually, following the curve of the hill. We picked up our pace, enjoying the vigorous walk and delighting in the beauty unfolding around us. An hour later, we spotted a lazy spiral of smoke curling upward just over the brow of the hill. When we reached the top, we traced the smoke to a small hut tucked within a grove of pine trees. A few other simple dwellings built of stone with slate roofs were clustered nearby. This was the hamlet of Chirbasa, named for the pine trees that grow in this area. On the last night, our hotelkeeper had told us we would be able to get a hot lunch at the roadside tea stall here.

A few minutes later, we were perched on rickety wooden benches in the tea stall, sipping hot, sweet tea from steel tumblers and deliberating about what to eat for lunch. Len and I were reluctant to try the spicy *dal* again and opted instead for *aloo parathas*, flatbread stuffed with potato and fried on a hot pan over the fire.

Refreshed and rejuvenated by our lunch stop, we set off on the trail again. As we ascended above 9,000 feet, the deodar trees gave way to stunted cyprus and spruce. By this time, we were beginning to feel the altitude and our pace slowed considerably. I was conscious of a mild headache and shortness of breath. We were heading for the pilgrims' hut at Bhojbasa where we would spend the night, still several kilometres away. It was late in the year for a pilgrimage and a cold wind began to whistle down from the mountains. Shivering, we pulled warmer clothes out of our packs and bundled up. We trudged along the path, focusing on putting one foot in front of the other.

We finally spotted the pilgrim hut in the distance, near a stand of the elegant birch trees that gives Bhojbasa its name. Arriving at our destination in the gathering dusk, we were greeted by an old man carrying a kerosene lantern. After showing us the simple room where we would spend the night, he said, "Now I will bring you something."

We fervently hoped that he had gone to get cups of steaming hot tea. But when he came shuffling back, I saw to my dismay that he was holding a sheaf of familiar forms. In India, tourists must fill out a registration form known as "Form C" whenever they stay in a hotel. These forms, filled out in triplicate, record information about the tourist in exhaustive detail. As I began this all-too-familiar task, I couldn't help giggling. "Form C" at 10,000 feet!

After we completed this essential task, the old man relaxed a bit and eventually brought us the tea we'd been craving. He told us that the pilgrimage season was almost over and he would be closing for the winter in a few days. We recognized the other guests in the hut—the two families from Rajasthan and the men who'd been riding ponies. Despite the biting cold, the Rajasthani villagers were in high spirits. They pushed some cots together, wrapped themselves in rough blankets, and began gossiping and laughing.

We slept well, exhausted from our day of hiking. The next morning, we prepared to make the final ascent to Gaumukh, still another 2,000 feet higher than Bhojbasa. We decided to leave our backpacks at the hut, taking just the bare essentials. I slung my trusty 35 mm Minolta camera in its bright red bag on my shoulder. My new passion was photography, and there could be no scenery more magnificent than this for an aspiring photographer. The air was clean and crisp, the sky a brilliant blue. We had passed above the tree line and the landscape became stark and barren.

The pilgrim's trail became more indistinct as we began to cross the rubble of the glacial moraine.

To our right towered the massive pyramidal mountain known as Shivling, the abode of Lord Shiva. Pradeep told us the mythical story of the goddess Ganga, who descended from the heavens toward the earth in a powerful torrent. Lord Shiva stepped forward to break her fall and the goddess was transformed instantly into the River Ganga, which flowed from the matted locks of Lord Shiva's hair. This sacred river is worshipped by millions of devotees all along its course, from the Himalayas to the delta in the Bay of Bengal. Lord Shiva is honoured in temples dotted all over the Himalayan region.

Directly ahead of us soared the Bhagirathi peaks, with the glacier that forms the source of the river crouching at the base of the mountain. By the time the sun was directly overhead, we could see the blunt snout of the glacier itself. Most of it is covered in fine gravel, but here and there rays of sunlight sparkled off the ice beneath.

By late morning we reached our destination, the sacred spot known as Gaumukh. The pilgrim trail ended beside a stream of turquoise water that poured out of a hollow in the glacier. This is called "the cow's mouth" by Hindu devotees, recalling the sacred symbolism of that animal as the nurturer of the human race.

Pradeep and I walked to a secluded place beside the water. We'd decided to take this opportunity to create our own unique marriage vows, ones that would have special meaning for us. Holding hands, we pledged to commit ourselves to our chosen path of social service and spiritual search. We promised to support each other in our journey of personal growth, encouraging each other to pursue the aims closest to our hearts. But we realized that pursuing our own aims could potentially lead to disagreement and discord, and so we made one final vow. If serious conflict arose between us, we would choose the path that would sustain the bond of our marriage.

As we walked slowly away from the glacier, my cup of joy was overflowing. At that moment, I felt that I was in "my place," the spot in the world where I was meant to be. No matter what the future would bring, I could store this precious memory in my heart forever. I thought of Emily Dickinson's lines:

> *Oh, better than the minting of a new-crowned King,*
> *Is the safe-kept memory of a lovely thing. . . .*

CHAPTER FOUR:

Stranger In A Strange Land

After Len had left for North America, Pradeep and I did a little more traveling—to the desert state of Rajasthan, and then to the famous temples of Khujaraho.

When we'd returned to Ghaziabad, Mummyji helped me purchase bedding and kitchen utensils for our new home. Loading all these purchases, our suitcases, and assorted wedding gifts into a taxi, we set out on the six-hour road trip to Rishikesh to begin our new lives as residents of Sivananda Ashram. On the way, Pradeep described the history of the ashram.

Swami Sivananda founded the organization, which he named the Divine Life Society, in the early 1930s. Over the years, it grew into a worldwide organization, with ashrams in many countries. The original ashram in Rishikesh began as a small collection of buildings clustered near the bank of the Ganga. Swamiji[4] had a powerful presence and great charisma and the little community grew rapidly. Two young men who joined the ashram in its early days took *sannyasa* (the vows of the renunciation taken when a

....

4   the honorific "ji" would always be added when referring to a swami.

Hindu spiritual aspirant becomes a swami). These two devoted disciples became known as Swami Krishnananda and Swami Chidananda, and they jointly took on the leadership of the ashram after Swami Sivananda's death in 1963.

Swami Sivananda had been trained as a doctor prior to taking *sannyasa*, and always maintained a commitment to medical care for the poor. He established a hospital soon after construction of the ashram in Rishikesh began. The hospital, originally an eye hospital, provided primarily cataract surgeries for anybody who needed them. But after Swami Sivananda's death, some of the energy behind the hospital waned. Over the next two decades, it was in use only intermittently.

In the early 1980s, Dr. Devaki Kutty joined the ashram as a permanent resident. She'd been the head of the department of obstetrics and gynecology at King George Medical College in Lucknow, where Pradeep had received his training and I had spent two months as a visiting medical student. A longtime devotee of Swami Sivananda, she'd made a vow to come and live in the ashram after her retirement. She was a remarkable physician, famous throughout the state of Uttar Pradesh for her diagnostic skills. Possessed of tremendous energy, she soon began to think about restoring Sivanand Hospital to a well-functioning condition. She planned to start a section for women's health and recruited Pradeep to introduce a general medical program.

"I've been working in the hospital for two years now. Patients are coming from far and wide," Pradeep said enthusiastically to me in the taxi, on our way up. "You'll like the hospital—there's always something unusual happening. And we'll be living right in the ashram, you know. We have a little flat in one of the new buildings."

"I'm really excited to see it. Our first home!" I said, happily.

"But I'm not sure what you'll think of the place," Pradeep replied, suddenly sounding tentative.

I squeezed his arm. "I'm sure I'll love it."

By mid-afternoon, we were nearing our destination. We crossed the town of Rishikesh, and drove along a road that followed the course of the Ganga. Pradeep instructed the driver to let us off by the main gates of Sivananda Ashram.

"We'll walk up to our new home—that way, you can see a bit of the ashram first," Pradeep said. "The hospital is right here, just beside the road."

Sivananda Charitable Hospital was a modest, two-story building located in the oldest portion of the ashram, built in the early 1940s. Between the hospital and the riverbank were clustered about a dozen small buildings, including administrative offices, residential buildings, and a printing facility. This area was separated from the central portion of the ashram by the Rishikesh road, which led from the town into the Himalayan foothills.

Crossing the road, Pradeep and I walked up a long flight of stone steps.

"This is the main part of the ashram, which was built a few years after those first buildings," said Pradeep. "Here, we have so many residences for the swamis, and then there is the library. And just in front of the library is the *satsang* hall, where the senior swamis give discourses every evening. Over there is the temple— I'll take you in there some day soon."

I tried to pay attention to Pradeep's enthusiastic commentary, but I was feeling overwhelmed by the sensory experience of simply being there. Noise assailed me from all sides: music blared from loudspeakers, temple bells clanged, and traffic roared on the road. Men in orange robes walked past, muttering, "*Hari Om!*" in greeting. A boy with a tin container of milk in his hands nearly collided with us. I saw only one woman, clad in white, who gazed down at us from a balcony. Cows wandered through the grounds, nosing through piles of food waste. My mind swirled in

confusion—the ashram seemed so alien, not at all how I'd imagined a spiritual community.

Seemingly oblivious to my discomfort, Pradeep said, "Come
this way. Do you see that path, just beyond the dining hall? At the
top of the hill, you'll see our new home. The taxi with all of our
luggage will be waiting for us there."

As we climbed the path, winding away from the central portion
of the ashram, I was relieved to notice that the hubbub began to
diminish. At the top of the hill there were two modern-looking
blocks of flats, backing onto forested land. This looks a bit more
promising, I thought.

Pradeep led the way to our apartment on the third floor of
the farther of these buildings. The first room was clean and airy
but completely empty. The second room was furnished with two
rough wooden cots with lumpy cotton mattresses, and a small
bookshelf. In the tiny adjoining kitchen, I found three cracked
porcelain cups, two metal plates, and a battered kerosene stove.
The bathroom had a toilet and sink, but the bathing arrangements
consisted of a cold-water tap jutting out of the wall with a bucket
beneath it.

Somewhat dazed, I stepped back into the bedroom. On the
wall hung a faded framed photograph of a stern-looking Indian
sage—Sri Aurobindo, the philosopher, whose work Pradeep
greatly admired. A door at the far end of the bedroom led off to a
small balcony with a view of the jungle beyond.

I had entered a monastic cell, not a cozy nest for a couple
of newlyweds.

"Pradeep," I said. "We are going to have to make some
changes here."

"Of course, of course," said Pradeep, hastily. "Whatever
you'd like."

Over the next week, we made trip after trip to Rishikesh,
exploring every inch of the bustling market. We also made a

shopping expedition to Dehradun, a city about forty kilometres to the west. Pradeep and I would then stagger up the stairs to our little apartment, laden with boxes and bags. The monastic cell was undergoing a design makeover.

Ten days later, I sat back with a sigh of contentment. The first room had been transformed into a simple but comfortable living room, with a daybed that doubled as a sofa, a wicker chair, a wooden bookcase, and a metal storage trunk covered with hand-dloomed fabric. On the wall hung two framed prints of rugged northern landscape done by the Canadian artist Lawren Harris, a wedding gift from my parents. The kitchen boasted a small modern refrigerator, a single-burner electric cooker, a set of steel plates and glasses, and two elegant china mugs. In the bathroom, a compact electric hot water heater had been attached to the wall to provide hot water for bathing. The bedroom now had a large bed with a good mattress. The bedcover patterned with traditional Indian designs added bright notes of colour to the room.

"What do you think?" I asked Pradeep.

"Well, it's beautiful. I just never thought we'd be needing so many things," Pradeep replied, hesitantly.

I still had one more suitcase to unpack, which contained some of my favourite books, books I felt I couldn't live without: *Out of Africa* by Karen Blixen, *The Stone Angel* by Margaret Lawrence, *Sunshine Sketches of a Little Town* by Stephen Leacock, *Meetings with Remarkable Men* by Gurdjieff, and *The Little Prince* by Antoine de Saint-Exupery. Out of the same suitcase, I withdrew several medical textbooks and my copy of *Where There Is No Doctor* by David Werner, about the provision of health care in remote parts of the world. Finally, I unpacked the personal journals I'd been keeping since I was a child of twelve. I knelt to arrange my treasures beside Pradeep's collection on the bookshelf in our bedroom. As I did this, I noticed with surprise that nearly every one of Pradeep's books had to do with Indian spirituality. I felt strange stirrings of unease.

"Pradeep," I asked, "Where are your medical books? And you must have books about health and development? What about books on Garhwal?"

Pradeep joined me beside the bookcase and replied, "I don't think I have any medical books. Wait a minute. . . . Here is one!" He pulled a slim volume with a cheap yellow cover off the shelf.

"*Orthopedic Appliances*," I said, reading the title. "Orthopedic appliances? What use would this be to you?"

"Oh, no use at all really," he said. "There was a doctor visiting who left it in the hospital. I've never looked at it. I no more have any interest in medicine—not for the last two years. Of course, I am continuously doing my medical work in the hospital, but that's not where my heart is. I am so much interested in my spiritual life."

A faraway look came into his eyes and he began to recount some of his experiences. In the past two years he had developed an intensive meditation practice, trying to achieve a state of bliss beyond mind and body.

Sivananda Ashram was a fertile field for such exploration. Swami Chidananda, the president of the Divine Life Society, was considered one of the greatest living Hindu sages in the world. Swami Krishnananda, the general secretary, was a scholar with a penetrating intellect, a leading expert on the ancient Vedanta scriptures. In this extraordinary atmosphere, Pradeep's fascination with spiritual philosophy flourished.

But the uneasiness within me began to grow. How well did I really know Pradeep? He had changed so much since I'd first met him. Gone was the fashionable young man in bellbottoms, smoking cigarettes, talking of Marxism. Now here was a serious young man wearing a simple cotton *salwar kurta*, who'd given up smoking and become a strict vegetarian. He seemed to have lost

interest in political ideologies, in Western literature and philosophy. He was still filled with passionate intensity, but now he spoke
only about his remarkable spiritual journey. When he described
his inner experiences and insights, I felt nothing but bewilder-
ment. No matter how intently I listened, I could not fathom the
depths of his spiritual life.

Soon after we'd settled into the ashram, Pradeep took me to
visit Sivananda Charitable Hospital. As we walked down the broad
stone steps leading to the main entrance, he told me that the busy
outpatient clinic was attracting more than a hundred patients a
day. We stepped into the central waiting area, which teemed with
activity. Village women clutched wailing infants, two orange-
robed swamis sat in stoic silence, an elderly man chewing betel
nut leaned against the far wall, a man in a tight-fitting polyester
shirt pushed his way through the crowd, ignoring the harried
swami at the registration desk.

I noticed two disheveled Western tourists standing hesitantly
on one side, a young man and woman wearing T-shirts and tattered jeans. The woman looked pale and exhausted, and I wondered if she was about to faint. The young man managed to find a
spot for her to sit, and she sank onto the bench, holding her head
in her hands.

An enormous portrait of Swami Sivananda dominated the
waiting room wall. Sitting cross-legged in his orange robes, he
beamed benignly down on the crowds below.

We threaded our way toward Pradeep's consulting room, the
crowd parting in waves to let us through. The room was furnished
with a heavy wooden desk and a row of chairs lining one wall.
A calendar with a brightly coloured picture of the elephant god
Ganesha adorned the far wall. On the desk lay a blood pressure machine, a jar of thermometers, a prescription pad, and a
stethoscope. I picked up the stethoscope. Its familiar weight and

contour was comforting, a precious talisman linking me back to a known world.

I sat next to Pradeep in the consulting room, watching closely as he conducted the morning clinic. I listened carefully to the conversations, but my grasp of Hindi was so poor that I understood only a few words.

Later that week, Pradeep took me to meet the two senior swamis of the ashram, Swami Chidananda and Swami Krishnananda. Swami Chidananda was deeply revered throughout India, an ascetic with finely drawn features and luminous eyes that radiated a gentle peace. He welcomed me to the ashram, and gave me a lovely woollen shawl.

Swami Krishnananda was quite different, his eyes bright with fiery energy and his manner abrupt. I was wary of Swami Krishnananda because I knew he had wanted Pradeep to take up the religious life, perhaps seeing a future for him as a senior swami within the ashram. He had been opposed to Pradeep's marriage, no doubt thinking married life was a waste of time for someone who had such spiritual potential. Pradeep had pointed out that the life of the householder, the *grihastha*, can be a challenging spiritual path in itself.

The senior swamis assumed that after Pradeep's marriage he would move out of the ashram and find accommodations in Rishikesh. But Pradeep wished us to continue to live within the ashram. Swami Krishnananda reluctantly agreed. We were the only married couple living in Sivananda Ashram.

I felt lost and disoriented in those early days. My surroundings were alien, the language incomprehensible, and the way of life unfamiliar. If I had hoped that life in the ashram would provide an easy path to understanding the Hindu religion, I was soon discouraged. The myriad images of gods and goddesses, the mystifying rituals, the chanting—all were bewildering.

"You can't be expecting to understand Hinduism in just a few weeks," said Pradeep. "It's a way of life really, not just a religion. Our music and art are all about the Divine. Even those Bollywood films—you've seen them—they're full of religious ideas."

I'd observed that spiritual ideas were intricately woven into the fabric of everyday life in India, in a seamless integration. But when I explored the borderland between spirituality and rationality, I felt profoundly unsettled. My Western education and upbringing had instilled within me a respect for rational thinking. Yet in Indian ways of thinking, rational explanations for many phenomena were overturned in favour of spiritual answers. For me, this devaluation created a chasm of cultural difference that separated me from my new world. Often, Pradeep himself stood on the opposite side of that chasm.

One morning, Pradeep said to me, "D'you know what? I can see your aura, all around your body."

"What do you mean, my aura?" I asked.

"Everyone has an aura—an energy field. The auras have different colours and you can tell a lot about a person from their aura."

"Really?" I answered, skeptically. "What can you tell me about me, then?"

"You have a deep blue and purple aura all around you. It tells me that you are a sweet, loving person who is very spiritual," Pradeep replied.

"Ha! You're just trying to butter me up," I said, trying to keep a light-hearted tone. "Of course, I agree I'm a sweet and loving person. But I'm not a spiritual person, not at all, really."

"Oh, yes, you are. I can see it," replied Pradeep earnestly. "And I can show you proof about auras. Look at this book I'm reading. It's about Kirlian photography. It's a special type of photography where you can actually see people's auras."

I picked up the book and glanced through it. Kirlian was a Russian chemist who accidentally discovered a process of "electrophotography." When photographs are taken in a high-voltage electrical field, coloured halos surround the human body. Apparently, many people believe that these halos represent auras.

"I don't think this is very convincing," I replied, with an edge to my voice. "It's probably just an artifact of the process he was using."

"No, his research has proved that auras exist," insisted Pradeep. "And, besides, when I look at someone I can see their aura myself. So of course this is a real thing."

I got up abruptly. "I'm hungry. Let's walk down to the Madras Café and grab something to eat."

Later the same day, I attended the gathering that Swami Krishnananda held for his devotees and visitors to the ashram. At eleven o'clock every morning, he gave a brief talk about some point of Vedantic philosophy and then answered questions. I followed the stream of devotees who filed silently into the room, and slipped to the back of the hall, trying to make myself inconspicuous. Pradeep had mentioned that some devotees from Japan were staying at the ashram, and about ten of this group entered the room and prostrated themselves before Swamiji.

I don't remember what point of philosophy Swami Krishnananda discussed that morning, but I never forgot the discussion afterward. I learned that the Japanese visitors belonged to a spiritual community in Japan and were on a pilgrimage to India to visit some of the great ashrams. One of them spoke in glowing terms about their own guru, the spiritual leader of their community.

"He is truly extraordinary," said the devotee. "He has many special powers—look at this!" He produced a photograph from within the folds of his orange robe and passed it around the audience. When the photograph reached me, I studied it with interest. An elderly man sitting in the classic cross-legged position of meditation—nothing special there. But then I noticed that he was not sitting on the floor. In fact, it appeared that he was floating a couple of feet above it!

When the photo reached Swami Krishnananda, he glanced at it briefly and handed it back to the Japanese devotee.

"Tell your guru that he is wasting his time," he said, in his abrupt way. "One can achieve many powers through meditation. But these powers are just a distraction. The seeker of the true path must turn aside from all of this. Seek unity with the Divine!"

Completely bewildered, I cast surreptitious glances around the room. Surely nobody really believed that the man in the photo was levitating? But everyone in the room was sitting silently, with beatific smiles on their faces. A few minutes later, the gathering ended. People prostrated themselves once again before Swamiji and filed out as silently as they had come in.

Walking away from the hall, I felt my head pounding and my stomach churning. Thoughts buzzed around my brain like hornets. *What is going on? Nothing makes sense to me. I feel as if I've entered a strange world where rationality has no place...*

Bells were clanging in the temple, mingling with the peculiar sound of a conch. The loud dissonance of the bells and the eerie sound of the conch evoked no spiritual feeling inside me; just a desire to get away from the noise. I hurried down the long staircase from the temple, not really knowing where I was going. The clanging began to fade, only to be replaced by the harsh dissonances of other sounds. Reaching the Rishikesh road, with the blare of truck horns and the spluttering of badly maintained vehicles, I took one look at the chaotic scene and quickly turned around to go back to the ashram.

Just then a voice called out, "You must be Pradeep's Canadian wife! Welcome!"

I whirled around, and saw a thin elderly man dressed in white, standing at the top of the flight of stone steps. He was smiling broadly and—wonder of wonders—spoke with an unmistakably Canadian accent!

Astonished, I walked over to introduce myself. "I'm Bill," he said. "My daughter, Susan, and I have been looking forward to meeting a fellow Canadian. Come and have a cup of tea with us."

I followed Bill to one of the older residential buildings in the ashram, where we entered a tiny room furnished with several rickety wooden chairs. Bill lit a kerosene stove and placed a pot of water on to heat. Susan, a woman about my age, soon joined us. Over cups of tea, Bill told me about the journey that had led him to India. He had worked for many years in Vancouver as a business executive in a financial company. His meetings with Swami Chidananda on Swamiji's visits to Canada had affected him greatly and, over the years, he became more and more drawn to the spiritual life. He told me a dramatic story about his decision to leave his life and his family. As his spiritual life deepened, he wondered whether he might leave Canada to follow Swami Chidananda to his ashram in India. But the idea seemed utterly impractical—he had a high-powered career, a wife, and four adolescent children. One morning while at work, an inner voice told him "QUIT NOW." The compulsion to follow this inner prompting was so strong that he handed in his resignation the next day. Within a few weeks, he arrived in India. Susan, who also had a strong spiritual calling, joined him several years later, and they had been living in the ashram ever since.

I shared a little of my story with Bill and Susan, talking about the parts of Canada I knew best. I'd grown up in Quebec, had attended university in Nova Scotia, and practiced as a family doctor in northern Ontario. Bill and Susan were from British Columbia, where I had been only once.

Before long, our conversation turned to an analysis of what we missed most about Canada (food seemed to figure largely in this discussion). What a relief it was to be with people from my own country again! Until that moment, I hadn't realized what a strain the past weeks had been for me, adrift in an environment where all familiar landmarks had disappeared.

The three of us soon established a habit of going for a daily walk followed by a shared cup of tea. One day, Bill asked me how I was finding life in the ashram. I didn't quite know where to begin. Hesitantly, I found myself talking about all the shocks I'd experienced since arriving, including the greatest shock of all—that the man I'd married seemed to be no longer interested in medicine.

"I thought that our life's work would be providing medical care to the poor and marginalized in the Himalayan foothills," I explained. "Yet Pradeep hardly thinks about this. He's a very good doctor—I know he is. But his heart is not in it. He's constantly thinking about spirituality, about meditation, about all kinds of philosophy that I don't understand at all."

Bill was silent for some time. Then he replied thoughtfully. "What you are telling me is that you had an expectation of Pradeep—a very clear expectation that he would share your passion for medical work. Am I right?"

"An expectation? Well, not exactly. I mean, I thought he did share my passion for medical work. He always talked about working as a doctor in the Himalayas. So I am just kind of shocked that he seems to have lost interest. How can you lose interest in your life's work?"

Bill nodded. "Do you think it's possible that things have changed? Perhaps he is on a new path, following a passion that is even deeper for him."

A long silence followed. Memories began to surface, creating a collage of images before my mind's eye. I recalled Pradeep sitting beside me on the steps of the tomb in Lucknow, saying, "I never wanted to be a doctor. I wanted to study Hindi literature and poetry only." I recalled him saying, "I hate God!" with an intensity that revealed a deeply held passion. I thought of his romantic letters, in which he shared the mythic image of the Cloud Messenger. Then I considered the choice he'd made to work here, in Sivananda Ashram, a community of seekers. I used to wonder what drove him, what gave him his inner intensity. Now I realized that his inner flame was his spiritual search. It always had been.

A sudden tide of anger surged within me. "Well, where does that leave me?" I asked bitterly. "I'm not interested in spirituality. And what about our medical work? And even our marriage itself—I don't want to be married to a monk!"

Bill looked at me compassionately. "Your work now is to understand the nature of your own discontent."

"What do you mean?" I asked in genuine puzzlement.

Bill replied, "So much of human unhappiness has to do with the failure of our expectations. We build up imaginary worlds in our minds, and then when we understand the illusory nature of these worlds we feel terribly disappointed."

"My relationship with Pradeep is not illusory. We really love each other," I said, heatedly.

"Of course you love him—but you also have a very specific idea of who he is. You are attached to that image you have created. But do you remember Swami Chidananda talking about the sorrows of attachment the other evening?"

"Yes, but I thought he meant being attached to wealth and status. Pradeep and I have given up all that."

"Wealth and status are attachments of a relatively superficial level. The deepest attachments spring from what we love, what we believe, what we dream about. You are attached to your idea of who Pradeep might be. When you discover that the reality is something different, you feel sorrowful. You feel angry. Your expectation of him has not been met."

"So what am I supposed to do?"

"Accept this new reality. Don't waste time grieving the failure of your expectations. That is not the spiritual life."

I sat silently, not knowing what to say.

Bill must have sensed my discomfort. "Pradeep is an excellent doctor. He's really respected here in the ashram. But I've seen great changes in him in the past two years. If you truly love him, you will support him on this path he has taken. And he will support you on yours, I'm sure. So now your task is to discover your own true path."

Silence fell. I gazed down into my cup of tea, thoughts whirling through my mind. *My own true path! How would I recognize it, and how would I know if I'd strayed from it? What if I never found it?*

I looked up, utterly confused. Bill gave me a compassionate smile, and said, "Why don't you participate a little in the life of the ashram? You could attend a morning class with Swami Brahmananda—I think he's one of the wisest swamis in the ashram. You'll learn a lot."

That evening, I thought about Bill's reflection about Pradeep and myself, turning his words over and over in my mind. I wondered if everyone has a true path in life, and if so, how many actually find it? What could I say about the path I was on? After pondering this point for some time, I finally concluded that, despite the confusion and difficulties of the past months, I had no regrets about coming to India. Whatever my true path was, it would be with Pradeep.

A few days later, I rolled out of bed at half past six. Leaving Pradeep peacefully asleep, I closed the door of our room quietly and crept down the stairs. Outside, it was still dark and icy winter air swirled around my shivering body.

Anybody who thinks India is always hot should visit the Himalayas in January, I grumbled to myself, pulling my shawl tightly around me. The ashram was already bustling with activity.

Many people had been up since 4:30, attending early-morning meditation in the *satsang* hall. As I walked down the steep slope to the main part of the ashram, I could hear the voices of women chanting *kirtan* in the temple.

Following Bill's instructions, I made my way to an older building where many of the senior swamis lived. A neat line of *chappals* was arrayed outside the door that led to Swami Brahmananda's room. I slipped off my sandals and stepped inside the little cell. Six people were sitting crosslegged on the floor facing an elderly, orange-robed man, who sat on his wooden cot with his eyes closed and hands folded. Beside the cot was a small metal bookshelf holding a photograph of Swami Sivananda and a large clay pot with a lid, on which was a brass drinking cup. I could see no shrine or religious image anywhere.

Bill had told me that Swami Brahmananda rarely left his room, living an austere, solitary life of contemplation. Unlike other senior swamis, he gave neither lectures nor public audiences. He was held in great reverence as a quiet, saintly presence.

I sat down on the thin mat behind the other devotees, closed my eyes, and waited. After about ten minutes of silence, Swamiji opened his eyes and murmured "*Hari Om*," the traditional greeting used in the ashram. All the devotees responded with the same words.

"Let us begin again," he said, picking up an old book with a worn green cloth cover. "We are studying the Katha Upanishad," he said, with a nod in my direction, acknowledging that I was new to the group. He began to recount a story from this ancient scripture, first reading from the Sanskrit text and then translating the meaning into English. I remember little about what he taught that first day. What lives in my memory is the remarkable aura of peace in that small room, enveloping us in an atmosphere of contemplation. Swamiji's voice was quiet and deep, and his command of English was nearly perfect. I enjoyed listening to the mysterious-sounding Sanskrit phrases, followed by Swamiji's fluid transitions from Sanskrit to English.

I began to attend Swami Brahmananda's class every morning, and soon I found myself drawn into the process of studying and discussing the text. The dialogue that followed his commentary was inevitably thought-provoking. I had never spent much time examining spiritual philosophy, but now I found myself drawn into these discussions about the deepest questions of life.

During one of my first visits, Swami Brahmananda asked me, "How did you come to Sivananda Ashram, on your spiritual journey?"

I replied earnestly, "Oh, Swamiji, I am actually not on a spiritual journey at all. I am here in India to do medical work, with my husband, Pradeep."

Swami Brahmananda looked at me curiously. Then a smile began to spread across his face, which soon turned into a chuckle. "Well, this is God's *leela* indeed," he said. "You have come to the holy heart of Hinduism and you do not even know that you are on a spiritual journey."

The word *leela* means "play on earth," and refers to a beautiful concept in the Hindu tradition that God enjoys playing with his human creations. For Swami Brahmananda, the idea that I was living in such a sacred place yet didn't perceive the spiritual nature of my journey was a lovely example of this *leela*.

Swamiji's comment gave me food for thought. I wondered if I was, indeed, on a spiritual journey, and that I might have something to learn in this ashram. By attending Swami Brahmanada's morning classes, a window opened in my mind, illuminating a world of ideas whose horizons were vast. The gods and goddesses of Hindu popular religion lived in this world, offering a portal into sacred space. Those people who chose to step through this portal could communicate with the Divine through symbols and rituals, drawn from an ancient mythological heritage. But

I realized that this sacred world had subtler dimensions as well, hidden behind the colourful images of the gods and goddesses. Scriptures dating back as far as 5000 BCE speak of the existence of a universal cosmic soul, the Brahman, which is beyond name and form. Then the goal of the individual spiritual seeker is to go beyond the material world in search of a mysterious union with that cosmic soul.

I realized that for a Vedantic scholar like Swami Brahmananda, the gods and goddesses of Hindu popular religion did not have much significance. His goal was to go beyond these names and forms in order to experience something eternal. As my understanding of Hindu philosophy deepened, I found it easier to talk to Pradeep about his experiences. I still didn't have much personal interest in meditation, but at least I had some way of comprehending Pradeep's passionate spiritual search.

After the early shocks of life in India had settled somewhat, my days in the ashram began to fall into a pleasant routine. The morning class was followed by a leisurely breakfast with Pradeep, which we often ate while sitting on our little balcony. Then Pradeep would go off to the hospital to begin his clinic. My priority was to learn Hindi, and I spent time every morning with Vijaya Mataji,[5] a long-term ashram resident. Her husband had been a devotee of Swami Sivananda and had worked in the ashram until his untimely death at a young age. Vijaya Mataji had lived in Sivananda Ashram ever since. She spoke no English, so initially our communication was challenging. My Hindi textbook, used in a well-known language school, provided the foundations of grammar and syntax. With the aid of a dictionary and sign language, I struggled to master conversational Hindi. Our lessons invariably ended with food. Vijaya Mataji brought out tea

....

5   Mataji means "mother" and is an honorific used for women living in the ashram.

and biscuits, or she prepared a delicious Indian meal. I marvelled at the gastronomic delights she could produce, squatting on the floor in front of a small kerosene stove.

In the afternoons, I walked down to the hospital to join Pradeep. I was able to put my feeble Hindi to the test by trying to take a medical history from patients in the clinic.

After the clinic closed, we often strolled down to the banks of the Ganga. Lining the near bank were scores of little shops selling books on spirituality, carvings of jade and crystal, Indian music cassettes, and innumerable cheap trinkets with a religious theme. The sensory experience of this walk by the Ganga overwhelmed me. We heard the blaring of Hindi devotional music, the imploring cries of beggars, the insistent cajoling of shopkeepers, the polyphonies of a dozen different languages spoken by pilgrims from all over the world. We saw the gaudy images of the Hindu gods and goddesses depicted in posters and on temple walls, the brilliant colours of clothing, the flashing of jewellery, and the turquoise blue of the Ganga. We smelled cowdung and dust, sandalwood incense and the spicy aromas of *samosas* and *dal*.

Pradeep and I would cross the bridge spanning the Ganga and roam along the opposite bank, sometimes sitting on the sparkling white sand. From this spot, I loved to watch the birds: swifts and redstarts swooping across the river, brown dippers diving into the water, and sandpipers pacing along the bank.

Two species of monkey shared our Himalayan domain. The langur monkeys looked like aristocrats wearing elegant grey fur coats, observing us with aloof disdain. The rhesus monkeys, on the other hand, were brash and bold. They roamed the ashram like terrorists, looking for unsuspecting victims.

One day we were walking home from the hospital, climbing a path up the steep hill that led to our home. A stone wall set against the bank of the hillside protected the path from obliteration during the monsoon season. I'd bought some fruit from the little market below the hospital, which I was carrying in a cloth bag slung over one shoulder. Pradeep and I were lost in a rarified world of spiritual philosophy, hardly noticing our surroundings. A sudden movement caught my eye. Before I could register what was happening, a monkey leaped off the wall and landed heavily on my shoulders. Gasping with shock, I lost my balance and stumbled forward onto the stony path.

Pradeep reached out to break my fall, while yelling furiously at the monkey. *"Bhaago! Hut jao!"*

Baring its teeth ferociously, the monkey yanked the cloth bag off my shoulder, bounded back onto the wall and then disappeared into the forest beyond.

"Are you alright?" Pradeep asked, helping me to my feet. Thoroughly shaken and close to tears, I brushed the dust off my clothes and tried to compose myself.

"I hate those stupid monkeys!" I exclaimed. "They are really dangerous. They bite and scratch and they even carry rabies."

"We should always be carrying a heavy stick with us," said Pradeep. "They usually stay away if they realize that we'll fight back."

"Why don't the ashram authorities hire someone to get rid of them? They should be destroyed. They're a real public health hazard," I said to Pradeep.

Pradeep looked shocked. "Oh no, that would never happen. Monkeys are sacred in India. You know that Hanuman, the monkey god, is worshipped. So how could we kill them?"

I sighed. *I should have seen that answer coming*, I thought.

Just a few days later, I had another encounter with a monkey. When I unlocked the door to our flat, I noticed that we'd left the door to the balcony open. I heard a scuffling sound in our kitchen, and approached cautiously. An enormous male monkey was sitting on the countertop, helping himself to fruit.

"Hey! Get the hell out of here!" I shouted. The monkey looked up indifferently, and then calmly went back to peeling another banana. Furious, I snatched a heavy book from the bookcase (it was Sri Aurobindo's *Adventure of Consciousness*) and flung it at the monkey. He ducked easily and the book slammed against the wall. The monkey gave an angry huff. Tucking several bananas under one arm, he hopped off the counter and waddled onto the balcony. He leaped onto the branch of a nearby tree with surprising agility, still keeping a firm grasp on his treasure of fruit. I retrieved the book from the kitchen counter and dusted it off with an apologetic glance at the portrait of Sri Aurobindo, who stared down at me balefully.

By the time Pradeep got home, I'd begun to see the humour in the situation. When I described the monkey's getaway, with the fruit tucked under his arm, we both burst out laughing.

Later that evening, we received a message that one of the elder swamis in the ashram was ill and required a visit. Swami Nadabrahmananda lived in a small set of rooms on the second floor of an older building in the ashram. He was in his late eighties, his mind sharp although his physical body was beginning to weaken. Blessed with great musical ability, he had been the court musician to the King of Mysore in his youth. He had married and had a family, but in midlife he had decided to take the vows of *sannyasa* and live in Sivananda Ashram. His brilliance as a musician, his spiritual depth, and his engaging personality made him beloved to a wide circle of devotees around the world. In his younger days, he had traveled widely.

When he heard I was from Canada, he smiled with delight and said, "Oh, yes. How I loved visiting your country!"

Pulling out a photo album, he flipped through some pages and then displayed photographs of himself in Jasper and Banff, with some of his Canadian devotees. There was Swamiji in a wintry Canadian landscape, wearing a bright orange parka and toque and smiling happily. The same infectious joy shone in his eyes now, despite his age and ill health.

Replacing the photo album onto the shelf, he asked me, "Would you like to see a moon rock?"

Without waiting for an answer, he opened the drawer of a small chest and removed an object wrapped in orange silk. A jet black, volcanic-looking rock tumbled out of the silken coverings. Apparently one of the lunar astronauts had been an admirer of Swamiji's and had given him this rock!

Pradeep finally brought us back to the original purpose of the visit—Swamiji's illness. Swamiji had been suffering from a bad cough with low-grade fever for the past few days. He had a condition known as bronchiectasis, in which pockets of tissue in the lungs become chronic sources of infection. Pradeep prescribed antibiotics and a cough expectorant, and said he would visit again in a few days. As we left Swamiji's room, my head was whirling. This world I had entered was confusing and mad—but how fascinating!

CHAPTER FIVE:

Learning To Dance

The reputation of Sivananda Hospital had been growing rapidly, and every day scores of patients lined up to be seen. Garhwali farmers and their families arrived from villages in the foothills on foot or by bus, local people came from the town of Rishikesh, swamis attended from the nearby ashrams. Dr. Kutty, the well-known specialist in gynecology, had a far-reaching reputation for treating women suffering from infertility. Elegantly clad wealthy women travelled across the country to consult her.

By the time I joined Pradeep in the ashram, he was seeing up to a hundred patients a day in the bustling outpatient department of the hospital. I wanted to assist him, but I needed a better grasp of Hindi and some practical knowledge of tropical disease and its treatment. To begin with, I simply sat next to Pradeep in his consulting room, listening to him as he took histories from patients. He would then translate for me and comment briefly on the diagnosis and treatment plan. Because there were so many patients to be seen, groups of eight or ten people were brought into the consulting room at a time. Nobody seemed to mind having their medical histories heard by the others in the room. Those who were waiting took a lively interest in the patient being seen, and often offered sympathy as well as advice.

Pradeep asked one patient, "So, you have worms? Are they long worms with round bodies or small worms with curvy bodies?"

The patient replied, "Long ones," indicating a length of about six inches.

The other patients waiting to be seen clicked their tongues in sympathy.

"Oh yes, I've had that kind," one of them said. "Nasty things!"

"Try eating *karela* (bitter gourd)," said another, eager to help. "That'll get rid of them."

As Pradeep wrote out a prescription for mebendazole, the antibiotic used to treat ascariasis (roundworms), I tried to prevent myself from giggling. The scene was so different from a consulting room in Canada.

During the first week I spent in the clinic, I saw conditions that I'd only read about in Canada. A mother brought in her two-year-old daughter who'd been suffering from high fever, a cough, and a widespread rash. Pradeep examined the child and showed me tiny white spots on the inner surface of her cheeks.

"They're Koplik spots, and so we know that this child has measles," he said. Noticing my surprised look, he said, "But you must have seen this many times before?"

In my Canadian practice, I had never seen a case of measles, a condition that has become rare ever since the vaccine against this disease was incorporated into routine immunization schedules.

The little girl in our clinic lay listless in her mother's arms. Her breathing was laboured and we wondered if she was developing pneumonia, one of the serious complications of measles. Without x-ray facilities, we had to depend on clinical judgment to make the diagnosis. We counted the child's respiratory rate and looked for indrawing of the muscles between the ribs, indicators of respiratory distress. Listening to her chest with a stethoscope, we could hear widespread crackles, another indication of pneumonia.

Pradeep prescribed a sulfa-based antibiotic, an inexpensive and effective treatment for most forms of community-acquired pneumonia in children. Liquid preparations of medications for children were beyond the budget of the hospital and our patients. Our compounder ground adult pills into a fine powder, worked out the dose according to the child's weight, and then packaged each dose individually into a small twist of paper. The mother could then mix the powder with a small amount of breast milk before administering it to her child.

After the woman and her child had left the consulting room, Pradeep called in the next set of eight patients. A young man dressed in a neatly pressed shirt and tightly fitting polyester pants walked in hesitantly and perched on the edge of the bench. I recognized immediately the universal bodily language of anxiety: his breathing was shallow and rapid, the tendons in his neck were sharply defined, his fingers were drumming restlessly against his leg. Our eyes met briefly, but he immediately looked away, blushing with embarrassment.

When his turn came, he pulled the stool close to Pradeep, and in a low, rapid voice, began to describe his problem. I lost the thread of the conversation almost immediately, and listened instead to the cadence of the dialogue. The patient's voice was strained and hurried, his words tripping over each other; Pradeep's voice was calm and reassuring.

The young man left, and we continued with the afternoon's patients: a child with dysentery, an adolescent with a chronic draining ear, an elderly man complaining of cough with bloody sputum, a boy with a gash on his leg. Pradeep dealt with each problem swiftly and efficiently—medications for the patients with dysentery and the draining ear, a chest x-ray for the man with the cough, a dressing for the boy with the gash on his leg.

"Well, that's it for today," Pradeep finally said, with a sigh of satisfaction. "We saw eighty-two patients altogether. Soon, we will be hitting our century mark every day."

After supper that evening, Pradeep and I took our cups of tea onto the balcony of our little flat. Pradeep began to read the latest issue of *The Times of India* while I dipped into Paul Brunton's book, *A Search in Secret India*. He was an English explorer who'd spent years in the Himalayas, meeting swamis and sages. He met some remarkable individuals, and his book about his experiences was enthralling. But that evening I couldn't concentrate.

"I still keep thinking of that little child," I said. "She was susceptible to disease because of her undernourished state, but also because she'd never been immunized against measles. Could we get a measles vaccination program going?"

"There is measles vaccine in our hospital. It's provided free from the government. And we are having all the other immunizations as well. But sometimes, parents refuse for vaccination. Especially for measles. Some people think that vaccination might harm their children. And other people feel that measles is an ordinary childhood disease and you should not prevent it."

Thinking about the afternoon clinic, I asked, "And what about that young man? He was so worried."

"He was feeling anxious because he was having nocturnal emissions of semen," replied Pradeep.

Puzzled, I replied, "But surely that's just a normal thing? Why would he worry?"

"Here in India, men are thinking that semen is something very precious. It is like the pure essence of the body. And they worry too much if they lose semen."

"So what did you tell him?" I asked.

"I asked him about his life. I knew that he must be going through many problems. His wife has TB and they can't afford the medications. He is afraid he will lose his job. And they have three daughters, but no sons. This is another worry for him. It always helps to talk about such problems, to relieve the mind of its burdens. And then of course I told him not to worry about the nocturnal emissions."

I lapsed into a thoughtful silence. I wondered if the complaint of nocturnal emission could be a sort of coded language of distress. Pradeep acknowledged the symptom, which was harmless, but then perhaps it served as a cue for him to probe more deeply into the man's life, and all its psychosocial problems.

Putting aside my speculations about the hidden meaning of symptoms, I went back to reading Paul Brunton's book. He wrote about swamis who practiced austerity for years, living in remote caves in the Himalayas, even during harsh winter weather. I thought it all sounded highly improbable.

"I find this book hard to believe," I said. "Did sadhus and holy men really meditate in caves in the Himalayas? Or is that more of a myth?"

"Oh, no, it's not a myth," replied Pradeep. "There's a cave not far from here where the famous sage Vashistha meditated for many, many years. It's a beautiful place. You will like it, I just know."

The following Sunday, Pradeep borrowed a motorbike from a friend, and we set off on our exploration. We followed the road that traces the course of the Ganga, the route we'd taken on our way to Gangotri. Along one side of the road stood huge *sal* trees, with their spade-shaped leaves, bearing silent witness to the beauty of the forest that once had been. Monkeys chattered from branches of oak trees entwined with creepers; birdsong filled the air. Far below us sparkled the turquoise river.

By noon, we reached the sacred site of Vashisth Gufa, the cave where the famous sage Vashistha lived and meditated, hundreds of years earlier. Pradeep pulled the motorcycle into some brush by the side of the road, and we picked our way down the overgrown path to the small temple near the mouth of the cave.

We slipped our shoes off and stepped into the gloom of the temple's interior. A stone *lingam* occupied the centre of the temple, marking this as a site for the worship of the god Shiva, creator and destroyer of the universe. Against the back wall, I could see a small recess in which were enshrined several sacred objects—a trident, a serpent, and a lotus. My studies with Swami Brahmananda helped me to understand the complex symbolism of these images, each representing a portal into sacred space.

Pradeep and I found a sunny glade just beyond the cave where we unpacked a picnic lunch. We sat in comfortable silence, enjoying the beauty of our surroundings. A grey hornbill perched on a branch of a nearby tree, its magnificent curved beak clearly visible against the dark green foliage. Tiny sunbirds flitted down from the forest canopy.

I finally broke the silence, saying, "Pradeep, the trip coming to this place was wonderful! Exploring this area by motorcycle is so different from travelling in a car."

"I want to go through the whole Himalayan foothills by motorcycle," said Pradeep enthusiastically. "Imagine—we will start in Sikkim or Bhutan, then we will travel to Darjeeling, then we'll drive all the way to this part of the mountains. And then we'd go on travelling to Kashmir."

"Yes, let's do it!" I replied, always ready for an adventure. "Maybe we could even plan it next year. You could find someone to take your place in the hospital for a few months."

That trip to Vashisht Gufa was the first of many short expeditions that Pradeep and I took during our first months of married life. The landscape surrounding Rishikesh was steeped with myth and legend. Every hill and valley had a special story.

A pilgrimage to this sacred land was a journey of significance for any devout Hindu, not just the wealthy and privileged. I often saw battered buses arriving in Rishikesh from faraway states, chartered by groups of pilgrims. These people were often very poor, but would save for years to afford a trip to this sacred place. There were several ashrams that offered accommodation for just a small donation, where people could unroll their bedding and sleep in huge open rooms.

At dawn, pilgrims rose early for the ritual bath in the sacred river, stepping carefully down the stone steps of the bathing *ghats*. The women managed to immerse themselves totally, without losing the slightest bit of modesty, by judicious draping of their saris. Later, they might visit some of the many temples clustered on both banks of the river, listen to discourses by both holy and not-so-holy men, and shop for little trinkets in the innumerable stalls lining the banks of the river. When they became ill, they would often find their way to Sivananda Hospital.

I enjoyed trying to guess which part of India the women were from by the style and manner of tying their saris. The Bengali women wore saris with beautifully patterned borders, the Rajasthani women wore bright cotton saris with tiny winking mirrors sewn into the fabric, and women from the western state of Maharastra draped the free end of the sari in front of the body rather than behind.

Seekers from Western countries also arrive in Rishikesh in search of spiritual sustenance, most of them poorly prepared for the rigours of life in India. They often came to the hospital with illnesses such as dysentery, jaundice, and malaria, and many were seriously ill by the time they came to consult us. Some of these seekers had drifted to India during the 1960s, when Maharishi Mahesh Yogi first constructed his ashram in Rishikesh. The Maharishi has long since left Rishikesh, but a few of those original seekers remain in the area. Living in caves or ramshackle huts along the beach, they had thrown away their passports long before and had no intention of ever returning to the West.

Late one afternoon, a young man arrived in the clinic for treatment of his chronic diarrhea. Wearing a thin orange loincloth, his hair matted into the locks of the wandering Hindu ascetic, he looked emaciated and ill. He had a parasitic infection and was clearly malnourished. He told us that he'd come to India from the US many years ago, but did not offer any further information about his life. I didn't press him for details about his spiritual practices. Perhaps through rigorous deprivation he was attempting to go beyond the physical body to an experience of pure spirit. This denial of the body is a theme within Hinduism that manifests as ascetic practices that have achieved worldwide notoriety. Some ascetics achieve remarkable control over their physical bodies through practices that seem to defy the limits of human physiology.

Could the young man in our clinic be following this ancient tradition of "mortification of the flesh" in his spiritual search? As Pradeep wrote out a script for medication to treat his parasites and offered suggestions about diet, I observed the man surreptitiously. *He just looks ill to me. His eyes are so vacant and dull. Surely this could not be a way to seek the Divine?*

I had no time to discuss this with Pradeep, because the next patient needed attention—he was an older man with an open, bleeding wound on his lower leg. In the four months since I'd begun my hospital work, I'd learned many medical terms in Hindi. I'd also learned the elements of grammar from Vijaya Mataji, my Hindi teacher. Now it was time to attempt to communicate directly with a patient using my meagre language skills. After examining this man's wound, I said to him, "*Ap dispensary jaiye— vahan patti lagwaienge.*" I was fairly sure that my instruction to go to the dispensary to have a bandage applied to the wound was grammatically correct, and I felt a flush of excitement at this first attempt at medical communication.

However, the patient looked bewildered.

"You've told him to go to the dispensary and have a leaf applied to the wound," said Pradeep, trying to hide a smile.

I had used the word *patti*, which can mean either leaf or
bandage depending on the way the T sound is pronounced. The
letters T, P, S, and R have several variants in their Hindi pronunciation, each with subtle differences. Without a grasp of these
nuances, the new learner will not just mispronounce words but
unintentionally say words that mean something entirely different from what was intended. As time went on, I learned to avoid
words that were particularly difficult to pronounce.

I continued to go to the hospital every day with Pradeep, and
often would also attend Dr. Kutty's morning clinic. I soon realized
what a remarkable opportunity that was, because Dr. Kutty was a
gifted teacher as well as a brilliant physician. By seeing patients
with her, I began to learn about a range of women's reproductive
health concerns in Garhwal. Many women had conditions I'd often
seen in my Canadian practice—menstrual problems, uterine pro-
lapse, menopausal syndrome, infertility. Although the treatment
approach was different in India, the underlying pathophysiology
was the same. However, other conditions were more difficult to
understand. Many women consulted us for an illness they termed
"safed panni" (white water). Their chief concern was vaginal discharge, accompanied by back pain, dizziness, and burning hands
and feet. I was puzzled by this condition, which did not seem to fit
any particular biomedical diagnostic category.

A thin woman wearing a faded cotton sari came to the clinic
one day, accompanied by her mother-in-law and husband.
Speaking in a soft whisper, she said that she was suffering from
"safed panni," and that she was getting weaker every day.

Dr. Kutty took her into an inner room, where she checked
the woman's heart and lungs and then did a pelvic examination.
Afterward, she called the woman's husband and mother-in-law
into the consulting room.

"Look at your wife!" Dr. Kutty shouted at the husband. "Can't you see how weak she's become? How are you treating her? Making her work day and night, I suppose?"

Turning to the woman's mother-in-law, she asked angrily, "And what type of food are you giving her? Dry *rotis* and tea?"

Dr. Kutty was a formidable character, and when she was in a rage she was terrifying. The woman's husband literally shook as he stood before her. The mother-in-law tried hesitantly to respond to Dr. Kutty's question, but she was silenced by a peremptory wave of her hand.

"Don't give me any excuses! I want to see some changes! You must make sure that this young woman gets enough food and enough rest. She must take this medication for two months and then I want to see her back again. Don't you know how dangerous *safed panni* is? Foolish people!"

Stunned, I watched as Dr. Kutty wrote out a prescription for calcium and multivitamins with iron. After the patient and her family had left, I tried to make sense of what had just taken place.

"What was wrong with her?" I asked.

Dr. Kutty replied, "These village people worry so much about these symptoms. They think they have a disease, so serious that they can die from it. The real problem is that these women are overworked and underfed. And of course their personal hygiene is poor. You'll see—she'll be much better in two months."

My brain swirled in confusion. I'd never seen a condition like this in my medical work in Canada, and the symptoms just didn't make sense to me. When I met Pradeep for lunch that day, I described the woman who'd attended Dr Kutty's clinic, and asked him for an opinion.

"This problem of *safed panni* is very common in India," he said. "In Lucknow we were also seeing many women like her."

"But a condition like that doesn't even exist in Canada," I said. "It's as if people's cultural background affects the way they experience their bodies – even someone's symptoms can be different depending on the culture they grew up in. Isn't that amazing?"

Pradeep replied, "Maybe it's because we people in India never used to think of the body like a machine with lots of parts. We think of the body as having flows of energy – something that is always changing. It's a different idea completely."

As we walked back down to the hospital, I was lost in thought. *Perhaps to become an effective doctor in India, I'll need to decipher the language of the body... I suspect this is a skill far more subtle than simply learning to speak Hindi.*

My musings about the cultural meaning of symptoms halted abruptly with the arrival of the first patient of the afternoon. A thin woman wearing a tattered sari walked hesitantly into the clinic, saying that her daughter was suffering from *kumjori* (weakness). The child lay against her mother's shoulder, her eyes dull and lifeless. She was wrapped in a ragged blanket that covered most of her body, but her arms encircling her mother's neck were emaciated. We asked the woman to undress the child so we could weigh her. When I saw her wasted little body, I tried to suppress a gasp of shock. She weighed a bare five kilograms, although she was nearly fifteen months old.

We learned that her family were refugees from Bangladesh, and they lived in flimsy shanties constructed on the banks of the Ganga just outside Rishikesh. These people had watched their land and homes wash into the Bay of Bengal when a terrible cyclone hit the coast of Bangladesh several years earlier. They eked out a bare living working as labourers in the area, and many of their children were malnourished.

"What are you giving her for her *kumjori*?" we asked.

"I have good medicine for her, very good, very costly," whispered the woman, taking a small medicine bottle out of the cloth bag she carried.

Filled with a bright red liquid, the bottle had a colourful label displaying a fat, healthy baby. I knew something about these "tonics", top-selling items in medicine shops across India. They contain a mix of multivitamins and minerals, although the vitamins contained in the tonic could be obtained for a fraction of the cost in tablet form. What these children really require is better food, and more of it.

The Bangladeshi refugee child did improve slowly. We treated her intestinal parasites and encouraged her mother to give her supplemental food in a form that she could digest. She gradually put on some weight and began to look more like a little girl than a wasted ghost. One day when Pradeep and I were walking to town, we passed the squalid refugee colony where this girl and her family lived. Shacks made out of tin and plastic sheeting clung to the sloping banks of the river, occupying land that nobody else would want to use. During the monsoon season these fragile dwellings could easily be washed away. I wondered what it would be like to live so close to the edge of disaster. But these people, having already faced the worst, seemed to have tapped into a core of resilience that allowed them to keep going in the face of all odds.

Just then we heard a voice calling a greeting, and we caught sight of the mother of the little malnourished girl waving to us. Picking our way across the muddy riverbank, we reached the shack where she stood, the child perched comfortably on her hip. She asked if we would have a cup of tea with her. We squatted outside the shanty, watching as she filled a battered pot with water and lit a kerosene stove. A neighbour's son was sent to buy two hundred millilitres of milk for the tea—a luxury that the refugees could seldom afford. We asked the woman to tell us about their long journey from Bangladesh. She told us about their trek, describing how they had travelled for weeks on foot across the vast expanse of North India, carrying their children and their meagre possessions.

"Why did you decide to stay here in Rishikesh?" I asked. She was silent for some time, and then suddenly smiled. "Look!" she said.

We gazed down the river in the direction she pointed. People with the pinched look of desperate poverty squatted outside ugly shacks crowded along the muddy riverbank. A few emaciated stray dogs nosed around heaps of refuse on the outskirts of the colony. But beyond the squalor of our immediate surroundings was the river Ganga. Shimmering blue-green water contrasted with dazzling white sand of the beaches on the far bank, where wild elephants still roam the dense forest. Following the sweep of the river, we gazed at the distant contours of the Himalayan foothills.

"It's beautiful, isn't it?" whispered the woman by our side.

We nodded slowly. Yes, to live near such beauty is indeed a privilege, even from the vantage point of that desperate poverty.

Pradeep and I walked back home quietly, both of us lost in thought. I felt as if I'd received a great gift from that woman, the insight that even in the face of gruelling hardship, beauty still has meaning.

A few weeks after this visit, Pradeep suggested that we make a trip to a hill village beyond Rishikesh. He was interested in extending the work of the clinic into the rural areas, and had been discussing this idea with the *sarpanch* (head man) of a village called Neer Gaon. One Sunday, we made plans to visit. We packed a medical kit with an assortment of standard medications, a field notebook, snacks and water for the journey, and my Minolta camera. After we'd traveled for about four kilometres by motorbike, we came to the start of a winding path leading up into the mountains. Pradeep parked the bike in a secluded spot just off the road. He had arranged to meet a village man at that same place, and he was waiting for us when we arrived. Two mules were standing by his side, their long ears flicking away flies.

Half an hour later, Pradeep and I were winding our way up a steep switchback trail on the backs of the mules, obliging creatures that knew exactly where they were going. As we climbed higher, we enjoyed splendid views of the Ganga, curving in sinuous loops through the forested land far below us. Lush green vegetation bordered the trail on both sides, and in the distance we caught glimpses of waterfalls. This village is blessed with abundant fresh water, unlike so many others in the region.

Pradeep told me that the last time he had come to this village a snake had slithered across the path right in front of him. The words from a guidebook to the Garhwal region flashed into my mind: "In Garhwal, there are approximately one hundred and five species of snakes. Only ten of these are deadly poisonous."

When we reached the village, we were greeted by the *sarpanch* and several other village men and women. We climbed a flight of narrow stone steps to reach the roof of the *sarpanch's* house, where an elderly man sat in the sun smoking a hookah. The *sarpanch's* wife appeared and offered us tea. I asked if I could have mine without sugar, an unusual request in Garhwal where the tea is usually served very sweet. Hundreds of red chillies were laid out on the roof to dry in the sun, and one of the women asked me if I liked chillies in my food.

"No, I can't eat food with chillies," I replied.

The old man smoking the hookah chuckled.

"Without sugar and chillies, what is the fun of life?"

This remark broke the ice, and before long we were all chatting comfortably. My Hindi was still too poor to follow most of the conversation, especially since we were not discussing purely medical matters. In social situations, I was only able to trot out a few stock phrases that I had learned for that purpose, though I had become quite skilled at inquiring about matters such as diarrhea and vomiting.

Pradeep remarked, "It must be difficult if somebody becomes ill in this village. It is a long way to reach our hospital, and even longer if you need to get to a big hospital where surgery could be done."

"That is true," said one of the men. "But don't forget, we have people here in the village who can do things. We have our *dai* who takes care of our women during delivery. She also makes medicine from herbs she gathers in the jungle. And the pundit of our village can do a lot. Today, he was treating a man who has fits. You can ask him how he does it."

After tea was over, one of the village men led us along the narrow path between the houses, which were mostly constructed with stone walls and heavy slate roofs. A few houses were built in a more modern style and had flat concrete roofs. Most of the traditional Garhwali dwellings were double-storied, with stables for the animals on the ground floor, and living quarters for an extended family above.

The pundit, a thin man in his late fifties, wore the homespun cotton clothes of the Garhwali villager. We spent some time exchanging greetings in the polite way that mountain people have. When we asked him if he could tell us a bit about his work with sick people, he readily agreed.

"Some get ill because of too much heat or too much cold. Others get sick because somebody else is angry with them and puts a curse on them. And then other people get sick because of a bad spirit. Maybe that spirit is from an ancestor who is angry about something that has happened in the family. Sometimes, we don't know why a spirit descends on the person and causes illness. But in these cases, my treatment is needed."

"But how do you know that an illness is caused by a spirit?" asked Pradeep.

"Many ways, many ways," responded the pundit, evasively. "Of course I know that you doctors do not believe in this. But I have seen the effects of bad spirits, and I know that I can treat them."

"Can you tell us what you do exactly?" Pradeep asked.

The pundit was silent for a few moments. Then he replied, "No, this is something that I cannot tell you. If someone falls sick and I am needed, then I can show you. But the power is not in the telling, the power is in the doing."

After this cryptic remark, he would say nothing more on the subject. I was intensely curious to learn more about this way of understanding illness, but I'd have to wait for another opportunity.

On our way down the mountain later that day, my mind was filled with thoughts about what I'd seen and heard that day. *I can learn so much about the women of Garhwal by making these village visits. I'll be able to see each woman in her own context, and learn about how she feels, what she loves, what she dreams about. Surely that will help me understand her health needs.*

The trail opened onto a small grassy patch of land, and we decided to take a break to stretch our legs. The mules were glad to be rid of their human burdens, and began to crop the grass contentedly.

Pradeep said, "Don't you think it would be good if we could extend our work into villages like these? It would be really good, especially for our TB program. You know, a lot of the patients we diagnose with TB stop the medication before the full course of treatment is completed. And it's not because of cost – the government provides TB medicine free. I think we need to follow up with people after they start treatment."

I felt a thrill of excitement. "Yes, what a great idea! It would be our first step to reach out to the villages. We must discuss it with Dr Kutty."

That evening, we relaxed on our balcony in a contented silence. I was excited about the events of the day, and particularly about my most recent conversation with Pradeep. *I think he really is interested in the health program. And he's such a good doctor – I am learning so much from him about medical practice in rural India.*

Every day, I observed Pradeep closely as he saw patients in the clinic. He had an excellent reputation as a physician, partly because of his natural rapport with patients and his gift of being able to explain a complex medical problem in simple language. Because my knowledge of Hindi was still fragmentary, I initially assumed that I wouldn't learn much from observing clinical encounters. Taking a medical history is all about language—or so I thought.

As a medical student, I was taught to sift through the patient's description of illness to glean clues to make a diagnosis. Our early interviews were done in the hospital, where we learned to narrow down a diagnosis through an increasingly sophisticated process of history-taking. Chest pain could be due to stomach problems, muscular strain, or a heart condition. Ankle swelling could be due to congestive heart failure or a kidney problem. By understanding patterns of symptoms, we usually could arrive at a diagnosis, even before any tests were done. We used language, but in a very specific way. While we learned to tease out a medical diagnosis, we were also learning to tune out details about the patient's experience of illness.

Even at that early stage of my training, I felt dissatisfied with this process of history-taking. *Where is the human being in these accounts of illness? Where is the richness of their story? I think patients want to describe their suffering, not just their physical symptoms. They want to describe struggles to overcome disability and loss, their defeats and their triumphs...*

At Sivananda Hospital, I saw the struggle on a patient's face as he tried to make sense of his suffering, and I watched how Pradeep responded to him. I began to see the medical encounter as a delicate dance, a subtle communication beyond language.

Both the patient and the doctor have roles to play. The initial steps are choreographed—the patient describes the symptoms of illness and the doctor asks for clarifying details. Then a new movement in the dance begins. The patient puts forth an idea about the cause of the illness, and the doctor offers a biomedical explanation. The dance takes on subtle dimensions as the patient and doctor search for a way to fall in step with each other. Even without understanding the intricacies of the Hindi dialogue, I could observe this dance unfolding before my eyes. The patient's questions swirled around the room—he wants to know what the illness is, and how he fell ill. But the more profound question hovers like a shadowy figure on the stage: Why has this happened? Why now in my life?

I studied Pradeep as he played his part in this dance, observing the subtle language of his body. Sometimes, he leaned forward to give a reassuring touch; at other times he drew back, a slight frown crossing this face. I listened to the tone of his voice—sometimes calm, sometimes soothing, sometimes challenging. He and the patient seemed to move together, in a continuous flow that had both rhythm and poise.

I recognized when the dancers reached an agreement and formed a plan—the moment was almost palpable. Observing the patient, I heard a deep exhalation and saw his neck and shoulders relax. A brief silence fell. Then Pradeep picked up his pen to write out a prescription and some instructions: the closing scene of the drama.

After the clinic was over, Pradeep and I walked across the bridge spanning the river. Reflections of the setting sun danced on the rippled surface of the water. As we sipped our tea at a riverside shop, I thought about my new perception of the medical encounter. The dance between doctor and patient seemed both profound and mysterious, opening lines of communication more eloquent than language.

My cross-cultural quest had taken on another dimension. I had begun to explore the culture of medicine, going beyond the boundaries of a purely biomedical view of the body to a more nuanced understanding of the human experience of living within a body, in all its mystery and depth.

CHAPTER SIX:

At Home In Garhwal

By early February, fresh green leaves were appearing on the trees behind our apartment block, and lilies and cosmos blossomed in the gardens. New life was springing up in our lives as well—I was expecting our first baby. When I realized I was pregnant, worries crowded my mind. *Wasn't this too early in our married life for a pregnancy? Would I be safe? How could I care for a baby in India?* These concerns buzzed around my head like angry hornets. Yet when I told Pradeep about the pregnancy, he simply said, "How wonderful!" As I relaxed into his embrace, I realized the truth of his words. Yes, this gift of new life is truly something wondrous.

I continued my routine of studying Hindi and going to the hospital, but I did cut out most of those early-morning classes so I could sleep a bit longer. I began to wear a sari every day, discovering they are very convenient garments for pregnant women. I had no need of maternity clothes. I could simply let out pleats as my belly swelled!

We spent hours talking on those long evenings, our conversation ranging from the mundane details of everyday life to the most esoteric experiences of spiritual life. Pradeep's passionate interest in life's great questions of meaning was deepening as each day passed.

"You know, when I first came to Sivananda Ashram, I started to attend some of Swami Krishnananda's lectures. I learned a lot from him about the philosophy of Vedanta. But my best teacher is Sri Aurobindo. He was a great master," he said, gesturing to the photograph hanging on our bedroom wall. I looked up at the photo of Sri Aurobindo, noticing his lined face, white hair and deep, serious eyes.

"I've tried to read his books, but his philosophy is way too obscure for me. And in that photo he looks so sad. Perhaps it's not a good idea to think too deeply about life," I said, a slightly flippant note in my voice.

Pradeep leaned forward, saying eagerly, "You must understand what he was trying to do. He was trying to explain how everything in this world links together. He was explaining the evolution of consciousness."

I found this concept mind-boggling. After some moments of silence I finally asked, "So is he your guru?"

"No, not at all. I will never have a guru, only teachers along the path. I want to explore on my own. That's what I learned from J Krishnamurti. Be your own guide!"

Several of J Krishnamurti's books lined our bookshelves. I'd read them, and they were a little easier to understand than Sri Aurobindo's writings. But I found all this philosophy esoteric, and I was unable to relate the concepts to my daily life. Yet clearly, Pradeep was finding his spiritual search of great practical benefit. He'd begun to experiment with meditation techniques, often spending many hours in intense practice. He experienced the profound effects of calming the mind, and discovered that meditation affected his body, as well. The headaches he'd been suffering for several years disappeared completely, and he felt much more centred.

He often tried to describe his rich inner journey to me. I listened with fascination, but I found his experiences difficult to understand. On one particular evening, we became entangled in an intense philosophical discussion that threatened to degenerate into an argument. Frustrated by my inability to understand his inner world, I walked out onto the balcony, my head spinning.

Pradeep joined me a few minutes later, and we said nothing more about spirituality or philosophy. Wanting to change the subject, I said, "Tomorrow's Sunday. The clinic's closed. How about if we go somewhere, do something different?"

Pradeep agreed immediately. "Why don't we go exploring? There's a village just a few kilometres from here, up on those hills behind the ashram. You get there by walking along a jungle trail. I'm sure it would be beautiful."

Aside from our visit to the village of Neer Gaon, I still had little experience of the lives of ordinary Garhwalis. Just a few days before, we'd seen a group of women carrying huge bundles of grass walking up a trail that led off the road behind the ashram. Talking this over, we concluded that must be the path to the village. I squeezed Pradeep's hand, my frustration about our earlier argument dissolving.

The weather was perfect on the day of our expedition, and I felt a thrill of joy as we stepped into the brilliant sunshine to begin our hike. We walked about half a kilometre along the road behind the ashram, and then set off into the jungle following the narrow path. Birdsong filled the air: the busy chatter of the babblers, the sweet notes of the thrush, and the cawing of the magpies. I spotted a magnificent Flame of the Forest tree, its orange blossoms just beginning to open. Pradeep pointed out a tamarind tree, which in several months' time would produce the long tamarind pods that are used to flavour many Indian dishes.

Just then we heard the sound of women's voices. A little farther down the path, we caught sight of two village women wearing bright cotton saris, standing at the foot of a tall oak tree. One of the women wrapped the free end of her sari around her waist and then between her legs, tucking it in at her waist. Her sari was thus transformed into a baggy pantaloon. Then to my astonishment, she began to clamber rapidly up the tree, using her small sickle to help her get a grip on the trunk. She climbed about thirty feet, eventually reaching a sturdy branch. Crawling along the branch, she began to hack at the leafy twigs with her sickle, sending them fluttering to the ground. With her task done, she climbed back down as quickly as she had gone up. Then, she unwound the end of her sari from between her legs and carefully re-draped it over her left shoulder.

"Can you believe that she just climbed a tree wearing a sari?" I whispered to Pradeep. "It's incredible!"

The second woman had been gathering the leafy branches into a huge bundle. She tied the load securely with rope and then hoisted it onto her back.

"You should feel how heavy those bundles are," said Pradeep. "The leaves of those branches are fodder for their animals."

The image of those hill women climbing the tree and then carrying that heavy bundle of leaves lingered in my mind, a poignant illustration of the drudgery that women in the mountains endure. Lost in thought, I followed Pradeep along the path as it wound slowly upward.

An hour later, we came across a clearing within the forest in which a *Peepal* tree stood. This tree is considered sacred throughout India and is always protected. Beneath the tree was a small shrine, which contained a crudely carved image of a Shiv *lingam*. Beside the image were offerings of fresh leaves and a few pieces of the white sugar candy called *batasha* that is often used in worship. The stone image glistened slightly, and I realized that it must have been recently bathed in water.

"Village women come and worship at little shrines like this one. You can find them all over Garhwal," murmured Pradeep.

I gazed at the shrine, thinking about the contrast between this simple worship of a sacred object and the lofty Vedantic concepts of Divine Unity, beyond all name and form.

"Hinduism seems like a huge tree whose trunk is the truth of Vedantic teachings, but that tree has hundreds of branches. Each of those branches is a different way of religious thinking," I said.

Pradeep's eyes lit up. "Yes, you are so right! And under the shade of that enormous tree, millions of people find shelter."

We sat quietly in that peaceful glade for some time until we noticed that the afternoon sun was beginning to fade. We started our journey back to the ashram, having decided not to continue on to the village. A wave of peace washed over me. Once again, I had the feeling of being "in place," where I was supposed to be in the world.

That evening, we sat on our balcony till long after sunset, listening to the noises of the jungle surrounding us. Monkeys chattered in the trees, and below us we heard the raucous cry of a peacock; a nesting pair lived behind our building. A tiny chirping sound came from just behind us, where sparrows had built a nest on one of our windowsills. The chicks had hatched a couple of weeks earlier, and we'd been watching them grow.

"India is just teeming with life, isn't it?" I said. "Wherever you look, you'll find some form of life, even on our windowsill."

"But you are not so fond of all forms of life," said Pradeep, with a grin.

He was referring to my nemesis, cockroaches. Our kitchen sink drained through a plastic pipe into an open drainage hole in the floor. Cockroaches would emerge from this hole and scuttle around the kitchen. I hated them. On the advice of a neighbour, I bought a Flit gun that had a plastic container that could be filled with insecticide connected to a spray nozzle. I would spray insecticide around the opening to the drainage hole. Any adventurous cockroach that ventured past the insecticide barrier would risk being stamped to death when I did my nightly cockroach patrol. Pradeep was puzzled by my vehement hatred of cockroaches, and asked mildly, "But surely all creatures have a right to live?" My withering stare silenced him, and he quickly retreated behind his book.

One night, I awoke feeling thirsty, and I padded to the kitchen to get a glass of water. I heard a faint rustling noise, and flicked on the light. To my horror, I saw dozens of cockroaches on the kitchen wall, each paired up and locked in an amorous embrace.

"No! No! Absolutely NO WAY!" I yelled furiously, and made a dive for the Flit gun. Pradeep, startled out of sleep, leaped from the bed to find out what disaster had befallen me. Frantically, I sprayed the cockroaches and then crushed them with a heavy steel container when they fell off the walls. Many escaped, scuttling down the drainage hole. I pursued them relentlessly, spraying insecticide recklessly around the kitchen.

Finally, the last cockroach disappeared. I put down the Flit gun and burst into tears. Pradeep patted my back sympathetically, wisely saying nothing about the sanctity of all forms of life. After this episode, word must have spread throughout the cockroach community. Never again did they return to indulge in orgies on our kitchen wall.

Though I hated cockroaches, I was fond of geckos, small lizards that live quite peacefully on the walls of Indian homes. We had a particularly fine specimen who'd taken up residence behind the tube light on our bedroom wall. I enjoyed watching him emerge from his cozy house and scuttle around the wall catching insects. One day, I'd been sitting on the balcony reading and enjoying the late evening breeze. As dusk fell, I picked up my book and walked into the bedroom, closing the balcony door firmly behind me. Looking down, I saw that our little gecko had also been outside enjoying the breeze. To my dismay, I realized that I'd closed the door on its tail, amputating it! The gecko, looking quite peculiar without this appendage, scuttled up the wall and disappeared behind the tube light.

Pradeep was unconcerned. "You'll see, he'll grow a new one before long," he said. Over the next few weeks, I watched with interest as the gecko gradually grew another tail. He didn't seem to bear a grudge against me, and continued to live contentedly in his home behind the tube light.

I continued my classes with Swami Brahmananda, and occasionally went to Swami Krishnananda's morning class. After this class one day, I heard participants talking about an upcoming event of great significance. In April, the *Kumbh Mela* was to be held in Hardwar, the sacred town just a few kilometres from Rishikesh. I learned that the *Kumbh Mela* is a religious gathering of epic proportions, attracting upward of fifteen million people.

The mythic origin of *Kumbh Mela* springs from an ancient tale about a great battle between gods and demons for possession of an urn (*kumbh*) that contained the nectar of immortality. During the battle, drops of this nectar fell at four places—Allahabad, Hardwar, Nashik, and Ujjain—and it is at these places that the Kumbh Mela is held, rotating among the four sites in a twelve-year cycle. Saints, *sadhus,* and sages from all over India attend the Mela, along with groups of their devotees. Pilgrims listen to spiritual discourses, join in prayers and the chanting of *kirtan.* The highlight of the pilgrim's visit to the *Mela* is a sacred bath in the Ganga, which is believed to sanctify one's life and thereby acquire good *karma,* or spiritual merit.

As the time of the *Mela* approached, Sivanand Ashram was charged with an atmosphere of excitement and anticipation. Since the Divine Life Society is so well known, a large camp would be set up in a prime location on the *Mela* grounds for those of us who wished to attend. Both Swami Krishnananda and Swami

Chidananda would be present, as well as the senior swamis from all the surrounding ashrams. It would be a rare opportunity to mingle with some of the most revered saints and sages of India.

The *Mela* began in April 1986, and continued until mid-May. I was already five months pregnant, but I felt well and looked forward to the event. Dr. Kutty offered to let us stay in her tent—luxurious accommodation for a *Kumbh Mela* pilgrim. An enormous tent city had mushroomed on the grounds near the banks of the Ganga, complete with roads, streetlights, food-distribution posts, and medical facilities. Wandering through the site on our first evening, Pradeep and I were swiftly drawn into a whirl of sights and sounds. The music of *kirtans* blared out from loudspeakers and hawkers enticed us with spicy *samosas* and *channa bhoona*. White-robed acolytes pressed religious tracts into our hands; men in ragged clothes sold balloons and toys.

Large open tents were set up for each spiritual teacher attending the *Mela*. Most were male swamis wearing the familiar orange robes, but there were some female teachers who attracted large crowds. In one tent, a white man with matted hair and orange robes was holding forth on some point of spiritual philosophy. He spoke in English and had an unmistakable North American accent. I wondered about his life's journey, and how he had found his way to this remote place.

We saw a thin young woman wearing a faded cotton sari shepherding her three young children through the crowds.

"Village people like her, how do they get here and where do they stay?" I asked Pradeep.

He replied, "You wouldn't believe it, but people from villages will save up their money for years so that they can come to the *Kumbh Mela*. They just sleep on the ground in huge encampments."

"What if one of those children slips out of her sight?" I asked. "In this crowd of millions of people, how would she ever find the child?"

"That happens quite often," said Pradeep. "D'you know that teenage boy who helps out in the ashram kitchen? He was a little boy who got lost in the *Kumbh Mela* that was held in Hardwar in 1974. Somebody brought him to the Sivananda Ashram camp. They were never able to find his family, and when the *Mela* ended, Swami Chidananda had to bring him back here. He's been living at the ashram ever since."

The next morning, the camp bustled with activity. Ashram residents prepared to join a huge procession through the Mela grounds, along with devotees from all the other ashrams. Swami Chidananda led the Sivananda Ashram contingent, walking with grace and dignity. Revered throughout India, Swami Chidananda attracted huge crowds of devotees who tossed flower petals in his path and prostrated themselves before him. Behind Swami Chidananda walked many of the other senior swamis of the ashram, followed by the younger swamis and then the white-robed spiritual aspirants who had not yet taken the orange cloth. After that came an assortment of other ashram residents, including Pradeep and me.

"*Hari Om!*" cried the pilgrims lining the path, bowing humbly and trying to touch the feet of all those in the procession. As they rushed forward to offer me their salutations, I tried not to giggle, feeling like an utter fraud!

From my position near the end of the Sivananda procession, I caught glimpses of many other processions converging from various parts of the Mela grounds. All had one destination: the bathing *ghats* beside the holy river. I recognized the banners of several other ashrams in Rishikesh, including the Yoga Niketan ashram just down the road and the Parmath Niketan ashram located on the other bank of the river. Pradeep nudged me, pointing out another procession approaching from a different direction. No colourful banners fluttered at the head of this extraordinary group, which was comprised of naked men smeared with ash.

"They are the *Naga Sadhus*," whispered Pradeep. "Most of them live by themselves in caves in the Himalayas. It's only during the *Kumbh Mela* that you ever see them together."

At the bathing *ghat,* each procession moved slowly down the steps to the water. As the participants immersed themselves in the holy Ganga, fervent cries of "*Hari Om!*" split the air. Observing the blissful faces of the people around me, I wondered if I could ever experience a spiritual moment in such a profound way. My Western brain, programmed into patterns of rationality and skepticism, may have lost forever the capacity to access this kind of pure ecstasy.

After our return to Sivananda Ashram, I realized that the profound religious experiences I had witnessed at the *Mela* had kindled a deeper interest in the Hindu religious tradition. By living in Sivananda Ashram, I had a unique opportunity. Swami Chidananda and Swami Krishnananda were considered to be two of the greatest living masters of the Hindu tradition.

I began to study some of the sacred texts, reading excerpts from the great epics such as the *Mahabharata* and the *Ramayana* and then studying Hinduism's most beloved scripture, the *Bhagavad Gita.* The *Gita* forms a small part of the *Mahabharata,* and represents an interchange between the great warrior Arjuna and Lord Krishna, who is his charioteer. It is the beginning of the Kurukshetra War, and Arjuna is about to go into battle. But he knows some of his own relatives are fighting on the other side, and the moral dilemma that he faces paralyzes him. Lord Krishna speaks to him about the necessity of *dharma*, or duty, and tells him he must take up arms and fight. The outcome of the battle must be left up to Divine will.

This puzzled me.

"But what would Mahatma Gandhi think of this? Surely his message was about non-violence, not about the validity of war?" I asked Pradeep.

"Well, Gandhiji interpreted Lord Krishna's message in a different way. He believed that battle was sort of a symbol of the struggle that goes on within each person's heart. You become attached to your ideas about yourself. When you are attached to your ego, you will face suffering and sorrow, sooner or later. And so Gandhiji said that people must dedicate every action to God, leaving the fruits of that labour to Divine will."

Later that day I met Bill and Susan for our afternoon walk. I was curious to know Bill's views about these central concepts of the Hindu faith.

"Pradeep was talking about the dangers of getting attached to the ego," I said. "But surely you have to depend on your ego in order to build the confidence to do anything meaningful in the world. You can't just deny the ego and accept whatever is happening in your life. Isn't that fatalism? From what I've read, fatalism is Hinduism's fundamental flaw. Fatalistic beliefs prevent people from taking effective action."

"That is a misinterpretation of Hindu philosophy," Bill replied. "You must accept what is, but then work hard, taking right actions according to your own inner direction. But remember: the fruits of your labour must be left to Divine will."

"What do you mean?" I asked.

"When we work hard and care about what we do, we inevitably want to see the fruits of our labour—the results of our action in the world. But there are spiritual dangers here. If you believe that you've succeeded in your chosen work, then you may fall prey to egotism. If you believe that you've failed, then you may risk disillusionment. Either interpretation will take you off your spiritual path."

We fell into a thoughtful silence as I pondered the implications of Bill's words. What could be the fruits of my labour here in Garhwal? Well, what I hope for is to create a health program that has a positive impact on the lives of Garhwali women! If I could achieve that, of course I'd be attached to it. Surely that's just natural?

"Tell me how your studies with Swami Brahmananda going," Susan said.

"Well, I'm enjoying it a lot more than I thought I would," I replied, glad to be thinking about something else. "It's kind of surprising, but my study of Hindu spiritual thought is encouraging me to re-examine my own Christian background. The concept of *bhakti*, devotional love, reminds me of the faith of Christian mystics like St Teresa of Avila. And of course *seva*, or service to others, is a theme that's common to both faiths."

I'd been reading *The Marriage of East and West*, a book written by the great interfaith explorer Bede Griffiths. He was a Benedictine monk who lived the last twenty-eight years of his life in India, using Hindu forms of worship in his profoundly inter-spiritual path. He lived in a simple hut he had built with his own hands, and worshiped in a tiny chapel that was equally austere. He began to wear the orange robes of the Hindu monk, took a Sanskrit name (Dayananda) and studied the Hindu Vedantic scriptures. I was fascinated by his writing, and Bede Griffiths soon became a much-beloved companion on my own spiritual path.

When Pradeep and I were out for a walk one day, I talked to him with enthusiasm about my discovery of several great Christian teachers who had explored Hinduism in depth. His response took me by surprise.

"Well, I hope they really were studying Hinduism," he said, skeptically. "I suspect they were just gaining surface knowledge in order to cover up their real intentions—to convert people to Christianity!"

"What are you talking about?" I replied, hotly. "Have you read any of their work? Why are you so suspicious?"

Our discussion degenerated into an intense argument, one of the first serious conflicts we'd ever had. As time went on, I gradually began to understand the reasons behind Pradeep's reaction to Christianity. Many thousands of Christian missionaries have come to India over the years, and conversion of Hindus to Christianity was always a top priority. In the eyes of the missionaries, Hinduism was often seen as a religion of idol worship. There was rarely any examination of the symbolism behind the pantheon of Hindu gods and goddesses, or any acknowledgement of the concept of Divine Unity as expressed in the Vedantic scriptures.

Many of the missionaries preached that Christianity represented the one true path to the Divine. Such an assertion would be anathema to those who understood the beauty and depth of the Hindu path. In Pradeep's mind, Christianity had come to represent the humiliation of his own religion and his people. This same sense of humiliation has soured relationships between Hindus and Muslims, dating back to the time of the Moghul invasion when many thousands of Hindu temples were destroyed all across North India.

Over the centuries, Hinduism has been remarkable for its ability to absorb and transform elements of other religious traditions rather than placing Hindu beliefs in opposition to them. Within this flexible idiom, seekers on the Hindu path have always acknowledged that people can find God through many religions.

As summer approached, the weather was getting increasingly hot. Pradeep suggested that I escape to Canada for the month of May, and spend some time with my parents. I knew that they were worrying about me, so the idea of a visit was appealing. Before this visit, Pradeep and I had to visit Narendranagar, the district capital, where the local branch of the Home Office was situated. Here, I was registered as a foreigner living in India, and every time I wanted to leave the country to visit Canada, I had to obtain a "No Objection to Return" certificate. Without this piece of paper, I could not leave India.

The Home Office was in a dreary concrete government building near the centre of Narendranagar, an equally dreary town. Open drains filled with filthy, stagnant water lined the main street. Two young men on a battered scooter roared through the market, narrowly missing an emaciated cow that was wandering across the road. A mangy stray dog with an ugly running sore on its hind leg nosed at a pile of garbage. Flies buzzed up from the garbage heap and settled onto the animal's open wound. I turned aside, sickened.

In my hand was a letter to my parents, in which I'd described the colour and bustle of the Indian market, the warm hospitality of my Indian family, and the exotic flavours of the food. But I realized that I was not painting a full picture of India. Somehow I must also find a place for this pitiful dog, the garbage heap, and that buzzing swarm of flies. An insidious pain began behind my eyes, which slowly developed into a pounding headache.

Pradeep and I climbed the crumbling steps of the Home Office building and asked for the foreigners' registration office. We were directed to a small room at the end of a hallway, where we sat on a wooden bench to wait. Half an hour crawled by. Finally, the door opened and an officious young man said, "The visa officer will see you now."

Middle-aged and paunchy, the visa officer was chewing on *paan,* which stained his lips and mouth an alarming red. He wore a heavy gold ring on one finger, and a tight polyester shirt that strained over his bulging belly. His battered metal desk was covered with piles of dusty files, tied in bundles with string. Behind him, long metal shelves containing overflowing boxes of files covered the cracked and damp-stained walls.

We greeted him with polite *Namastes.* Pradeep told him about our marriage in Ghaziabad, our registration at this office after settling in Rishikesh, and our work in Sivananda Hospital. Then I handed the man my Canadian passport with its visa stamp inside, and I said, "I'm planning to visit my family in Canada, and I'd like to request a 'No Objection to Return' certificate."

The visa officer studied me closely and then breathed a deep sigh. "This is a difficult part of my job, you know. Here in the Home Office, we have to be so very careful about foreigners."

Surprised, I asked, "Oh? But why?"

"Spies," replied the officer, sternly. "It is well known that the CIA plants foreigners in this area. They may seem like the most innocent people—but we soon realize they have other reasons for being in India. Spying."

"But what does this have to do with my wife?" Pradeep asked, indignantly. "She's married to me, an Indian citizen, and we live in Sivananda Ashram working as doctors."

"Ah, yes, of course, of course. It's very noble work. But all the same, I have a job to do. I have government responsibilities. I can't just grant your wife a 'No Objection to Return' certificate without doing a proper investigation."

"An investigation? To see if I'm a spy?" I asked. The idea that I could be involved with espionage for the CIA was so ludicrous that I was speechless for a few moments. Finally, I spluttered, "I am certainly not a CIA spy. For one thing, I'm Canadian, not American." I realized that it was a ridiculous reply to an even more ridiculous query.

The visa officer's face was expressionless. He said nothing for a few moments, and then shrugged his shoulders. "Madam, what can I do? I have my duties to perform."

Pradeep sighed, audibly. Then he turned to the visa officer and said, "To do your investigation, you'll obviously require some money. How much do you need?"

The visa officer smiled slightly. He leaned back in his chair and said, "Well, of course there will be some travel expenses. And food. It will be several days' work."

Pradeep nodded. "Yes, I see. Well, perhaps five hundred rupees would cover it?"

I stared at Pradeep, open-mouthed. He pulled out his wallet and handed over five hundred rupees. The visa officer said, "Very good, then. I will have your certificate ready in a few days. In fact, I'll bring it to you in Rishikesh."

We got up to leave. On our way out, I hissed to Pradeep, "What was all that crap about the investigation? You just gave him a bribe, didn't you?"

"Yes, I did," replied Pradeep. "And I can tell you that we were never going to get that certificate without it."

I sat silently all through the bus ride back to Rishikesh. The idea of having to bribe someone to do his assigned duty was anathema to me, yet Pradeep seemed to accept it as a matter of course. This clash of values resulted in another series of arguments, similar to our conflicts over religion. We gradually realized that in order to maintain a harmonious relationship, we would have to examine all of our attitudes and values. With time, both of us were able to challenge and set aside many notions that had arisen simply from cultural conditioning. For example, some of Pradeep's views on countries of the West were negative stereotypes, attitudes that gradually changed as he got to know people from those countries on an individual level.

On my part, I began to question my own attitudes toward marriage. Like most white Canadians, I went into marriage with a sense of optimism that the marriage would be strong. However, I also believed that if things didn't work out, we could always separate. But I soon realized that for Pradeep, marriage was a sacred bond that should never be broken. If problems arise, as they undoubtedly would, both people would put the marriage first, above all other priorities. We vowed to do this, trying always to make decisions that would provide mutual support of each other's goals. For Pradeep, the spiritual quest was at the centre of his life's journey. For me, an exploration of intercultural differences most engaged my heart and mind.

We also acknowledged that a time might come when we had different ideas about what path to take. In such a case, if one of us felt strongly that he or she could not continue along a certain path, the other person would agree to follow.

Both of us reaffirmed our commitment to a life of exploration, a life of inquiry into the complex questions of living. As Henry David Thoreau once wrote: "I went to the woods because I wished to live deliberately, to front only the essential facts of life, and see if I could not learn what it had to teach, and not, when I came to die, discover that I had not lived."

CHAPTER SEVEN:

Welcoming A New Traveller

Summer begins in North India in mid-April, and by May the heat on the Indian plains is scorching. The summer of 1986 was the first I spent in India, a gruelling experience. The temperature rose to 40° C most days, and the heat was often accompanied by a hot wind that sucked the moisture out of every pore of the body. We lived on the top floor of a concrete apartment building, where the temperature was even higher than outside. By this time, I was seven months pregnant, and the heat made the small discomforts of late pregnancy even more difficult. Our electricity supply was erratic, and when the power failed, the heat became unbearable. I would sit naked in the bathroom, dripping water onto my head and fanning myself. Poor Pradeep felt terribly sorry for me, and would anxiously scan the sky each morning for signs of a cloud.

"The monsoon can't be too far away," he'd say hopefully.

Later that year, he told me this was the first summer he'd ever felt the heat. Listening to my groans and moans, he became painfully aware that India is indeed a hot country. Until that time, he had simply accepted the heat as a part of the natural order of things, and it had not troubled him.

In the hot season, the hospital closed at one o'clock so everyone could go home to eat a midday meal and rest. At four o'clock,
when the worst heat was over, the hospital opened for another
three hours.

During those suffocating afternoons, Pradeep tried his best to
distract my attention. He brought me tapes of Hindi love songs,
hoping the magic of music would transport me to a more pleasant world. Lying on our bed under the spinning ceiling fan, we
listened to everything from lively Bollywood tunes to elegant
ghazals of devotional love. *Prem Geet* ("love song") was our favourite, the theme from a film we had watched soon after our meeting
in 1981. That familiar melody never failed to lift my spirits.

I tried to listen to the lyrics of the songs and decipher their
meanings. My Hindi was passable by this time, good enough for
casual conversation and for medical history-taking. But when it
came to the words of Hindi film songs, I was often stumped.

"*Jab se dekha maine tujhko, Mujhko aashiqui aa gayi!*" I repeated
thoughtfully. "OK, I understand the first line. It means, 'Ever since
I saw you.' But that second line—what does *aashiqui* mean?"

"Oh, it means love," replied Pradeep. He jumped from the bed
and whirled to face me, striking a dramatic pose. "Ever since I saw
you, love has come to me," he sang.

"I thought *prem* was the translation for the word love," I
replied, giggling at his antics.

"Hindi has so many words for love," Pradeep said. "*Prem* is
perhaps the most commonly used word, but don't forget *pyar*—
such a nice, cozy word. And *anurag*—another beautiful term for
love. And then there's *sneh,* meaning the love between friends,
and *mamta,* the love of the mother for her child. If you are speaking of your beloved, there are lots of great words taken from Urdu,
which is such a poetic language. You could use *mohabbat,* or *ishq,*
or *aashiqui* . . . take your pick!"

"Wait a second! Let me write these down," I said, seizing the notebook in which I kept track of all the Hindi words I was learning.

"Here's another one," said Pradeep, bursting into song again. "*Yeh rang na chootega, ulfat ki nishani.*" *Ulfat* is used for the love between husband and wife."

"What was the meaning of that line?" I asked.

"It means 'This colour will never vanish, the mark of our love,' and it refers to that red spot on the forehead of married women, the *bindi*."

"Love between husband and wife—do you mean sexual love?" I asked.

"No, not really, we've got other words for that kind of love," Pradeep said with a sudden gleam in his eye. "There's *vasna* and of course *kaam*, as in the *Kama Sutra*."

"I see! Well, with so many words for love, I guess Hindi speakers must be a loving and sexy bunch," I said, squeezing his hand.

"No doubt about that!" Pradeep replied, and we had a good laugh.

When evening came, we took our supper onto our balcony in hopes of catching an evening breeze. Our simple meal consisted of *kitcheree*, made from lentils and rice, and a salad made from fresh ripe tomatoes. Golden mango slices dripping with sweet juice made a delectable dessert. After the meal, I leafed through the weekly newsmagazine *India Today*, while Pradeep read *The Times of India*. In 1986, Rajiv Gandhi was the prime minister, and a sense of hopefulness and vibrancy was in the air. Declaring his commitment to root out corruption from government institutions, he earned the nickname "Mr. Clean." He was also committed to modernizing economic institutions, paving the way for India to play a larger role in the global economy. Reading about his vision for the future, both Pradeep and I sensed the power and excitement of this new emerging India. In May, the prime minister introduced a new national policy on education, which included expanded educational opportunities for Indian women and scheduled castes. I knew that "scheduled caste" referred to people on the lowest rung of Indian society, who are often discriminated against by Hindus of higher caste. Proactive government policies since the time of independence have made a great difference in the lives of people of scheduled caste. Despite this, many people from this group still suffer from social disadvantage.

Another focus of Gandhi's policy was to improve the quality of primary education and health care. Pradeep and I were well aware that in many parts of India, access to good primary health care was sorely lacking. Doctors at rural primary health centres were often absent. The health centres themselves were poorly equipped and often lacked essential medication.

"You know what I was reading the other day?" I asked. "There are some non-governmental organizations in different parts of India that have come up with really good ways of delivering primary health care in rural areas. Maybe someday we'll get a chance to work in the villages . . . see if we could figure out some system that would actually work."

I lapsed into silence, my imagination beginning to spin a future for us. *Suppose we moved to a remote rural area in Garhwal, and tried to create a model primary health care program. . . .*

"What are you thinking about, so deeply?" asked Pradeep.

"I am building castles in the air," I said, dreamily.

"Castles?"

"It's an expression—it means that you are imagining something very beautiful for the future—something you will create."

"So tell me about your castle," said Pradeep, intrigued.

"Well, I was thinking about villages in Garhwal. It sounds like there is really a need for basic health care, just simple things, like treatment of wounds, medication for a few diseases, immunizations, contraception—am I right?" I asked.

"Of course, that is so necessary," said Pradeep. "Most of what village women need is not five-star medical care, it is simple things. But still you are not telling me about that castle you are building in the air? I want to know what this castle looks like, and who lives in it."

"What does it look like? Let me see. I think my castle is built out of shimmering, shining glass. It is built in a remote area of Garhwal, and when we look out of its windows we see the whole range of the Himalayas. And who is living in it? Well, of course, you and I are there, and our children—quite a few children, maybe six or so."

"Six children?" gasped Pradeep.

"Just kidding!" I said with a giggle. "And also living in our castle are many young people. Each one of them has been trained to be a health worker. They can recognize and treat basic diseases, and they know a lot about prevention. They would go everyday to the villages to give the care right where it is needed."

"What about you and me, what would we be doing?"

"If the patient had a serious illness like TB, we would see them and arrange the proper treatment. And of course we would be busy setting up systems and training our workers. Then we need to think about pregnant women—who looks after about them when they give birth?"

"Most villages have a *dai*—an older woman who has a lot of experience about childbirth. She is the one who comes to attend the birth. But most of them don't have any proper training. They just learned from other *dais*. In medical school, I saw so many women who had given birth in the villages, and sometimes they had bad problems—you know, like postpartum hemorrhage or childbirth fever or obstructed labour."

I said eagerly, "You know, I've read about many places in the world where traditional birth attendants like the *dais* get training.

It's a basic three-day training course about safe delivery practices. Maybe we could do that, too?"

"I think the government of India has a program like that, but probably it has not spread to remote parts of Garhwal."

"So we must invite lots and lots of *dais* to our castle," I enthused. "This will be a wonderful way to improve women's health."

A breeze suddenly sprang up, bringing a breath of welcome coolness with it. The heavy leaves of the *sal* trees behind our building began to rattle with the wind.

"Can you smell the rain?" said Pradeep excitedly. "The monsoon is coming at last!"

A few moments later, a torrential rain began, drawing a dark curtain across the land. We stayed on our balcony till late that night, delighting in the sound and smell of the first monsoon rain.

By mid-July, after two weeks of oppressive humidity, the earth had begun to cool. The daytime temperature dropped to about 35 °C, and with a ceiling fan the heat was more bearable. I was now in the last stages of pregnancy, and Dr. Kutty had become concerned about the baby's size. I had not gained much weight and my tummy seemed small for a nine-month pregnancy. Her concern worried us both. The hospital where I would give birth had minimal equipment for newborn babies.

The night of August 22 was a wild one, with heavy monsoon rains pelting down. I went into labour in the evening, and by midnight I was having regular contractions. Pradeep went to call Dr. Kutty and they returned to pick me up in the ashram's minivan. Despite my condition, I enjoyed the sight of the orange-coloured van with the ashram's logo "Serve, Love, Meditate, Realize" emblazoned on the side. What an unusual vehicle for a labouring woman!

By the next morning my labour had not progressed well and Dr. Kutty became concerned about the baby's welfare. She decided that an urgent Caesarian section was necessary. I felt perfectly calm, with a strange sense of serenity that I often feel at times of crisis. Pradeep was far more alarmed than I was.

Fortunately, all went well. Our daughter Sonia tipped the scales at a mere six pounds, but much to our relief she was vigorous and healthy. I had only minor post-operative complications, and Pradeep finally began to relax. He hurried off to send telegrams to both sets of parents. I instructed him carefully about the wording of the one to my parents. It read:

> *Healthy six-pound baby girl born Aug. 23.*
> *NO STRIPES.*

Pradeep's parents arrived a day later, traveling from Ghaziabad by bus. Despite their long journey, they looked quite fresh—Papaji in a neatly pressed shirt and pants and Mummyji in a sari that fell in perfect folds. Pradeep touched their feet in greeting and welcomed them with relief in his voice. Mummyji came over to give me a kiss, and then lifted baby Sonia into her arms. "*Arre, beti, tum kitni sunder ho!* How beautiful you are, little daughter!" she exclaimed. She handed the baby to Papaji to admire, and then immediately set to work reorganizing the hospital room.

I watched the proceedings through half-closed eyes, marvelling at her brisk efficiency, not a movement wasted. She tidied and dusted while simultaneously directing Pradeep and Papaji to move Sonia's crib away from the window and put a small table in its place. Then she opened a bulky package containing a battered pot and a kerosene stove wrapped in newspaper. She set up the stove, directed Pradeep to fill the pot with water, and then began to unpack the contents of another shopping bag. Soon we were all enjoying afternoon tea with biscuits, *namkeen,* and *parathas.* For me, she had brought a special treat: sweet round *laddoos* made with the edible gum of a tree. Pradeep explained that these sweets are given to women who've just had a baby.

During the time I spent in hospital, I had a chance to get to know my parents-in-law better. I wanted to know more about their lives, and about the India of their childhood. Mummyji spoke no English, and though Papaji understood English well, he felt more comfortable speaking Hindi. So Pradeep translated, and the stories that emerged created vivid portraits of their lives. Papaji grew up as the only child in a household filled with a harsh struggle for survival. His father had died at age thirty of tuberculosis, and his mother had to depend upon the charity of relatives. She loved her only surviving son with a fierce devotion, and Papaji said that it was this devotion that led to his determination to succeed. He completed high school and then got a job with the Indian Railways, where he gradually rose to a position of assistant stationmaster.

Mummyji took up the story at this point. She'd had a happy childhood, a younger daughter in a large, well-to-do family with many female children. Because there were so many girls in the family, not all of them could be married to well-off men—the dowry demands would have destroyed the family's wealth. Though Papaji's income was low, he was recognized as a responsible and determined man, and so their marriage was arranged.

After their marriage in 1955, Mummyji had to struggle to adjust to a life where every rupee was precious. Recalling those times, a faraway look came into her eyes. "*Mere jivan main bohot farak aa gaya. . . .* So many changes came in my life." She explained that she'd had little experience of cooking or managing a household. But she said that she was always supported by the love of both Papaji and Ammaji, her mother-in-law. With time, she became an expert manager, running a household that included Ammaji and an elderly set of great-grandparents as well. Soon children began to arrive—Pradeep, Piyush, and then Nimmi.

Pradeep took up the thread of the narrative, describing those years of hardship and struggle. He described Papaji's yearning to gain some higher education, and the determination he showed when he enrolled in a local college and attended evening classes year after year, eventually earning an MA in English literature. He kept on studying, sat for the Indian civil service exam, and was subsequently selected for a position as sales tax officer in the state government—a real achievement. It was a job of dry facts and figures, one in which corruption was rampant. However, Papaji managed to maintain his honesty, not stooping to the corrupt practices that characterized so many of his colleagues' work. During those busy years, he ensured that each of his children had an education, and he arranged his daughter's marriage to a responsible young man. Because he was considered a man of wisdom, the extended family often sought him out for advice. Pradeep concluded ruefully, "In fact, in our extended family, if there was a child behaving badly, he was sent to live with Mummyji and Papaji for a few months or even years, just to get sorted out!"

What a great solution to the perennial problem of the misbehaving adolescent, I thought, with a smile. I reflected on Pradeep's family, so different from my own privileged circumstances in Canada. For us, higher education was always part of our future, not something we'd have to struggle to achieve. We never had to think about money, because there was always enough.

Both Papaji and Mummyji were delighted to have a granddaughter, the first girl to be born to one of their children. Sonia was an alert and active baby, viewing her new world with curiosity. She was born on Pradeep's thirtieth birthday—an unforgettable gift!

When I was discharged from the hospital, we brought baby Sonia to our home in Sivananda Ashram. Papaji returned to his job in Ghaziabad, but Mummyji stayed with us for a week to help with Sonia's care. She must have been shocked by the kitchen arrangements in our little apartment. I am not much of a cook, and Pradeep and I had been getting our meals mostly from the ashram kitchen. It was a dull diet, with virtually the same food being served every day. Pradeep's mother soon changed that! A succession of delicious dishes began to appear—different types of *dal* (the lentil soup that is the staple protein of India), *muttar paneer* (my favorite Indian dish made of peas and cottage cheese), many other vegetable curries, and of course rice and hot, fresh *rotis*, the round flat bread that is so typical of the North Indian diet.

I am also not much of a housekeeper, and our apartment tended to be untidy, despite Pradeep's valiant efforts to maintain order. Within a few days, our little home underwent a transformation under Mummyji's efficient management.

I found this sudden change in our domestic arrangements delightful. Some women don't like to have another woman take over their domain. But my view is that if someone is willing to cook, she is free to do whatever she wants in my kitchen! Mummyji prepared every dish from fresh ingredients and not a scrap of food was wasted.

"Pradeep, look at how much better off you would be if you'd married a nice Indian girl who could cook and keep house properly," I said one evening. My dear husband bravely assured me that he did not regret his decision to marry me.

I also enjoyed watching Mummyji take care of Sonia. She bathed her by squatting on the floor of the bathroom, extending one leg and placing Sonia over her ankle, with her back against Mummyji's foot. Thus stabilized, Sonia would receive a thorough bath despite her wails of protest. Toilet training starts early in India. Mummyji would hold Sonia over the toilet every hour or so, making a soft whistling noise as she did so. Babies apparently learn quite quickly to associate the whistling sound with urination. Once I saw this process in action, I began to understand why I would seldom see Indian babies wearing diapers.

After Mummyji left, Pradeep and I began to face the daily complexities of parenthood. In India, everyone who has had a child feels they must give advice to the new mother. I was bombarded from all quarters, with pointers about feeding, about sleep routines, about the importance of covering a baby's head in any weather condition. The woman employed to sweep the apartment halls suggested that I apply a round black mark of *kajal* somewhere on Sonia's face, to ward off evil eye.

One of our neighbours in the apartment building was Lata Mataji, a woman who had decided to take up the spiritual life after retirement from teaching. Her elderly mother lived with her, a kind-hearted woman we called Ammaji. They were delighted to have a baby next door, and Ammaji in particular loved to come and visit. In those early days, Sonia developed the habit of wanting to sleep all day and play all night. Pradeep and I were getting increasingly exhausted. Finally, I suggested that we let her cry herself to sleep one night, and then try to keep her awake the next day. When Sonia realized that we were not going to pick her up, she began to let out a series of lusty yells. We tried our best to ignore her. But within a few minutes there was an agitated knocking on our door. Ammaji burst into the room, brushed past us and went straight for Sonia's bassinette. Picking her up, she began to coo softly to soothe her. I tried to explain our strategy, but was met by an uncomprehending gaze.

"Babies must never be left to cry," murmured Ammaji.

When Sonia was two months old, we employed a young woman named Laxmi to come to our apartment in the afternoons so that I could return to hospital work. I enjoyed being back in a medical environment after months away. At six in the evening, Laxmi would arrive at the hospital with Sonia. Tucking her into a little blue baby carrier, Pradeep and I would leave the hospital and go for a long evening walk, often crossing the bridge over the Ganga to sit on the white sandy beach.

Pradeep and I took Sonia on her first trip in October, to visit Mummyiji and Papaji at their home in Ghaziabad, and celebrate the festival of *Diwali*. On the evening before the festival, people light tiny clay lamps and place them all around the periphery of their homes. This symbolizes the ancient myth in which people lit lamps to welcome Prince Rama and Sita, his wife, back to the kingdom after a long exile. *Diwali* is an occasion to wear new clothes, eat sweets and special foods, and visit friends and family. Happy shouts of children mingle with the crackle and bang of fireworks.

Pradeep's parents had much to celebrate this *Diwali*, with two new grandchildren joining the family. Sonia was born in August, and Pradeep's sister Nimmi gave birth to a second son just a few months later. Nimmi and her husband Anil also lived in Ghaziabad, and they arrived for afternoon tea, with their son Raja and the new baby.

As we sipped our tea, I glanced over at Ammaji, who was holding baby Apoorv on her lap. She'd known much sorrow in her life, including the deaths of many loved ones. But fortunes had changed dramatically since those difficult days, and now prosperity and health blessed every branch of the family. Her face, usually so worn and tired, was creased with smiles as she welcomed these tiny children into the family.

During those days of family togetherness, Pradeep shared memories of his childhood passion for kite-flying. His family struggled to make ends meet, but there always seemed to be a few rupees to spare for Pradeep to buy a little paper kite which he would fly from the roof of his house. He enjoyed creating "fighter" kites by coating the string in a mixture of cut glass and glue. Challenging another boy to a battle, he'd usually succeed in cutting the string of his opponent's kite. Pradeep became a master at this art and accumulated many trophy kites.

One of his elderly aunts would scour her neighborhood for lost or damaged kites. She'd bring them home and carefully repair them. When Pradeep came to visit, he would ask her with a sparkle in his eyes, "Auntie, do you have anything special for me?" She had very little money, but her gift of piles of refurbished kites was more precious to Pradeep than any other. Pradeep often told me that although his family was materially poor, his childhood was nevertheless filled with joy.

When the *Diwali* festivities were over, we prepared to return to Rishikesh. With Sonia's birth, I felt a part of Pradeep's family in an intimate way. In another month, we'd be celebrating our daughter's *naam karan sanskaar,* a naming ceremony performed when the child is several months old. Most often, the parents pick the name that appears on their baby's birth certificate, but a pundit or swami gives another name that has a special spiritual significance. Pradeep had asked Swami Chidananda if he would perform Sonia's naming ceremony, and he'd graciously agreed.

A baby's naming ceremony was a rare event in Sivanand Ashram, since Sonia was perhaps the first resident baby. On the morning of the event, Pradeep, Sonia, and I were surrounded by well-wishers—Lata Mataji, Ammaji and Vijaya Mataji, Dr. Kutty, and several of the ashram swamis. Pradeep's parents and his uncle attended the ceremony, and many friends from Rishikesh also came to celebrate.

At the *naam karan sanskaar,* Swami Chidananda spoke about the significance of the ceremony in the Hindu tradition. The name must be chosen with care, because it should reflect the child's individual spiritual essence. The child can use this name for inspiration and guidance in life. As Swamiji was speaking, he was observing Sonia closely. She was bouncing happily on Pradeep's lap, pleased to be the centre of so much attention. Swamiji reached out his hand to pat her plump cheek. She seized his finger and promptly began to chew on it.

Swamiji smiled with delight. "Yes, now I recognize you, little daughter. You will be the one who protects others, the one who is as firm as a thunderbolt, whose sword of knowledge cuts through ignorance. Your name will be Katyayani, one of the names of the Goddess Durga."

In the Hindu pantheon, Durga is revered as the goddess who protects her devotees from the evils of the world. She carries weapons in her eight arms—a thunderbolt, a sword, a bow and arrow, and a conch shell, whose sound recalls the sacred name of God. She rides upon a lion, representing power, determination, and will.

After the ceremony, the story of Swami Chidananda giving the name of Katyayani to Sonia spread quickly through the ashram. Many of the swamis would stop to greet Sonia, who was always happy to bestow her blessings upon her ever-widening circle of devotees. Our little family was at last becoming part of the ashram community, and I felt more at ease.

Christmas was coming, an occasion that is always celebrated in grand style in Sivanand Ashram. Swami Chidananda had a long-standing commitment to interfaith dialogue, and he had a special reverence for Jesus and his teachings. Bill and Susan were always in charge of the festivities, and I soon became involved in the preparations. Many Western seekers come to the ashram in December, knowing that Christmas and New Year are special times.

We decorated the hall with flowers, streamers and a Christmas tree hung with handmade ornaments. The program began with an hour of meditative chanting of the name of Jesus, attended by both Westerners and Indians, including some of the senior swamis. Bill read the Christmas story from the Gospel of Luke. Speaking from an interfaith perspective, he said that the birth of Jesus could be seen as a symbol for the birth of hope in a time of darkness.

A professional musician from an American symphony orchestra was visiting the ashram that year. He played the flute beautifully, and organized a musical program of remarkable beauty, weaving the familiar and beloved music of Christmas into elegant patterns of harmony. As the evening drew to a close, a quiet joy flooded my being. The experience of participating in the worship of Jesus in a Hindu ashram was profoundly moving.

Christmas morning dawned clear and cold. We dressed Sonia in a warm red jacket topped by a cap with a bell, so that she would look suitably festive for her first Christmas. We had offered to help with distribution of Christmas fruitcake to ashram residents, a tradition that Swami Chidananda had begun years ago. As we strolled through the ashram wishing everyone a happy Christmas and giving out cake, I thought of how my mother would have enjoyed the past two days. As a devout Christian, she had found my decision to marry someone of a different religious background difficult. If only she and Dad could get to know Pradeep better.

I suddenly thought about Piyush's upcoming wedding. "Pradeep, why don't we invite my parents to the wedding?" I asked. "Mum and Dad could meet my Indian family and see Sonia for the first time. I bet they'd love it!"

"It's a wonderful idea," replied Pradeep. "But what would your mom and dad think of the mess and chaos of India? Don't you think it would shock them?"

"Mum is an adjustable kind of person. She'd be OK. As for Dad, he copes with stress by drinking tea. If you provide him with a continuous supply, he will be able to cope with just about anything," I said with a giggle.

Piyush and Suchitra would be getting married in the city of Agra, where many members of Suchitra's extended family live. In Indian families, it is the bride's family who usually hosts the wedding. Suchitra's father had been seriously disabled by a stroke, but her mother, brothers, and sisters did an admirable job of organizing the ceremonies.

Because Pradeep and I were part of the groom's family, we joined the *barat*, or wedding procession, in which the groom arrives at the wedding hall riding on a white horse. As Piyush rode along, Sonia sat in front of him on the saddle, thrilled by this new adventure. This ancient tradition of having a young child accompany the groom probably symbolizes fertility in the wedding union. Suchitra looked lovely in her wedding finery, and all the ceremonies went off beautifully.

At the wedding reception, I became better acquainted with members of Pradeep's extended family. By this time, I could speak Hindi reasonably well and I began to enjoy learning the intricacies of family relationships. When Pradeep introduced me to his *Mausiji*, I knew that I was meeting one of Mummyji's sisters (she had nine). Her two brothers were introduced as *Mamaji*, maternal uncle.

Pradeep has many cousins, and he is older than most of them. This puts us in an enviable position in the family hierarchy, where age demands respect. Younger relatives addressed me as *Bhabhi*, and Pradeep as *Bhaiya*, and treated us with deference. An earnest adolescent waylaid us and launched into a long conversation with Pradeep. I soon lost the thread of the conversation, but I learned afterwards that he was asking advice about his future—should he join his father in the family business, or should he follow the longing of his heart and study Hindi literature? Other young cousins sought our advice about marriage, job prospects, and health concerns. Their trusting faith in us as mentors alarmed me. I knew very little about the realities of growing up in India and Pradeep, ever the rebel, was inclined to offer radical advice.

As my husband's younger brother and his wife, Piyush and Suchitra were now known as my *devar* and *devrani*. Traditionally, this is a very close relationship, and I was thrilled at the prospect of having a *devrani* to love and cherish in the years to come.

After the ceremonies were over, my parents spent a delightful three weeks with us. They were enchanted with Sonia and impressed with their son-in-law, who was a splendid tour guide. Pradeep took my comments about providing Dad with a continuous supply of tea seriously. Tea is available just about anywhere in

India, but Pradeep was not taking any chances. On our travels, he carried a little kerosene stove with all the equipment for making my father's favourite beverage. In our photographs from that trip, Dad always has a cup of tea in his hand.

My parents visited Pradeep's parents, and were treated to an elegant feast. The next day, we enjoyed another delicious meal with Pradeep's sister, Nimmi, and her husband, Anil.

Our plan was to travel to Jim Corbett National Park, a game sanctuary named in honour of a famous hunter. On the way to the park, we visited relatives of Pradeep's in the crowded city of Moradabad. Moradabad is dirty, noisy, industrial, and never included on a tourist's itinerary. We had to abandon the taxi near the centre of town because of the density of traffic—a car simply could not get through the crowd. Instead, we climbed into two flimsy bicycle rickshaws that began to weave their way through the chaotic melee. Just then I heard the banging of drums and the sounds of a mournful dirge being sung. A funeral procession appeared, with four men pushing their way through the heaving sea of people, carrying a corpse wrapped in a white sheet on a bamboo stretcher. Dad lifted his hat in his own cultural gesture of respect for the dead, his other hand gripping the wildly rocking rickshaw. For me, it was an oddly touching moment.

In Jim Corbett National Park, we gazed at elephants and crocodiles; in the hill town of Nainital, we rowed across a sparkling lake; in Agra, we admired the Taj Mahal. My parents returned to Canada feeling much happier about their daughter's choice of a husband, and thrilled about their first grandchild. They proudly displayed photos of their trip to friends and described it with enthusiasm. One of my father's colleagues mentioned that he'd been thinking of making a trip to India himself.

"How should I prepare for my trip?" he asked.

My father replied, "The first thing you must do is to get yourself an Indian son-in-law!"

Wedding

On the path to Gangotri

Garhwal Scene

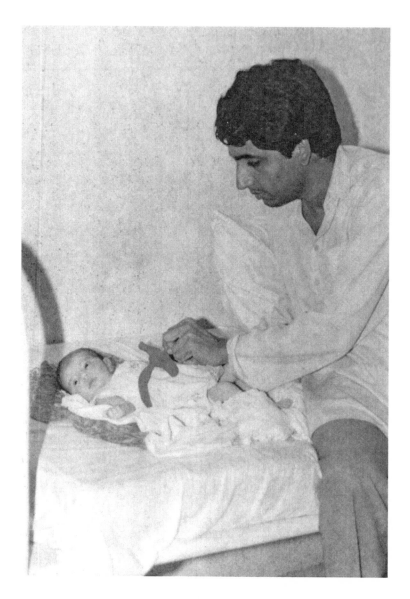

Pradeep's 30th birthday present: Sonia!

Our little family in Rishikesh

Swami Chidananda at Sonia's naming ceremony

CHAPTER EIGHT:

A Bend In The Road

One day in April 1987, I received a letter from the Voluntary Health Association of India inviting us to attend a health conference in Lucknow. There, we'd have an opportunity to meet health activists and leaders of NGO health programs from all around the country. The possibility excited me. In our hospital at Sivananda Ashram, we rarely had the opportunity to share ideas with others who had similar ideals.

"Let's go to this conference, Pradeep," I said.

"Why bother?" replied Pradeep. "It'll probably be very boring—a whole lot of people trying to impress each other. Long speeches and no action."

I felt a surge of irritation. "Don't you think we have anything to learn? There will be people who've done amazing things in the field of health. Maybe we could even go and visit an NGO that's done some fantastic work."

"To me the only interesting thing is the place—Lucknow," said Pradeep. "I will like to go and explore all those places where we first met."

We registered for the conference and made train reservations. Pradeep wrote to friends in Lucknow, saying we would be coming for a visit. As our date of departure drew closer, Pradeep became quite enthusiastic about the trip. However, I suspected his enthusiasm had nothing to do with NGO work and everything to do with visiting Lucknow, a city that held precious memories.

In Lucknow, we enjoyed many walks down memory lane, beginning with a visit to the exact spot in the pediatrics department where we had met in 1981. Tracing some of our early explorations together, we wandered through the grounds of the old British Residency building, where the siege of Lucknow took place in 1857. Behind the Residency is an old cemetery, where crumbling gravestones marked the last resting place of many soldiers and civilians from the days of the British Raj. We ended our day at the Clark's Avadh restaurant, where we had spent happy hours with Pradeep's good friends, Mahesh and Wasim.

The conference began the following day, opening with speeches from a seemingly endless parade of dignitaries who offered welcoming remarks. Pradeep nudged me and rolled his eyes.

"What did I tell you? Long speeches, no action," he whispered.

"Shh! Pay attention!" I hissed back at him.

Over the next couple of days, we listened to presentations from people doing health work in voluntary organizations throughout India. I took copious notes, and picked up pamphlets and newsletters from various NGOs. During the tea break one day, a tall, handsome man clad in white traditional clothing came to speak to Pradeep and me.

"A friend told me you're interested in working in Garhwal," he said. "I live in a part of Garhwal that's really been neglected. Our NGO has a project that's really taking off."

The man was Cyril Raphael, an Anglo-Indian who had lived in many parts of the world including England and Canada. He told us that he had been traveling through Garhwal when he'd met a remarkable man named Swami Manmathan. A charismatic social reformer from Kerala, he had founded an organization called Bhuwaneshwari Mahila Ashram in a remote part of the district Tehri Garhwal. Swami Manmathan had invited Cyril to join him, and for the past several years the two had worked together.

Cyril spoke about the successes they'd had in greening the barren land, and starting a dairy and a fair price shop.

"We are now moving into the field of education. We're planning to establish a school. People are noticing our work and we're beginning to get the funds for expansion."

He was passionate about his work, and Pradeep and I were soon drawn into a conversation about our own ideas for health work in Garhwal.

"Come and visit us!" said Cyril. "You may find a great base for your own work. And I think we will have the resources to support whatever you want to do."

Cyril's warm invitation intrigued us, and before the workshop was over, we had promised to take a trip to the village of Anjanisain to visit his organization.

On the train journey home from Lucknow, Pradeep and I talked about our meeting with this unusual and charming man. Curious about his work, I opened the envelope he had given us describing his organization. We read about the origin of the name Bhuwaneshwari Mahila Ashram (BMA). Bhuwaneshwari was the name of a goddess who is worshipped in that remote part of Tehri Garhwal, and *Mahila* means "woman," highlighting the organization's focus on women. The word "ashram" is usually used for a spiritual community, but in BMA's case, the word was used more broadly to mean a community of people working together for social good. BMA's founder, Swami Manmathan, was not a swami in the religious sense, but he had acquired the name because of his single-minded devotion to social work.

"Pradeep, I really like BMA's focus on women," I said. "And this organization is truly working from the grassroots. Swami Manmathan started with nothing, and look how the organization has grown. This may give us exactly the opportunity we've been looking for."

By this time, we had spent nearly two years in Rishikesh. I had learned a tremendous amount about life in Garhwal. I could speak Hindi adequately, and I had learned much about disease patterns in the Himalayan foothills. I knew how to treat common conditions in a cost-effective way, and I also understood the possibilities and limitations of treating more complex conditions. Both Pradeep and I were beginning to feel that it was time to move on, and we'd been looking for the right opportunity to make a move into the interior of Garhwal.

Pradeep's brother Piyush and his new bride, Suchitra, were planning to visit us in June. "Perhaps we could take them on a little trip into the mountains, and visit Cyril's organization at the same time," I suggested to Pradeep, who readily agreed.

I was looking forward to Piyush and Suchitra's visit. This would be our first opportunity to get to know our new sister-in-law. We planned to spend a few days in Rishikesh and then to set off into the mountains.

Sonia gave an enthusiastic welcome to her *chachaji* and *chachiji,* terms that identified Piyush and Suchitra as her father's younger brother and his wife. As parents, we were convinced she was the most adorable child imaginable, outgoing and expressive. On that trip, Sonia thoroughly enjoyed herself, revelling in the company of her doting *chachiji.* Our photos from that trip feature Sonia in almost every frame.

One image shows her in Suchitra's arms in front of the Chandrabadni temple, at the top of a hill very close to Anjanisain. This temple is one of five in Garhwal—all goddess temples that honour Parvati, the consort of Lord Shiva, each at the summit of a dramatic hill. At Chandrabadni, pilgrims come from many parts of Garhwal to worship at the *Devi* temple. For many years, village people sacrificed goats and buffaloes at the temple, but Swami Manmathan had opposed this practice and had put an end to it. Cyril told us that Swami Manmathan believed it was a superstitious ritual that had no place in a modernizing society.

After our visit to the temple, we traveled on to Anjanisain along a narrow, rough road. We soon spotted a cluster of white-washed buildings clinging to the side of the steep hillside, and guessed that this was Bhuwaneshwari Mahila Ashram. Our driver pulled to the side of the road and leaned on his horn. People soon began to emerge from the buildings around us, calling out greetings. High on the hill above us, Cyril appeared and waved to us. We unloaded our luggage and began to climb a winding path to join him.

That day, Cyril showed us around the ashram and regaled us with stories about the work in progress and ideas for the future. At one point, far away, we saw a thin figure clad in white garments, directing a group of labourers who were levelling some ground.

"That's Swami Manmathan," said Cyril. "He'll meet us later, I expect."

Darkness was falling, and a cold breeze began to blow. We hadn't brought warm clothes, because Rishikesh was baking in the June heat. Shivering, we wrapped ourselves in blankets and accepted another round of steaming tea.

Later that evening, Swami Manmathan suddenly appeared. He was a slight man with dark skin, tousled white hair, and a beard. But what struck me at that moment was not his physical appearance, but the strange electric energy he seemed to radiate. Cyril began to introduce us, but Swamiji interrupted him.

"Yes, yes, I know who they are," he said, abruptly. His piercing gaze swept over Pradeep and me. "Have you ever worked in the mountains?" he asked.

Pradeep told him about our work in Rishikesh and our plans to move to a more remote area of Garhwal. I described our meeting with Cyril in Lucknow, when he had invited us to visit BMA.

Swami Manmathan made no comment, but continued to stare at us intently. Being subjected to that interrogating gaze was a peculiar sensation. Finally, he said, "Well, let's see." With that cryptic remark, he turned abruptly and left the room. That was the last we saw of Swami Manmathan on that first visit.

Cyril chuckled comfortably. "Don't worry about Swamiji's manners," he said. "The man thinks only of his work. He's a genius, you know. Come now, let's have dinner."

The following morning, Cyril introduced me to two nurses who worked with BMA. "They're fine women, but they desperately need more guidance and training," he said. "I can imagine how well you could work with them."

We talked about the problems of women in the mountains. Already burdened by long hours of grinding physical labour, they also faced social oppression and lack of educational opportunities.

"We have formed women's groups in the villages, and we are developing opportunities for them to earn some income. Many are interested in learning to read, and of course they would all like access to better health care," Cyril said.

Cyril's words hit a responsive chord in my heart. How I would love to work with these women! When we left the ashram, both Pradeep and I were feeling that perhaps we had found the next destination on our life's path.

After our return to Rishikesh, we plunged back into our work in the hospital. Many good changes were taking place. Reviewing the hospital registers, we realized that we were seeing more than fifty thousand patients per year. The reputation of Sivananda Charitable Hospital had spread, and village people from all over Garhwal were coming for consultation. Dr. Kutty's clinic attracted women from far and wide, drawn by her remarkable reputation for having "the power of the hand"—the expression used for a physician with particular healing abilities. Women from the slums of Rishikesh wrapped in torn cotton saris stood in line with elegant women from Delhi dressed in shimmering silk. I often worked as Dr. Kutty's assistant, and I enjoyed watching the colourful parade of patients.

Dr. Kutty charged nothing for her services. However, her wealthy patients often stuffed bank notes into the hospital donation box, and with this money, Dr. Kutty had an operating theatre constructed on the second floor of the hospital. Here, she could perform gynecological procedures, and soon, visiting surgeons were coming from the city of Dehra Dun to do orthopedic and ophthalmic surgery.

The inpatient wards of the hospital had been renovated and refitted, and we were now able to accommodate twenty patients in two large wards. We had managed to recruit two more doctors to help us cope with the ever-growing demand for services. One of these young men was on a passionate spiritual search, and he decided to make a long-term commitment to Sivananda Ashram as a spiritual aspirant. Dr. Babu became a long-serving and well-respected member of the staff.

Not long after our visit to Lucknow, I discovered that I was expecting our second child. When I was about three months pregnant, I developed a high fever and shaking chills. The diagnosis was malaria, a disease spread by the bite of the *Anopheles* mosquito. Malaria can be prevented by daily or weekly doses of antimalarial antibiotics, but I had decided against taking continuous medications since I would be living in India long-term. I had consulted a tropical disease specialist in Toronto prior to leaving for India, and he had advised, "Don't take malaria prophylaxis. You'll get a few bouts of malaria and gradually you'll develop some natural immunity." Unfortunately, while developing my immunity,

I had to endure several bouts of malaria. I tried to protect myself against mosquito bites, but it was not easy.

My latest battle with malaria left me weak and shaky. I had become anemic, and I had to cut down my hours in the hospital. Pradeep was very busy there, and would come home looking exhausted. That year, we'd had an outbreak of dysentery and then hepatitis A, which particularly affected ashram residents. Hepatitis A is a viral infection of the liver that cannot be treated by antibiotics. Most patients recover, but this disease can be deadly.

A German guest in the ashram consulted Pradeep when he'd fallen ill with jaundice, diarrhea, and vomiting. Pradeep admitted him to the hospital and treated him with iv fluids, but his condition steadily deteriorated. Pradeep became increasingly concerned, and decided to transport him to a larger medical centre in Dehradun.

A day or two later, Pradeep came back from his hospital rounds looking drawn and exhausted.

"He's dead," he said, collapsing onto our bed with a deep sigh. "I found out from his girlfriend. She was with him to the end."

I gasped in horror. It seemed so tragic to think of that earnest young man who had come to India on a spiritual search, only to die of a preventable disease.

"It's a waterborne disease, and he was staying here in the ashram," I said. "We must get the ashram water tested."

Pradeep was silent for some time. "I don't know where to get a test like that done," he replied. "I am not sure if there are labs in this area that could do the testing. And if you do get it tested, well, people here may not believe that anyone could get sick from the water. They think water from the Ganga is always pure."

"Oh come on, surely nobody believes that," I said, impatiently.

"You'd be surprised," he replied. "People have deep beliefs about this river—it is sacred to all Hindus. Anyway, I think we should try to get the water tested and see what happens."

I wrote to an Indian friend working in public health in Delhi, and found out that the water could be tested in a lab at a university in Srinagar, about three hours' drive from Rishikesh. We made contact with the lab and arranged to have water samples sent. When the reports came back, it was just as I had suspected. The water in the ashram was unsafe to drink, with very high bacterial counts. Pradeep and I went to talk to the swami on the ashram management committee who was the person responsible for the drinking water.

When we told him about our concerns and showed him the lab report, his face remained impassive.

"So, you believe that people can get sick by drinking the water of Mother Ganga?" he asked, a flinty look in his eyes.

"Well, yes, Swamiji," I replied, "The lab report shows contamination. But of course the water could be treated by chlorination to make it safe to drink."

"I wouldn't pay much attention to that report," he replied, getting up, abruptly. It was clear that the interview was over.

Nothing was done about the ashram water and people continued to develop diarrhea. I spoke to Swami Saketananda, who was responsible for the administration of the hospital.

"At least we should get the hospital water treated," I said. "Then visitors to the ashram could also get safe drinking water. "

Swami Saketananda was in his mid-thirties, a powerfully built and handsome man who looked more like an athlete than a spiritual aspirant.

"This is not your responsibility," he said, angrily. "Just leave this matter alone."

I had always sensed that Swami Saketananda resented my presence in the hospital. From this day onward, he would barely acknowledge me. I began to feel rather uncomfortable in the hospital, but I still felt determined to do something about the water quality. I spoke to Dr. Kutty about the issue and even to

Swami Chidananda, the president of the Divine Life Society. Still, nothing happened.

Pradeep said, "I am sure that the senior people in this ashram realize that you are right about the water, but perhaps this is not the right time for a change. In India, things move slowly."

I tried to put aside my frustration and focus on work. But I was feeling increasingly restless in the ashram hospital. Treating people when they fall sick is necessary, but it can also feel like a never-ending task. So much of the illness was preventable by simple means—clean water, better nutrition, immunizations. I longed to work in a different setting where we could focus more on prevention rather than treatment.

One cold day in early December, I joined Pradeep for the evening clinic. He was sitting silently at his desk, staring at a piece of paper. When he saw me, he abruptly balled up the paper and hurled it into the wastebasket.

"What was that about?" I asked.

"I'll tell you after the clinic's over," Pradeep replied in an uncharacteristically curt voice.

Later that evening, we walked across the bridge to our favourite spot on the beach, a flat rock near the water's edge. The sparkling white sand offered a stunning visual contrast to the turquoise water of the Ganga. I slipped off my *chappals* and buried my feet in the sand, still warm from the day's sunshine.

"So, what was that note about?" I finally asked.

Pradeep explained that it was from Swami Saketenanda. As administrator of the hospital, he had decided that he no longer wanted me to attend the clinic. Pradeep could continue his work, but without my assistance.

"It's all about the water issue, isn't it?" I exclaimed, feeling a surge of anger, followed rapidly by an intense feeling of humiliation. *How could he do something like that? Had my work not been valued at all?*

I looked over at Pradeep. His body was rigid with tension, his hands clenched. He said, tersely, "We can fight this, I'm sure. He's taking on much more authority than he really has."

I was silent, staring at the tumbling water of the river. The sun was setting, casting shafts of golden light over the river and creating dancing highlights on the waves. Somehow, the beauty of the scene intensified my inner pain. I got up abruptly, hot tears pricking my eyelids. Pradeep and I walked back home in silence.

After supper, we sat out on the balcony, the special place where we'd so often shared ideas and debated points of philosophy. Warm quilts and cups of hot tea provided comfort against the winter cold. We talked about the events of the past few weeks, trying to make sense of all that had happened. Finally, unable to clear the confusion in my mind, I asked Pradeep what we should do next.

He reached for my hand, and said quietly, "I think it's time we left Sivananda Ashram. We both want a change. You are not well, and the baby is due in just a few months. Why to stay here and fight a stupid battle with that man?"

I had been planning to go to Canada for the birth of our second baby because of the complications I'd encountered during the first delivery. I desperately needed to regain my health and strength.

"After the baby is born and you are back to health, we could take up Cyril's offer and work in BMA. We'd be working in a much more rural part of Garhwal, as we'd always imagined," said Pradeep.

He resigned from his post in the hospital the next day.

As our life in Rishikesh moved rapidly to a close, my mind was whirling with confusion. I spent hours with Bill and Susan, talking about the sequence of events that led to our decision to leave the ashram. My initial feelings of anger at Swami Saketenanda were being replaced by a pervasive sense of sadness about the situation. Perhaps it had been inappropriate to make an issue of the water problem. They must have perceived me as an arrogant Westerner who thinks she has all the answers.

Bill's opinion was different. "God has other plans for you now," he said. "And when He wants you to make a move, you will know about it!"

Bill always interpreted every event as a manifestation of Divine will. His faith in God's goodness illuminated his life and shaped every decision. My own faith in the Divine had much more shaky foundations. Perhaps we were meant to leave the ashram at this time, but I just wished that our reasons for going had been more positive.

As we prepared to leave, I became aware of how many friends we had made, both in the ashram and in Rishikesh itself. On one of our last days, we took our customary walk along the bank of the river, across the bridge, and to the little restaurant where we had so often enjoyed a snack after our evening clinic. A policeman from the station nearby called a greeting. We inquired after his wife, whom Pradeep had recently treated for dysentery. Near the bank of the river, we met the kindly old swami whom we had secretly nicknamed "Cricket Swami," because he always seemed to have a radio close to his ear so that he could listen to the latest match. He was fond of Sonia and always took time to tickle her cheeks. Coming close to the bridge, we heard someone say, "*Namaste*, Dr. Sahib!" Looking down, we saw a thin, one-legged beggar dressed in rags crouched under the bridge. I recognized him as one of our regular patients.

Pradeep's reputation as a compassionate and skilful physician had made him well known in our little community. Before returning to the apartment, we dropped in to say goodbye to Dr. Kutty. As we sipped our tea and chatted, I noticed the sadness in her eyes, and realized that she would grieve our departure. She had never married, and in some ways thought of Pradeep as a son.

They had worked together for five years, transforming Sivananda Hospital from a defunct institution into a thriving medical centre.

I went to say goodbye to Bill and Susan the day before we left. They had been true friends to me over the previous two years, always able to provide a sympathetic ear and wise counsel.

As we drank our tea, Bill said to me, "As far as the water problem is concerned, you wait and see. I bet that within a few years, changes will happen. But I think that change will only come about when the time is right."

Those words were prophetic, and a few years later a safe water system was indeed installed at the ashram, along with many other improvements in sanitary facilities.

But all of that lay in the future. When we left Rishikesh in the spring of 1988, I struggled with feelings of disillusionment and frustration. My quest for cross-cultural understanding had ground to an unexpected halt.

CHAPTER NINE:

A Time Of Transition

I flew back to Canada in March 1988, and Pradeep joined me six weeks later. In late June, our son Raman was born in a hospital in Hamilton, Ontario. Sonia was delighted with her baby brother and promptly dubbed him "New Baby." This nickname followed him for several years, first being shortened to "Newby" and later to "Nubhi," a more Indianized version. He was a peaceful and serene baby, quite different from her lively older sister. We stayed with my parents during the days leading up to his birth and for several weeks afterwards. Their new grandson was a source of great delight.

Pradeep and I had decided to spend a few more months in Canada after Raman's birth, intending to replenish our depleted financial coffers. I was offered a position in a community clinic in the small mining town of Ignace, in northern Ontario. Pradeep had the opportunity to experience life in Canada, and I was able to regain my health and to enjoy Canadian medical practice once more. Those months were a delightful interlude in our lives, a time to be with each other and to enjoy the children. That winter, the temperature dipped to -45 °C, one of the coldest years on record in northern Ontario. We experienced fierce snowstorms in which wild winds buffeted our house and snow blanketed the town. But our snug home felt like a haven and we revelled in the joys of family life.

Still, we had not forgotten our dream of working in rural Garhwal. While we were in Ignace, we received a letter from India congratulating us on Raman's birth and officially inviting us to join BMA to head their health team. Swami Manmathan himself had signed the letter. Its friendly and open tone was quite at odds with the strange impression of Swamiji that we had received on our visit to the ashram. We felt pleased, though rather puzzled. Cyril had also included a brief note, repeating the invitation and expressing his eagerness to meet us again.

By early 1989, we were back in India and decided to accept Cyril's offer to work with Bhuwaneshwari Mahila Ashram. Initially, we planned to live in Mussoorie, a town that had been one of the old British hill stations. Mussoorie is on a ridge high above the town of Dehradun, overlooking a magnificent range of Himalayan peaks. Neither Pradeep nor I was keen to live at BMA's headquarters in Anjanisain, which had no accommodation suitable for a family. Pradeep had a friend in Mussoorie who was able to rent a cottage for us near several good schools. Sonia would soon be ready for kindergarten and, like so many other parents in India, we were already concerned about her education.

Our arrival in Mussoorie in June remains etched in my mind. We were travelling up the narrow, winding road to the town in a taxi packed high with our possessions, including all the paraphernalia required when travelling with two young children. Unbeknownst to us, Raman and Sonia had been exposed to chickenpox shortly before leaving Canada, and now they had both broken out in the itchy, blistering rash. Sonia was sobbing miserably and complaining about how bad she felt with "tickle pox." The oppressive heat of the plains was beginning to lift as we made the ascent into the mountains, but soon, dark monsoon clouds began to roll ominously over the ridge above. Suddenly, a clap of thunder split the air, and sheets of rain began to pour from the heavens. Both children began to wail simultaneously.

At that moment I had a flashback memory of Pradeep soon after we'd met in 1981. He had been describing his dream of living in the Himalayan foothills one day. He told me about the little cottage he would have overlooking the mountains, and the bench outside where he would sit and play his sitar on serene evenings.

"So, Pradeep, your dream is finally coming true. Here you are, moving to your cottage in the Himalayan foothills," I said, teasingly.

He managed a rueful smile and said, "This is not quite what I imagined."

Things did improve once we had settled down in the cottage and the children had recovered from chickenpox.

Soon after our arrival, we made another visit to Anjanisain to meet Swami Manmathan and Cyril. On this visit, Cyril told us the story of how BMA was established. Originally from the southern state of Kerala, Swami Manmathan was a fiery social reformer with a legendary capacity for hard work. He had been given a tract of barren hillside in Anjanisain by a retired army general, and here, he established an institution that he named Bhuwaneshwari Mahila Ashram, where he began his bold social experiment.

The mountain dwellers of the Garhwal Himalaya are generally noted for their honesty, courage, and hospitality. However, the Anjanisain district of Garhwal had a reputation for lawlessness. Deforestation had stripped the hills bare, most fresh-water sources had dried up, and people scratched a meagre living from the land. Alcoholism among men was a scourge, with its attendant problems of unemployment and violence against women.

Into this grim atmosphere came Swami Manmathan. Those early years must have been difficult, as he struggled to establish a community and make ends meet. But over the period of a decade, he began to achieve remarkable results. At the ashram itself, a young green oak forest was springing up where once the hills had been barren. Income for the ashram came from trees laden with apricots, plums, and walnuts and from a small dairy stocked with cross-bred cattle. During this time, Cyril Raphael paid a visit to the ashram, and he was so inspired by Swami Manmathan's work that he decided to join him.

Swami Manmathan challenged corrupt local politicians, and exposed their duplicitous habits of skimming off government money. Grants for government-development programs were now being used for their intended purposes, and access to clean water and sanitation facilities in the villages was improving.

The early successes of BMA attracted the notice of Save the Children Fund, and in 1988, SCF had granted a large sum of money to BMA for integrated development programs, including income-generating projects, environmental work, children's education, and health. Swami Manmathan's vision was to establish five small subcentres in remote parts of Garhwal where these development programs could take root.

As the new leaders of the health program, Pradeep and I had a generous budget to work with and freedom to develop an integrated primary health-care program in the way we wished. We plunged into the work with tremendous enthusiasm, beginning to organize a system of clinics in each of the five subcentres, which would serve as bases for health outreach work in the surrounding villages. Because the subcentres were so farflung, Pradeep was away from home for long periods as he worked to establish the health program. We soon realized that living in Mussoorie was not practical, as it was located too far west of BMA and its subcentres. Just a few months after our return to Garhwal, we moved to the hill town of Pauri, about 150 kilometres to the east of Mussoorie. Accompanying us was a young man named Teeka Ram Bhatt. We'd known Teeka since he was a teen, and we'd always been impressed by his eagerness to learn and his honest nature. When we'd returned from Canada, he'd expressed his desire to work with us. We welcomed him, sensing that he would become an integral part of our family in the years to come.

Pauri was an ugly town—an assortment of poorly constructed cement buildings, straggling down the slope of the mountain. The streets were filthy, and water and electricity were in short supply. The land around Pauri had been badly deforested and natural springs had dried up, making it progressively more arid. As the productivity of the land declined, many farms were abandoned. People migrated to the plains of India to seek work in factories or in the army. Literacy in this district of Garhwal is relatively high compared to other districts such as Tehri and Chamoli. Higher literacy opened the doors for better job opportunities elsewhere in India, another factor that made migration an attractive option.

Pradeep found us a house to rent that had been empty for several years. The place was a little out of town, high on a hill, above an old mission complex where American Methodist missionaries had settled years ago. The Methodists had left long before, but there was still a community of Indian Christians living near the complex. Not far from the house was St. Thomas School, founded and run by nuns. Outside the house was a verandah and a small open patio paved with flagstones. Surrounding the patio was a low brick wall, crudely built and crumbling in places. Inside, the house was fairly spacious, though the rooms that backed onto the hillside were dark and damp.

"I wonder why this house has been standing empty for so long," I said. "It's quite a big place, and housing is always in short supply."

"I heard that some years ago, two men were murdered in this house," Pradeep replied. "They had a lot of money with them. Someone broke in, and robbed and then killed them. I think people are superstitious about renting this place."

I felt a chill down my spine. "How awful," I murmured.

"I'm afraid there's not much else available to rent around here," said Pradeep, apologetically.

Trying to look on the bright side, I said, "Well, never mind. I think this place will be OK. Look at the beautiful view—that compensates for a lot."

From the spot where we were standing, we could see a vast range of Himalayan peaks. Pradeep named some of them—Chaukumbha, the massive mountain with four peaks; Kedarnath, the sacred pilgrimage site; Nanda Devi, the highest peak in Garhwal; and Trishul, shaped like the trident of the god Shiva.

"You can even see the mountains at Gangotri, just to the west of the Kedarnath peaks," said Pradeep. I gazed at the faraway peaks, thinking of the journey Pradeep and I had taken just after our marriage. I remembered the vows we'd made beside the glacier, promising to stay true to our chosen path and to support each other through all difficulties. *That was only three years ago. . . . How far we've travelled since then—a journey with many struggles and disappointments. But we have wonderful memories, too, and we've learned so much.*

"Do you still think we are staying true to our chosen path?" I asked Pradeep.

"Oh yes. It's time for us to experience Garhwal in a different way—to work right at the village level. It's what you've wanted for so long."

We spent the next few days getting settled. Teeka unpacked all the pots and dishes, organized the dark, cramped kitchen, and managed to cook delicious food. But he was strangely quiet, not like his usual cheerful self.

"Madam, I don't like this place," he said one morning. "Did you hear that two men were murdered? Right here. Right in this room. You should never live in a house where such a thing has happened."

"Oh come on, Teeka. You don't believe in ghosts, do you?" I teased.

Teeka turned away and said nothing. A few days later, I saw him standing on the patio staring morosely toward the range of snow clad Himalayan peaks.

"Great view, isn't it, Teeka?" I said, hoping to cheer him up.

"It's just mountains," he replied. Another heavy silence followed.

Finally, I said, "Teeka, why do you hate this place so much?"

"It's so different here," he said, slowly.

"In what way?" I asked. "Pauri Garhwal looks pretty much the same as Tehri Garhwal, as far as I can tell. What's so different about this place?"

Teeka said nothing for several moments. Finally, he said, "It's the cows. In Tehri Garhwal the cows are white. And here they are black."

I stared at him, wondering if he was joking. But he said nothing more—simply heaved a sigh and went back inside.

Pradeep was often away, working on setting up clinics at the various subcentres. With two children aged three and one, I found no time to feel bored. Though the demands of motherhood occupied most of my day, I still managed to work on the development of ideas for our health program. At that time, we had twelve young health workers, both males and females. The women all had training as "auxiliary nurse midwives" (ANMs) and, in theory, their training had included information about the treatment of common diseases, as well as prevention. However, their knowledge and skills varied greatly. Several of them were from South India and had been trained in a well-reputed NGO that gave excellent training. But others had received their ANM training from the government, and these training programs tended to be of a much lower quality.

Until recently, the city of Dehradun had been the only place where ANM training was available in Garhwal, and it was not easy for a young woman from a low-income family to live in the city. We had few Garhwali ANMs among our group of health workers, likely related to the lack of training opportunities in the hills.

But recently, the Pauri government hospital had started an ANM program, and we had just hired one of their first graduates, a young woman named Savitri. When Pradeep and I interviewed her, I'd been impressed by her passion to serve the people of the villages.

One morning, sitting on our patio working on the curriculum, I saw Savitri walking up the winding path to our house. She was taller than most Garhwali women, with an engaging smile and a spring in her step. Her hair was plaited into a long glossy braid down her back.

"*Namaste*, Madam," she called out.

I smiled and asked her to join me. She sat down shyly and I began to chat about our health program, asking her more about her training at the Pauri hospital. I'd developed enough facility with the Hindi language to detect that she spoke with the accent of Garhwal.

"Madam, I am sorry to tell you that I do not know much about health work, really. I am afraid that I am not a good nurse," Savitri said, her eyes downcast.

"Why is that, Savitri?"

In a burst of emotion, Savitri began to tell me more about her longstanding dream to become a nurse. She had grown up in an impoverished family in a small village near Pauri. Her father was dead and her mother had endured much suffering.

"And there are so many other families like mine in Garhwal. So many people who are poor and sick. I always thought—if only I could learn how to help them! This is what I want to do with my life."

"That is such a good ambition," I replied, encouragingly. "And now you've completed your training at the government hospital. That's an achievement."

Savitri glanced at me, with a woebegone expression. "But, Madam, the training was not good. Often, our teachers did not come and we had no books to study. I have not learned what I want to, and so that is why I am telling you I am not a good nurse."

Impulsively, I reached out to grasp her hand.

"But Savitri, you certainly seem to have the heart to be one."

"Oh yes, Madam," she replied with conviction. "I do have that."

I picked up the sheaf of papers in my lap. "I'm working on a training program for all our nurses," I said. "We don't expect you to know everything. We'll keep on working with you, and you must also tell us what you want to learn."

Savitri's face glowed. "You wait and see, Madam. I will learn everything you teach me!"

We plunged into a conversation about the health problems of the villages, and I showed her the outlines of the curriculum I was working on. Sparks of enthusiasm began to fly, lit by the fire of passion we both felt for health work in these hills. Savitri's desire to serve was tangible, and I was certain that she would become one of our most dedicated employees.

Pradeep arrived just then, and we all shared a cup of tea. We talked about our first training for health workers planned for early the following month. Three-day blocks of intensive instruction would be followed by two-month periods in the field. Each block would build on the one before, and the training would be practical and focused. In the two months between blocks, the trainees would have assignments to work on that they could share with the others at the next session.

After Savitri left, Pradeep and I reviewed the curriculum we'd developed to that point. We were discussing the schedule of the training sessions when the shrill ringing of the phone interrupted us. We rarely received calls, as the phone service in Garhwal was unreliable. Through the crackling static on the line, Pradeep heard his father shouting his message in brief phrases—Ammaji had suffered a serious heart attack the night before. Within an hour, we hastily packed, and managed to hire a Jeep. Tucking the children into the back seat, we began the twelve-hour journey to the home of my parents-in-law.

When we arrived, Pradeep's father came out to meet us. His head was completely shaven. Seeing him, I knew at once that Ammaji must be dead. Pradeep and I touched his father's feet, and then we unloaded our luggage and bundled the sleepy children out of the Jeep. Mummyji came to greet us, tears running down her face. As we made our way to the house, she began to tell us the story of Ammaji's final illness. She had developed chest pain and shortness of breath, and had been taken to a small private hospital nearby. The pain subsided, but she'd become progressively weaker. In the early hours of the morning, she had passed away peacefully, with Pradeep's father at her side.

Papaji and several other male relatives had already taken the body to the burning *ghat* for cremation and the performance of last rites. Papaji had not waited for Pradeep's arrival, because cremation is usually done as soon as possible after death. Women do not participate in Hindu cremation ceremonies, though they are an important part of all the other grieving rituals.

We settled in at my parents-in-laws' home to await the most important ceremony, which is held on the thirteenth day after the death. Piyush and Suchitra had already arrived with their baby Suyash. The days between Ammaji's death and the final ceremony were quiet ones. Papaji, as Ammaji's son, had special grieving rituals to follow. He wore the white clothes of mourning, slept on the floor, and spoke very little during those days.

During the quiet afternoons of this mourning period, Pradeep recalled precious memories of his childhood in which he described Ammaji's special place in his life. Mummyji was busy caring for the whole family that included an elderly set of great grandparents. Ammaji was the one Pradeep had sought out for comfort. She fed him, bathed him, and cuddled him at night. Well known throughout the extended family for her ability to remember stories from Hindu mythology, she would recount these fabulous tales to Pradeep as he lay snuggled beside her in bed. Pradeep is now the keeper of that vast treasure house of stories.

On the morning of the thirteenth-day ceremony, members of Pradeep's extended family poured in from all over the state. Mummyji had hired a cook, who set up several kerosene stoves in the courtyard and began to prepare vast quantities of food to feed the guests. Pradeep's sister, Nimmi, had arrived earlier that day. After she and Mummyji greeted an arriving group of family members, they both began to weep. Mummyji recounted the last day of Ammaji's life, telling the details of how she died. The other relatives comforted her. Then more relatives would arrive and Mummyji and Nimmi would do the same thing again. It seemed an important part of the grieving process—to repeat again and again the events of the day of the death.

In the late afternoon, the pundit called us for the final ceremonies. A massive iron cauldron was placed in the centre of the living room, which had been cleared of all its furniture. Sacred threads were tied around the wrists of the mourners, a ritual which forms part of many Hindu ceremonies. Then, the pundit lit the sacred fire, and while he chanted the ancient Sanskrit verses, he poured offerings of *ghee* into the fire. Up to that point, the ceremony was similar to many others in which I had participated. But then the pundit abruptly doused the fire with milk, extinguishing it. Next, he turned to Papaji and snapped the thread from his wrist. All of we other mourners then followed suit, tearing the sacred threads from our wrists. It was a powerful moment, symbolically releasing us from our connection with the deceased. Pradeep said afterwards that it was at that moment he most keenly felt the loss of his beloved Ammaji.

Two weeks later, we set out on our return journey to Pauri. As we travelled, we reflected on all the transitions in our lives over the past year-and-a-half. We'd spent some happy and productive months in Canada, and had returned to the mountains of Garhwal. We'd laid a solid foundation for our health work in the villages. Our family had changed, as well, first with the arrival of our son Raman and now with the death of our beloved Ammaji.

As we traveled, I thought about Ammaji. I had often observed her sitting silently, her face inscrutable, her gaze turned inward— perhaps to the past? To all her losses? So much of her life had been a harsh struggle for survival. Her husband had died at the age of thirty, and four of her five children had died before they reached adolescence. Unimaginable tragedies! Things improved when her son married and had his own children, though the family was still very poor. However, in the last decade, the family fortunes had taken a dramatic upward turn. She had lived to see her three grandchildren married with children of their own.

As I thought of our relationship, memories of Ammaji crowded into my mind. I saw her placing the little image of Jesus in her shrine after our wedding, I felt her hand on my head as she blessed me each time we left Ghaziabad, I tasted the *kitcheree* she cooked for me when I was nauseated in pregnancy. I remembered her words of caution and disbelief when Pradeep described our plans for a life of voluntary poverty. I remembered her whispered words of blessing when she held our babies in her lap. I remembered her indulgent chuckle when Sonia snatched the sugar candy offerings from her shrine.

Raman was the first "son of a son of a son" to be born to Ammaji, and a year later Suyash was born to Piyush and Suchitra. At the naming ceremony for Raman and Suyash just two months previously, Ammaji's face had been filled with a quiet joy. Perhaps this affirmation of life's continuity had healed some old wounds.

Ammaji's life could not have been more different from mine. She grew up in a traditional Hindu household in a desperately poor family, and had very little formal education. By contrast, I grew up in the Christian tradition in a wealthy Canadian family, and had two degrees after my name. Yet we'd created a bond of love that transcended all boundaries, a love that was deep and true.

CHAPTER TEN:

Water From A Mountain Stream

Our house in Pauri was usually bustling with activity, as workers from BMA came to discuss ideas and plan programs. One of the first projects I attempted in those early days was to meet the group of traditional birth attendants who worked in our health centres. These women are intimately connected with village women, and are respected authorities on health at the village level. Each of our health teams included a local village birth attendant, or *dai*, as they are known in Garhwal. Wanting to know more about these women, I planned a two-day workshop to be held at our house.

The World Health Organization has published a curriculum for a three-day training program for traditional birth attendants that has been used in many parts of the world. Nationally, the Indian government has also instituted training programs for *dais* in many parts of India. I had a copy of both these curricula, and considered adapting them for use in Garhwal. However, I wanted to first meet the *dais* from our subcentres to get a sense of their existing knowledge about childbirth.

Five women came to that workshop, one from each of our subcentres. They were women in their fifties and sixties who had learned their craft from an older woman in the village, often their mother-in-law. Also, these women had taken a three-day government *dai* training program several years ago. Now they were a part of the health-care team at each subcentre.

That weekend, the *dais* provided me with a fascinating window into women's health in Garhwal. They shared stories about their daily lives, and talked about their work. Curious to know more, I asked them to tell me about birthing practices in Garhwal. One of them laughed and said, "I'll show you, but you will have to be the woman in labour. We are all too old to give birth!"

She promptly manoeuvred me into a squat, the preferred position for childbirth in this area, and explained that the labouring woman would hang onto a rope suspended from a ceiling beam while another woman provided her with back support. The *dai* squatted in front of the woman, and helped to ease the baby's head out.

On our last afternoon together, the *dais* suggested that we go into the forest in search for the herbs that they use for women during pregnancy and childbirth. We took a two-hour walk through the dense reserve forest high on the ridge above our house. The women collected the seeds and leaves of numerous plants, describing the way they would prepare and use these traditional medicines. When we returned to the house, we laid out the plants to be dried in the sun.

That weekend marked the beginning of my interest in the work of the traditional birth attendant in Garhwal. Over the following months, I took road trips to visit our subcentres, often accompanied by Leela. We spent time with the health workers, checked the clinic's equipment and supplies, and made village visits. I always asked to speak to the *dai* of the village, and invariably she taught me something new about the lives of village women.

On one memorable trip, Leela and I traveled to a little place called Guptkashi, high in the hills of Chamoli Garhwal. The word

"Guptkashi" means "the hidden sacred place." A green valley dotted with fruit trees stretched below the town, and a vast range of the Himalayas shone in the distance. We could see the massive mountain known as Chaukumba, with its four peaks that look like the turrets of a castle.

The town of Guptkashi had a high school, one of the few in this remote area. The principal visited me at our centre, and invited me to speak at the graduation ceremony the following day. I spent the evening feverishly composing a speech in Hindi, using the Roman alphabet to approximate the sounds of the words. Though I could read the Devnagri script, I still could not write it. The workers in our centre listened to me practice and helped me with grammar.

The next day I stood in front of the graduating class, a large crowd of eager young people seated on mats on the beaten earth in front of the school. Almost all were boys, I noticed. In these remote parts of the foothills, girls rarely had the opportunity to complete high school. I managed to get through my speech without too much difficulty, and I hoped that they could understand my peculiar pronunciation. I would never find out what mistakes I made, because people in Garhwal were invariably appreciative of my meagre language skills.

Later that day, Leela and I accompanied the health workers to a nearby village, where we planned to attend a meeting of the local women's organization, the *Mahila Mangal Dal,* to talk about women's health. The path to the village led through groves of orange trees. The fruit was ripening, glowing with colour in the morning sun. *What a feast for the senses! This green valley, the orange trees, and the lofty peaks of Chaukumba in the distance...I can't think of a more beautiful spot in the world.*

When we reached the village, we were welcomed by a woman with an air of natural authority, with striking dark eyes and a confident posture. I learned that she was the leader of the *Mahila Mangal Dal,* and that she was a tireless advocate for women in that area. As we walked through the village I explained that I wanted to learn more about why women in Garhwal suffer ill health.

"Of course, of course," she replied. "The women will explain everything to you. Come and see where we'll be meeting."

She led us to an open area near the centre of the village, shaded by a huge tree. We sat on the wooden bench that encircled the trunk of the tree, and before long a young girl appeared with cups of tea. Leela talked with the health workers about their latest challenges, while I sat quietly absorbing the atmosphere of the place.

Village women began to gather in the open area around the tree. Chatting and laughing with each other, they settled themselves in a semi-circle around us. One of the health workers introduced me to Beena Devi[6], the *dai* of that village. She was a woman of about sixty with a weather-beaten face and piercing black eyes, a keen intelligence evident in the way she spoke.

The leader of the *Mahila Mangal Dal* welcomed the women to the meeting, introduced us and explained that we wanted to understand more about why women in Garhwal fall ill.

Beena Devi replied at once, "Of course, it is mostly because we have to work so hard—too hard! We get up before the sun has risen and we give food to the animals. Then we drink a cup of tea with one dry *roti*. Next, we have to walk for hours to reach the jungle. Every year, we women have to walk farther to get wood for our fires and fodder for our animals."

Another woman nodded and said, "Don't forget the problem of water. Some villages have a tube well or a natural spring. But quite often there is no water in the village, and we have to walk to collect water as well. This is our biggest headache."

A woman sitting beside me said, "Let me tell you a funny thing. In our village, when a marriage is being arranged for a girl, she

....

6   Many women in India do not use surnames, but rather use their first names followed by "Devi", an honorific meaning goddess.

right away asks her parents—Is there water in that boy's village? Imagine! She doesn't even ask about the boy, is he handsome, does he have a job, is he kind-hearted? She asks—'Is there water in his village?' Because she knows that she will have great trouble and hard work for many years if there is no water in the village."

"What about the family?" asked Leela. "I suppose that if a woman has many children, she is burdened with too much work?"

"Yes, that is true," replied a middle-aged woman wearing a large nose ring, traditional jewellery in this part of Garhwal. "In days gone by, women had very big families, sometimes eight or ten children. Nowadays, we women do not want to have such big families. The best family size is three children: two boys and one girl."

Other women in the group nodded in agreement and a vigorous discussion began.

"We must have a son," explained an elderly woman, who was wearing the white sari of widowhood. "Our daughters are only travellers in our home. Their true home is with their future husband. It is our sons and their wives who will care for us in our old age. And when we die, our land goes to our sons."

"Without a son, who will light our funeral pyres?"

"Without a son, who will plough the fields? This work is too heavy for us, even though we are strong."

"But why is it necessary to have two sons?" I asked. "What about one son and one daughter?"

The old woman in the white sari said, "We have a saying in Garhwal that goes, 'Ek ank se kya barosa—do ank hona chayiye.' This is why it is necessary always to have minimum two sons."

I learned that this saying means, "How can one trust only one eye—one should have two eyes." Infant mortality is still high, and many women had personal experiences of the death of a child. At least two sons should be born to ensure the survival of one to adulthood.

Then a younger woman broke into the conversation. "But Didi, will it always be like this? Why can't our daughters light our funeral pyres? Why can't we invite our son-in-law to live with us? Why can't we hire our neighbour to plough our fields?"

Leela said, "You are right, and this is beginning to happen nowadays. I heard of a family in Pauri that had just two daughters. The girls were educated and had good marriages. When the parents became old, one of the girls invited them to live with her family. And her husband welcomed them."

The woman with the nose ring said, "In a village not far from here, there lives a strong-minded woman who never cares what people say. When her mother died, she and her eight-year-old son performed all the death rituals for her mother. People in the village were shocked! They criticized her a lot. But she told me that several days after the ceremonies were complete, her mother appeared to her in a dream and told her that she had done the right thing. Then her heart was at peace."

"After hearing about the dream, the villagers also came to accept her actions, " said the elderly woman.

I asked, "How do people feel when a daughter is born?"

One of the younger women replied, "Usually, when a girl is born we do not have any big celebration within the family like we do after the birth of a boy. You know that we still give dowry for our daughters at the time of marriage, and so people worry they will have a lot of money problems if there are many daughters."

"And if you can believe it, we women are often blamed if many girls are born to us. The man might say that you have some deficiency; that is why only girls are born," said a woman sitting at the edge of the group who had been silent so far.

"Ha!" snorted Beena Devi. "I would say to him: 'Listen, whatever seed YOU sowed so will be the plant. . . .'"

All the women burst out laughing. Beena Devi, like so many other village midwives, seemed to be the one who could voice a protest about cultural values that were demeaning to women. I found it fascinating to hear how these women resist gender discrimination using humour and storytelling.

A few months after the Guptkashi visit, I had the opportunity to spend some time at the BMA headquarters while Pradeep looked after the children. I decided to visit a *dai* in her own village, observing her life and work and discussing women's health issues with her. I set off early one clear February morning, backpack on my back. The first part of the trek took me through a forest of soaring *chir* pines. Beyond the forest, I could catch a glimpse of Chandrabadni Devi, a small, glittering temple at the top of the tallest hill in the area. This is one of five sacred temples in Garhwal dedicated to the goddess Parvati, all dramatically located on hilltops. Beyond Chandrabadni Devi, I could see shimmering rows of snow-capped Himalayan peaks. The joy I have felt so often in Garhwal—the joy that always draws me back to this remote corner of the world—seized me once again.

Rajni Devi was a *dai* I'd met at a recent meeting. In the usual hospitable way of Garhwali villagers, she'd invited me to her home. Now as I reached her village, she came running out to greet me. We walked together through the village to her home, an old traditional Garhwali house built of wood and stone. We sat down on the verandah, and tea appeared almost instantly, brought by a shyly smiling girl of about ten.

Later in the afternoon, Rajni Devi asked me to visit some women in the village who were having health problems. She led me along narrow paths between the houses, holding my hand when we had to negotiate a steep or broken section. We visited five or six women that evening, some with relatively minor illnesses and others with serious health problems. The last woman we visited, Janaki Devi, asked us to come inside her home. The room we entered was dark and smoky, lit by a single kerosene lamp. It took a few minutes for my eyes to become accustomed to the dim light. The room was furnished with two *charpoys*, the traditional rope beds that are still used in many parts of India. A large metal trunk covered with an orange cloth occupied one corner of the room. These trunks are used to store blankets, winter clothes, and sometimes a precious possession such as a carefully preserved wedding sari. On the wall above the trunk was a brightly coloured calendar displaying an image of the goddess Laxsmi.

Janaki Devi sat down on the *charpoy* opposite us and began to tell her story, hesitantly at first.

"My problem is a terrible one," she murmured, softly. "It began nine years ago, after my last baby was born. I have five children and I've never had any trouble with the births before. But with that baby, something went wrong." Her eyes welled with tears. Struggling for composure, she draped the free end of her sari over her head and hid her face from view.

"My pains were very strong, but the baby could not be born. We tried many things." Here she looked over at Rajni Devi, who began to look rather hesitant. Finally, Rajni Devi said, "You know, Madam, here in our Garhwal we have many beliefs when a baby is slow to be born. The pundit came and did a ritual. We sacrificed a goat. And, finally, I went and called Dr. Pal, who is the *chota* doctor working in the next village. He came and gave her an injection that made the pains even stronger. But nothing worked."

I knew about *chota* doctors in Garhwal. These practitioners have worked as assistants to licensed physicians for some years, though they have no formal medical training. Then through a Government of India program (since discontinued), they are eligible to apply for a certification that enables them to work in remote areas of the country. They are generally well accepted by the village people and they are accessible in cases of emergency. However, their practice of medicine can be dangerous, since they rely heavily on injectable medications and on the administration of intravenous fluid. In Janaki Devi's case, Dr. Pal must have given an injection of oxytocin, a powerful uterine stimulant.

Janaki Devi took up the story. "When the injection didn't work, Rajni Devi told me that I must go to hospital. But it is not easy to do that! We must walk for one hour to reach the road, and we have no vehicle. And my father-in-law said that it would cost too much. We village people can be cheated by people in the city. Most of all, I was afraid of going to the hospital."

"So another day went by," said Rajni Devi. "But finally, on the third day, I insisted to the family that she must be taken. And so with great difficulty, four men of the village carried her up to the road. We were lucky that a truck came along within an hour or so, and the driver agreed to take us to the hospital in Srinagar. When we reached there, the lady doctor said that a Caesarean section must be done. We were all afraid of this, but we agreed. What else could we do?"

"The baby was born dead," whispered Janaki Devi. "I was very weak but I knew that I would survive. And so I left the hospital as soon as I could. But ever since that baby was born, I have been unable to hold my urine. It is dripping out of me all the time. It is a matter of great shame to me." She began to weep silently.

I realized that she was suffering from vesico-vaginal fistula, an abnormal connection between the bladder and the vagina caused by the pressure of the baby's head against the mother's bladder during an obstructed labour. The continuous urinary incontinence is distressing for the woman, who finds it impossible to keep herself clean and dry. I had been noticing a foul, musty odour in the room, mingled with the smell of wood smoke, and I now understood its origin. What a torment this condition must be for this poor woman.

In those remote parts of the world where obstetrical care is difficult to obtain, vesico-vaginal fistula causes a great burden of suffering among women. When I discussed this further with Janaki

Devi, she said that she had not consulted a doctor because she felt too ashamed of the problem. She also thought that little could be done. I described the operation that can be done to correct the problem. It is not an easy procedure, but it is usually successful.

Janaki Devi called her husband to come and join the discussion. Surgery would mean a trip to Dehradun and considerable expense. However, the gynecologist in Dehradun who did these procedures was a classmate of Pradeep's, and would always reduce her fees for those who are not well-off. Yet Janaki Devi's husband replied, "Even if I have to sell our buffalo, I think we must go. This is a terrible problem for us."

Later that evening, I wondered how many other women in these hills were suffering silently with this problem. Perhaps the way to find out would be through the *dais*, women like Rajni Devi who have such intimate knowledge of women's health problems. These women seemed to hold the key to local understanding of women's health issues in these villages.

When we returned to Rajni Devi's house that evening, she and her neighbours picked up large brass pots and set off to fetch the evening supply of water. We walked steeply downhill for about half a kilometre to an ancient stone temple. It looked to me that it had been built in about the eighth or ninth century, a time when small but magnificent stone temples were constructed all over Garhwal. Flowing out from underneath the building was a clear stream of water, emerging from the mouth of a stone lion. It was the festival of Shiv Ratri that day, so all the women went into the temple to worship and make offerings of a few rupees and some fruits. This small, sacred site has been a place of worship, and a source of water, for well over a thousand years.

As I watched the women making their offerings, I noticed a whistling thrush perched on a branch overhanging the little stream, its glossy blue-black wings folded over its deep purple body. Its song begins with brief trilling notes, stops abruptly, and then starts up again, in a breathtakingly beautiful cadence. There is a legend in this part of India that a little boy had been very fond of whistling, trying to imitate Krishna's flute. Lord Krishna, furious at this effrontery, turned the boy into a bird—the whistling thrush.

When the women had filled their brass pots with water, we began the long, slow climb back up the hill. As we walked, the woman ahead of me discussed the problem of her daughter-in-law, childless after eight years of marriage. Infertility is a devastating problem for a Garhwali woman, and all too often she is blamed without having had any investigations done. However, in this case, the husband and wife had been to a well-known gynecologist in Dehradun. Once I got back to the house, I looked through all the investigations and reports. Even a specialized test called a hysterosalpingogram had been done, which showed that the fallopian tubes were blocked. The gynecologist had said nothing could be done. I asked the family about the possibility of adoption, although I knew that the answer would be an emphatic "No." Raising a child not of one's own blood is considered an undesirable and risky undertaking. The mother-in-law said, "No, I realize that there is only one answer. My son will have to marry again." The childless daughter-in-law, a beautiful woman of about twenty-six, stared down at the ground, her hands twisting in her lap.

I felt a rush of pity for this young woman, realizing the precarious nature of her place in the family. I didn't know what to say, and an awkward silence ensued. I felt relieved when Rajni Devi entered the room to call us to the Shiv Ratri feast. Rajni Devi's family was already seated in the main room of the house, waiting for us. The women had been fasting all day, and would now break their fast with a specially prepared meal. A particular delicacy for this day is a root found deep in the jungle. Rajni Devi and her sister-in-law brought out the large metal *thalis* on which the food would be served, and gave one to each man sitting in the main room. They would eat first, followed by the children, and last, the women.

I slept that night in a narrow cot, across the room from Rajni Devi with two of her grandchildren. The last sound I heard before sinking into sleep was the strange call of the nightjar—a peculiar "tonk, tonk" that sounds like a hammer striking a plank. I slept soundly, awaking soon after dawn. It was the last day of February, my birthday, and I could not think of anywhere else I would rather be than here in this village. Rajni Devi and the other women had already left the house to go on their long walk to the forest to gather firewood. Rajni's elderly mother-in-law brought me a breakfast of *roti* dipped in sweet tea. We sat in comfortable silence under the shade of a tree, each lost in her own thoughts. Before my mind's eye floated the image of the stone lion below the temple, with a stream of fresh water pouring from its mouth. Who had carved that lion, and how long ago? That unknown artist had been inspired to create something of beauty as a way to worship this mountain stream. What a symbol of hope, and of life itself!

The harsh caw of a crow shattered my peaceful reverie. The sun was rising high in the sky, and Pradeep would be waiting for me at noon, in the little town by the road. I got up abruptly, hastily stuffed my belongings into my backpack, and bade farewell to the old woman. Though I knew the way back, an elderly man from the village insisted on accompanying me. His face was weatherbeaten, with a web of wrinkles around his eyes and deep lines carved across his brow and down his cheeks. He was probably not more than fifty-five, but a tough life had aged him prematurely. He told me that he had served in the Garhwal Rifles, the regiment of the Indian army that draws its recruits from this region.

We reached the road just before noon. The Jeep was parked beside a teashop not far away, and I could see Pradeep sipping tea with the driver. We tossed my bag into the back of the Jeep, and began our journey. Pradeep wanted to meet a man who was

involved in a local NGO in the town of Tehri, the old capital of
the district of Tehri Garhwal. On our way, we passed through the
Bhilangana valley, an unusually fertile region whose broad fields
shimmered with waves of winter wheat.

I had read about this place in a book about Mahatma Gandhi's
life. One of his closest disciples was an English woman who had
taken the name "Mira Behn." Some years after Gandhi's untimely
death, Mira Behn had come to this valley and established a
spiritual community called Gopal Ashram. This community was
modeled on Gandhian ideals, and became a place where many
idealistic young people from Garhwal studied and worked. Mira
Behn was passionate about social justice and the empowerment of
women. She was also an environmentalist, one of the first to write
about the ecological threats facing Garhwal. In the early 1950s,
she was writing articles raising concerns about the deforestation
that was occurring in the mountains.

We rounded a sharp bend in the road, and before us, the
valley spread out in all its beauty. In the broad, terraced fields, the
mustard and wheat created a tapestry of gold and green. Women
wearing bright cotton saris moved slowly through the shimmering
fields, using handheld sickles to cut the crops. The winter harvest
had begun. Far above us, a group of three women were making
their way down a winding path toward the village in the valley,
each with a load of firewood on her back. From this distance, the
scene below looked tranquil, almost idyllic. Yet how well I knew
another reality. The women would have all risen before five in the
morning, balancing their responsibilities of work in the jungle
and in the fields with animal husbandry, childcare, and home-
making. They would be working all day and would eat very little.
If one of them fell from a tree or cut herself with the sickle, health
care would be difficult to obtain. Within the home, she may be
facing an oppressive husband or mother-in-law, and might have
the responsibility of caring for both children and elderly relatives.

Our Jeep slowed suddenly. We had reached the place where the path from the jungle above us crossed the road. The driver had spotted a woman coming down the path, a heavy load of wood on her back. He stopped the vehicle to let her pass. As she walked in front of the Jeep, she and I exchanged a glance. I smiled at her and held my hands up in the traditional gesture of greeting. For a brief moment, we regarded each other with careful attention. Then she smiled back at me, shifted the burden on her back slightly, and stepped onto the path heading down toward the village.

It was only a moment, probably of little significance to her. But it fanned a flame of desire within me, that same desire that had compelled me to leave Canada four years earlier. I wanted to create a connection with her, to learn from her, and to be useful in some way to her and other women of Garhwal. This small moment symbolized my life's project—to create heartfelt connections across the barriers of culture, country, and class.

CHAPTER ELEVEN:

The Gathering Storm

By the end of our first year with BMA, Pradeep and I could look back with some satisfaction. We'd been pouring heart and soul into our work, and now had functioning health centres established in five different parts of the Garhwal Himalaya. We had a core team of twelve health workers trained in prevention and treatment of common illnesses, and outreach teams of village health workers and traditional birth attendants. Two health workers were young widows, women who otherwise would have no means of earning a living and little social status. As they acquired knowledge and skills about health, they began to blossom visibly before our eyes. They were becoming valued members of village communities, earning a living and providing an essential service.

Of those twelve, there were some women with whom I became especially close. Leela was our nurse. Originally from Kerala, she had had an unhappy first marriage, and had decided to leave her husband—never an easy choice for a woman in India. I don't know how she made her way to BMA, in this remote corner of Garhwal so far from her native place. But I do know that when she met Cyril, he immediately saw her potential and encouraged her to stay. Garhwal must have been a strange environment for her, a place where she didn't know the language or understand the customs. But within a remarkably short time, she became a highly respected nurse in BMA. I admired her superb organizational skills, and I loved her steely determination to forge a path for herself.

Then there was Savitri, our first Garhwali ANM. When she joined BMA, she was very young, with little experience and not much health knowledge. But what commitment she had! As I'd guessed at our first meeting, she became one of our most dedicated health workers. She was always willing to take on the toughest jobs, and her energy and enthusiasm were infectious.

Another woman I loved was Unita, whose husband had died some years previously in a tragic accident. She had three children, and no means to support them. She had done ANM training, and so left her children with her in-laws, and joined BMA. She rarely had an opportunity to visit them. I admired her for the way she bore these hardships without complaint, working hard to become a strong member of the team.

Besides our health workers, I formed friendships with many others in the ashram. Usha was a tiny woman who'd been born with a badly deformed foot, and walked with difficulty. She worked in the main headquarters in Anjanisain, mostly in the library. She had a special sweetness and a quiet strength.

"Do you think I'm foolish to care so much about these women?" I asked Pradeep one day. We were travelling in a BMA jeep, on our way to Anjanisain for team meetings.

"Of course not," replied Pradeep. "That is your true nature, to love others in a transparent way. You can see their hearts. That is your gift."

I pondered this for some time. A light rain had fallen the night before, and the mountains were draped in misty veils of cloud.

"Bill once said that I must find my own true path in life," I murmured. "When I am with those women, I feel as if I am walking on that path."

"That is wonderful," replied Pradeep, squeezing my hand.

Sonia and Raman had fallen asleep on the seat beside me, and Pradeep and I were enjoying this rare opportunity to share ideas. We always had something to talk about, with topics ranging from the mundane tasks of the day, to passionate debate about cross-cultural values, to thoughtful exploration of spiritual ideas.

When we reached Anjanisain, it was late afternoon. Rays of sun were breaking through the clouds and casting long shadows across the valley below the ashram. We saw Cyril striding down the path to meet us, accompanied by two boys and a younger girl who were waving and shouting greetings. Cyril had adopted these orphaned children some years before, and they were flourishing under his loving care. The two boys helped us unload the Jeep and carry our bags up to the guesthouse. Wide awake by this time, Sonia laughed with delight when she saw Cyril—he was a great favourite of hers.

The following morning, the team meeting began, with leaders from all project sites coming together to report on progress. Cyril spoke about his vision for BMA in the upcoming year, encouraging us to imagine future possibilities and inspiring us to shape our dreams into realities. We heard about the work of each subcentre from the team leaders. At Guptkashi, BMA was partnering with a local man on a venture to produce juice from *maltas*, the oranges that grew abundantly in that area. At the subcentre in Gairsain, the women's group had suggested developing a cottage industry to produce products from bamboo. The children's daycare programs seemed to be running well at all the centres, and were much appreciated by village women. Pradeep and I talked about the evolution of the health program, and discussed an upcoming training program for all the health workers that would be held in Anjanisain.

Swami Manmathan did not attend the meeting, leaving that work entirely up to Cyril. He was still a mysterious figure to me, and I wanted to get to know him better on this visit. I had hardly exchanged more than a few sentences with him since we had met. Pradeep and I sought him out one evening, finding him drinking tea in a small room off the ashram kitchen. He looked up abruptly as we came in. I am usually a good judge of character, but Swami Manmathan was impossible to read. He had an intense presence that I found disturbing, rather than appealing. We had a brief conversation in which he told Pradeep about a health problem that one of the office staff was having. Pradeep said that he would check her the next morning.

I asked him a question about the villages of the Anjanisain area, and he replied, "This area is full of crooks. Useless people mostly." With that, he got up and turned away from us, walking rapidly out of the room without any further comment.

"What a strange man!" I said to Pradeep. "Have you had any opportunity to really talk to him?"

"Not much," said Pradeep. "I always get the feeling that he is trying to test me. Last time I was in Anjanisain, he told me that there was a sick woman in a village at the very top of the mountain. He expected me to go immediately to see her. It was already beginning to get dark. Anyway, I did go. I climbed for nearly two hours and when I got there, I found that there wasn't much wrong with the woman. I had to stay that night in the village and come back the next day. You know, I think he made me do it just to show his power. I don't like him and also I don't trust him."

"And yet, think about that nice letter he sent us when we were still in Canada, inviting us to join BMA," I said.

"I doubt that was actually his letter. I think Cyril wrote it, and just got him to sign it," replied Pradeep.

As soon as Pradeep said this, I realized he must be right. Perhaps Cyril felt that it was all right to write that letter in his role as Swami Manmathan's PR man. Still, that little incident made me strangely uneasy.

Our stay in Anjanisain was nearly over. Before we left the BMA headquarters, I walked down to the clinic to say goodbye to Leela. As usual, the clinic was in perfect order. I reviewed the register she kept that contained details of the patients she had seen and the treatment she'd dispensed. She was making visits to the villages surrounding BMA as well as holding regular clinic hours. She'd established a prenatal clinic and was encouraging pregnant women to come in for iron supplements and a tetanus shot during pregnancy. When we began to discuss the care of women at the time of childbirth, Leela said, "Madam, recently a great tragedy happened in a village very near to the ashram."

She began to recount the sad story, hesitantly at first. She had been clearly affected by the experience, since she had been intimately involved.

She told me that Meera was a twenty-two-year-old woman who was expecting her second child. Late one evening, about a week before her due date, she developed sudden, painless bleeding. When it did not stop, the *dai* decided to call the pundit from a neighbouring village, who was known for his abilities to call the *devi*—the goddess worshipped by the village people. The pundit arrived, and for eight hours, various rituals were performed. Still the bleeding did not abate. The *dai* then decided that Meera should be sent to a hospital, and discussed the situation with family members. Meera's father-in-law was concerned about the difficulties and expense of the journey. However, eventually the family agreed, respecting the *dai's* assessment of the situation.

Four men carried Meera on a cot from the village up to the road. From there, she was taken to the clinic in the ashram where Leela assessed her. Realizing the seriousness of the situation, Leela prepared rehydration fluid and arranged for one of BMA's vehicles to take her to the nearest midsize town. But at their small government hospital, no doctor was available due to a doctor's strike. The group had to go on to Rishikesh, three hours away, where they consulted a female gynecologist. She was shocked at Meera's condition, blaming the group for their delay in bringing this woman to the hospital. For Meera's treatment, she recommended a blood transfusion followed by a Caesarian section. Since there was no blood bank in this hospital, she told them to go on to Dehradun, the regional referral centre, another hour's drive away. The family left the hospital, bewildered and upset. Meera's father-in-law had objections to both the blood transfusion and the surgery. Leela persuaded them to continue on to Dehradun, but before they could reach the hospital, Meera died. She had been bleeding for over twenty-four hours.

By the time she finished the story, tears were trickling down Leela's face.

"It was so sad, Madam. Such a young woman! And we did try hard, but there were so many problems."

Listening to the story, I surmised that Meera's biomedical diagnosis was placenta previa, in which the placenta was abnormally positioned behind the cervix, making vaginal birth impossible. The treatment for the condition is a Caesarian section, done as soon as possible. With timely treatment, mother and baby are usually fine.

As we drove back toward Pauri, I kept thinking about Meera, who had died because she had not reached a hospital in time for a Caesarian section. Could the outcome of her illness have been different? I realized that it was the *dai* who eventually made the decision to seek hospital care. I wondered how the *dais* decide when to seek emergency care, and which type of practitioner to consult. She would likely try home remedies first if a problem was thought to be of minor significance. If she believed that the problem was caused by evil spirits, then she would consult a ritual practitioner rather than a biomedical doctor.

Meera's story inspired me to start *dai* training programs at each of our subcentres. I thought I had a reasonable understanding of the work of the *dais* based on the first workshop I'd held in Pauri. Since then, I'd developed a curriculum based on a WHO model that Pradeep had helped me translate into Hindi.

By May I was ready to conduct the first workshop, to be held at the BMA headquarters in Anjanisain. Word had gone out to all the villages in the area about the upcoming training program, and sixteen participants had said they would come.

Savitri and Leela assisted in conducting the workshop. I felt a thrill of excitement when I realized I could communicate effectively in Hindi with these women. My grammar was often fractured and I still had difficulty pronouncing some words, but I could definitely make myself understood. We shared stories about difficult deliveries we had attended, and I gradually began to understand more about the way these women practice their craft. I discovered that there is a referral system that the *dais* had set up themselves.

Ujjala Devi was the *dai* who worked with our local health subcentre in Anjanisain. She explained to me, "We call on Kamla Devi when we have a problem with a delivery. She is very expert in many things. You must ask her when she comes about what she can do."

Kamla Devi arrived about an hour later than the rest of the women, walking into the room with an air of authority and easy confidence. All the other women moved aside to let her sit at the front. She was clearly held in great respect.

She told me that she was an expert in turning breech babies before birth. Whenever a pregnant woman was suspected to have this problem, she would be called in when the woman was about eight months pregnant.

"Then I apply mustard oil to the woman's tummy, and after that, I turn the baby slowly and carefully until it moves to the proper position," she told me, demonstrating the manoeuvre with her hands.

This fascinated me. In a remote region like Garhwal, the birth of a breech baby could certainly result in complications. Manual version of a breech baby to the vertex (head-down) position can also have complications. Sometimes the cord can be twisted or the placenta damaged. However, the overall risk to mother and baby is probably reduced by turning the baby prior to the onset of labour.

Kamla Devi also told me that the village *dai* is called in when animals had difficulties giving birth. She described a recent visit to a village where she had to deliver a breech buffalo. She said, "First, I put my hand into the birth passage and I felt the tail and rump of the calf. I knew it could not be born if it was lying that way. So I pushed the rump higher up, and then looped a piece of twine around one leg. In this way, I could pull that leg into the birth passage. Then I did the same for the other leg. Then when the mother buffalo had her next pains, I could see two little hooves coming out. And then the whole calf was born—alive!"

Following Kamla's lead, the other *dais* began to share stories. One woman told me that she'd delivered a set of quadruplets, each of whom was not much bigger than her hand. All of them died soon after birth, not surprisingly. Another *dai* described a woman with prolonged obstructed labour, which had tragically resulted in the death of both the baby and the mother.

Several of the *dais* recounted stories about women who had had postpartum hemorrhaging. I listened attentively, knowing that this is one of the major causes of maternal mortality world-wide. I noticed with surprise that none of the women perceived bleeding after a birth to be dangerous.

"It's good to bleed after a birth—you get rid of that bad, contaminated blood," said one elderly *dai*. The other women nodded in agreement.

I shared a story about a delivery I had attended when I was working in northern Ontario the year after I completed my training. The woman's labour had been progressing well, and she felt the urge to push. Suddenly, I saw a loop of umbilical cord appear at the vaginal opening.

"What do you think about that?" I asked the women.

"Very dangerous," Kamla Devi replied, promptly. "Most likely, this baby will die."

I continued my story, telling them we had called for the obstetrician to perform an immediate Caesarean section. I had gently pushed the cord back into the vagina and kept my hand there to prevent it from being crushed. We got the woman into the operating room within twenty minutes, and the baby was born alive and well.

"Imagine that," said the woman sitting next to Savitri. "If somebody has a problem, you can get help so quickly—even get an operation!"

"In our Garhwal, this doesn't happen," said Aarti Devi, a *dai* who worked in a village near Anjanisain. "Here, we are in God's hands, and if it is His will, we live. Otherwise we die."

By this time it was nearly 1:30 and we were ready for lunch. Plates loaded with *dal*, rice, and vegetables appeared from the ashram kitchen, and we were soon tucking in, chatting, and laughing as we ate. I felt excited about the morning session. We had developed a good rapport by sharing our stories about childbirth in Garhwal, and I looked forward to introducing some training material from the WHO curriculum in the afternoon.

Our first topic was the care of women during pregnancy. It soon became clear that prenatal care in the villages of Garhwal is quite different from that in my Canadian clinic. The *dais* talked about the need for strict regulation of diet during pregnancy, specifically the avoidance of any food considered "heating" to the system. This concept links to humoral understandings in which health is maintained by a proper balance between hot and cold in the body. I asked the women which types of food would be prohibited in pregnancy. They generated a long list that I scribbled down in my diary. "Hot" foods included meat, eggs, particular types of *dal,* and even certain fruits such as mangoes. Spices were also considered heating to the system and should be avoided.

"But I think it is very important for pregnant women to eat eggs, *dal,* and even meat, if possible, for the best possible nutrition," I said earnestly.

"No, no, absolutely not!" the women replied.

"You see, if a pregnant woman eats those types of food, her baby will be big and strong," I said.

"Ha!" replied the woman sitting beside Leela. "We do not want big and strong babies. We want small and lively babies."

I must have looked puzzled, because Kamla Devi intervened.

"You see, Madam," she said, "here in our Garhwal, we do not want to have big babies. This is dangerous for us. Do you know, there was once a woman in my village who became very big in her pregnancy. And when it was time for her to deliver, the baby's head popped out but its shoulder got stuck. I had a lot of trouble getting that baby out. For us, it's better to have small and lively babies."

In Canada, I was used to encouraging pregnant women to eat a high-calorie and high-protein diet to maximize the growth of the baby. Research worldwide has shown that low birth-weight babies do not thrive as well as bigger babies. But as I listened to Kamla Devi, I wondered if the researchers studying the correlation between birth weight and health of babies had ever considered the complications of delivery that can occur with large babies. I shuddered inwardly at the thought of having to manage the complication described by Kamla Devi in a Garhwali village. Known as shoulder dystocia, this condition results from the baby's shoulder getting jammed against the woman's pelvic bone during labour. Delivery of the baby becomes fraught with peril.

Anemia in pregnancy is a common condition among low-income Indian mothers, and the government of India provides free iron tablets to pregnant women throughout the country. We had stocks of these tablets in our clinic. I launched into a discussion of strengthening one's blood by taking iron tablets during pregnancy, and showed them the brown pills we kept in the clinic.

One of the *dais* clicked her tongue disapprovingly. "My daughter-in-law took those pills in her first pregnancy," she said. "And do you know what happened? She became very constipated and her poop turned completely black!"

In India, people's bowel habits are very well regulated and constipation is a condition that is universally disliked. The other *dais* shook their heads.

"No, we would not give this pill to pregnant women," they said.

I didn't seem to be getting very far with my discussion on nutrition in pregnancy. I looked down at my notes, and saw that the next topic was entitled "neonatal tetanus."

"Have you ever seen a baby that had fits when it was about ten days old?" I asked.

"Oh yes," replied several women.

Aarti Devi said, "This is what happens. The baby stops feeding well and becomes irritable and its muscles twitch. Then . . . I'll show you what happens next." She arched her back sharply and clenched her jaw muscles. "After that, the baby has fits and then it dies."

I was fascinated by this accurate description of the natural history of neonatal tetanus. This condition is caused by unhygienic treatment of the umbilical cord after birth. If the cord is cut with a dirty or rusty blade, the baby can develop neonatal tetanus. In places like Garhwal, this condition would be almost universally fatal.

"What do you think causes this illness?" I asked.

"It is due to possession by an evil spirit," one of the women replied. "We do rituals to try to chase away the spirit but in babies it doesn't usually work. Their bodies are not strong enough to resist the power of that evil spirit."

Pradeep had told me that these women likely would not subscribe to the germ theory of disease. In fact, he warned me, they would not even understand the Hindi word for germ.

"If you want to talk about germs as the cause for illness, you had better use the word *keera* which means worm. Tell them that germs are like very tiny worms," he suggested.

I took out my flipchart about neonatal tetanus that I had ordered from the Voluntary Health Association of India. Savitri and I worked our way through it, describing the way knives or sickles can carry *keera* into the baby's blood.

"These tiny *keera* are the cause of that disease in babies. It can be prevented by cutting the cord with a new razor blade," I said.

The women looked mystified.

"Are you trying to make a joke?" asked a *dai* named Vimla Devi. "How can there be such a thing as a worm that is so small that it is invisible?"

"What about the evil spirits? Does the worm call to those spirits?" asked another *dai*, incredulously.

With Savitri's help, I tried to explain once again the role of *keera* in neonatal tetanus. But I was fighting a losing battle. The women turned to Kamla Devi for her opinion.

"This illness is certainly caused by evil spirits," she pronounced. "I have seen many cases in my lifetime and I know how dangerous it is. Only an evil spirit can take the lives of so many babies. We all know about worms. Worms are unpleasant but they do not take lives. And as for a tiny worm, so small that it cannot be seen? No, Madam. Such a thing could not cause an illness as bad as this one."

Satisfied, the women nodded to each other. At that point, a young woman came into the room bearing a tray filled with glasses of tea, and soon the women were chatting cheerfully amongst themselves. I sipped my tea, my head spinning. So much for the authoritative voice of biomedicine, I thought, wryly.

That evening, Kamla Devi said to me, "Now Madam, we must show you some nice things from Garhwal. We will show you how we can dance."

Ujjala Devi settled herself in a corner of the room with a *dholak* in her lap, a traditional drum that is common in this part of India. She beat a slow rhythm, and one by one the *dais* got up and began to dance. The rhythm grew more rapid and insistent, and before long, the women were dipping and swirling around the room. The energy and joy of the dancing women coursed through the room, touching each of us.

Over the next two days, I plugged along with the training program and managed to work through the material that I had prepared. As the final day came to a close, I realized that I had learned a tremendous amount about childbirth in Garhwal. However, I was doubtful about how much the women had learned from me.

On the last day of the training, I had prepared a gift for each of the *dais*, handwoven cotton bags that each contained two dozen tiny birthing kits. Each kit contained a sliver of soap, squares of gauze, string to tie the cord, and a new razor blade.

Kamla Devi came over to look at the bags. She pulled out one of the little kits and inspected it closely. I could feel a blush spreading over my face.

Eventually, Kamla Devi said, " Madam, I can see that you very truly believe in these razor blades."

"Well, yes, I do," I replied, feeling ridiculous.

"Then in that case, we shall certainly use them!" she said. "Don't worry, Madam. I will explain everything to the women."

We walked back into the training hall together, our arms laden with the brightly coloured cotton bags. Kamla Devi showed the contents of one of the kits to the women, speaking rapidly in the local Garhwali dialect. I could hardly understand a word, and I knew from the puzzled look on Leela's face that she couldn't understand either.

"There we are!" said Kamla Devi, turning back to us with a satisfied air. "Everyone is going to use those little kits."

Completely bemused, I helped Leela and Savitri distribute the bags. There was much chattering and laughing among the women, and several of them patted my shoulder.

A *dai* wearing a large nose ring said, "Madam, I want to tell you that we enjoyed this training very much."

"Let's have another one soon," suggested another woman, and the others enthusiastically agreed.

Then they gathered up their belongings and we said our *Namastes* to each other.

After everyone had left, Leela, Savitri, and I started to tidy up the room, putting away the flipcharts, models, and diagrams that we'd used in the training program. I felt totally confused, and very relieved that the whole thing was over.

"Savitri, what did Kamla Devi say to those women?" I asked. Since Savitri was herself Garhwali, I knew she would have understood the conversation.

But Savitri was strangely reticent on the subject. I never did find out what convinced the *dais* of Anjanisain to use the razor blades!

The following day, I went out for a stroll along the Anjanisain road. I met Aarti Devi walking toward her village, not far from the ashram. I greeted her cheerfully and fell into step beside her. Soon, I was talking about the ideas Pradeep and I had for BMA's health program, filled with my usual enthusiasm for the work. I asked what she thought about our plans.

After a long pause, she said, "Madam, listen to my advice. Don't work here anymore. Find somewhere else to go. Too much blood has been shed."

"But that is all in the past, isn't it?" I asked, with surprise.

"The land remembers," she muttered. "Violence is all around this place."

She said nothing more, and we walked the rest of the way in silence. The conversation had given me a peculiar, uneasy feeling that was hard to shake. Back at the ashram, I told Pradeep about Aarti Devi's cryptic words.

To my surprise, Pradeep answered slowly, "I think I know what she means. Haven't you felt something strange in the atmosphere around Anjanisain?"

For the first time, I began to think carefully about this. The BMA headquarters were expanding rapidly, with more staff being hired and new buildings being constructed. Yet there was definitely something uncomfortable about the atmosphere around the ashram. I was often aware of an almost palpable sense of foreboding as we turned the curve around the mountainside near the ashram. Village people, usually so open and friendly, were not like this in the villages around Anjanisain. They stared darkly at the vehicle and I perceived hostility in their gaze. Pradeep said that he had noticed this from the first time he had come to Anjanisain. He knew that the area had been crime-ridden for years, but had assumed that the situation was improving since Swami Manmathan's arrival.

As I pondered Pradeep's remarks, I realized that I, too, had noticed worrisome signs—something dark sliding away from my view, the averted eyes of a village woman when asked about the ashram, an abrupt remark by a village elder.

Some months later, I met Aarti Devi once again. She was caring for a pregnant woman who seemed large for her dates, and she felt that the woman was carrying twins. She asked me to come with her to the village and give my opinion. I took my stethoscope, potent symbol of biomedicine, and tried my best to hear two heart sounds on the woman's bulging belly. I could hear only one, and made my pronouncement. I turned out to be wrong—the woman was delivered of healthy twins a few weeks later. Aarti Devi and I shared a hearty laugh when I heard about the twins, and we sat down to a companionable cup of tea on the roof of her house.

This time I pressed her—"What do you mean when you say this place is not good? What is wrong with the ashram?"

Averting her eyes, she said, "Swami Manmathan has made many enemies around here."

"Why?" I persisted.

"People in this village think that he is only interested in power. And there are a lot of people in the ashram who are afraid of him, you know."

"But look at the changes in the ashram. Don't you think he's done some good work?" I asked.

The *dai* shrugged. "Most of us just don't trust him. And Cyril Sahib—he can fool anybody, you know."

With these cryptic remarks, she abruptly changed the subject. I puzzled over her words, trying to decipher their meaning. Why were people afraid of Swami Manmathan? Was it simply his gruff exterior, or was there something more sinister about him?

I knew that his challenges to local traditions had inflamed tempers in the area around Anjanisain. He was not a tactful man, and I could well imagine him insulting influential people in the villages. I had also heard that local politicians were jealous of his growing influence in the area. Over the past year and a half, money had been pouring into the ashram from Save the Children

Fund and BMA was becoming a prime piece of real estate in this impoverished area.

I told Cyril about Aarti Devi's veiled remarks about Swami Manmathan.

"What did she mean when she said that people in the ashram are afraid of him?"

Cyril brushed my question off with a laugh. "Nonsense! Don't listen to that old gossip! Swamiji may be a rough diamond, but he has the best interests of these people at heart."

The delight I felt with these women contrasted sharply with my feelings toward certain other people in the ashram. Some of the male employees were brash and belligerent, and used their power to put down women. Worst was a man named Dhanesh Balodi. He had been in the Indian army, but had been dishonourably discharged because of his violent and unruly behaviour. Cyril told us that Dhanesh had been strategically hired by Swami Manmathan in order to keep certain dangerous village people in check. Swami Manmathan's morals and methods seemed questionable. Yet, as my level of commitment to the work of BMA deepened, I simply tried not to think about Swamiji at all. I rarely met him, as he was always in the ashram headquarters and Pradeep's and my work was mostly in the field sites.

Cyril continued to be warm and personable, extending his full support for any program that we would like to implement. He was adept at deflecting any concerns that we had about BMA, and instead encouraged us to plan ahead to create a bright future for the organization. Looking back, I realize that Cyril was always able to spin a shimmering web of possibility that was beautiful to behold yet insubstantial. But in those days, I could not perceive this, for I was already hopelessly entangled in the gossamer threads of that web.

CHAPTER TWELVE:

Inferno

In the late winter of 1991, I received the news that my father had developed cancer of the bladder and would need major surgery. Pradeep suggested that I go to Canada to be with him, taking Raman with me, while he and Sonia stayed in Anjanisain. I knew that Sonia would be delighted to stay in the ashram, surrounded by her many admirers. So in late February, Raman and I flew to Canada and spent three weeks with my parents, supporting them over the period of my father's surgery and his recovery.

Pradeep and Sonia spent that time in Anjanisain as planned, and then returned to our home the day before my arrival. As the Jeep drove up the winding hill to Pauri, I was filled with excitement. I'd only been gone for three weeks, but how I'd missed my husband and daughter! Sonia gave us a joyous welcome, flinging herself into my arms. Pradeep gave Raman and myself a hug, but I noticed almost at once that he seemed rather subdued. That evening when the children had gone to bed, we sat down in the living room and began to talk.

"Something's wrong, isn't it?" I said, noticing the lines of worry furrowing his forehead.

"Yes," he said slowly, heaving a sigh. "I just feel that something is not right in BMA."

"Not right? What do you mean?"

"I can't explain you exactly, but it is like there is electricity in the air. Everybody is tense."

"Has something happened?"

Pradeep was silent. "No, I don't think so. But listen to this. I went to that village below Anjanisain to see a sick old man. He has TB and we are giving him streptomycin injections. He is usually so happy to see me. But yesterday he seemed different—didn't want to talk much. He just kept telling me to be careful."

"Careful about what?" I asked, my heart suddenly pounding.

"I don't know. I just don't know," replied Pradeep.

An uneasy silence fell. Pradeep sighed deeply, turning to look away from me slightly. He took a brown cardboard file out of his bag, withdrew a sheaf of bills, and began to sort them into neat piles. His movements were jerky and stiff, robbed of their usual fluid grace. I noticed the rigid set of his body, the taut tendons in his neck. A cold knot of fear coiled within me.

The shrill whistle of a pressure cooker shattered the silence. Startled, Pradeep dropped a handful of bills. They fluttered to the floor, and I bent to help him retrieve them.

Teeka appeared in the doorway, wiping his hands on a tea cloth.

"I am making *toor* dal tonight—you remember Savitri brought it for us from the village? It's a special *dal* from Garhwal," he said.

"Good, good," said Pradeep abstractedly, shuffling through the papers we'd picked up.

Desperate for some distraction, I followed Teeka back into the kitchen. I watched him make the *tarka,* the mix of spices that would be later added to the *dal.* As the oil was heating in the *karai,* Teeka studied the array of spices neatly organized in his round spice tray. He tossed black mustard seeds into the hot oil, where they sizzled and sputtered furiously. Then he added coriander, cumin, and a little red chili powder, frying them lightly in the oil. Finally, he added a pinch of *hing,* and its pungent smell blended with the more subtle aromas of the other spices.

"How do you decide which spices to use?" I asked. Every *dal* that Teeka made was slightly different but always delicious.

"Oh, there are so many different ways to make the *tarka,*" Teeka replied. "Dr. Sahib was complaining of stomach pains this morning, so that's why I am adding *hing*—it's good for digestion."

Teeka opened the pressure cooker, stirred the *dal,* and then added the *tarka.* The hot oil sizzled and spat. Teeka added some fresh cilantro leaves and then tasted the *dal,* nodding with satisfaction. He lifted the lid off the second pot on the stove, and the fragrance of basmati rice floated through the air.

I helped Teeka set the table, musing that I had never noticed so acutely the various smells of Indian spices. Since that disturbing conversation with Pradeep, all my senses seemed heightened. I was aware of each movement of my hands as I laid the dishes of food on the table; I noticed a tiny crack in one of the serving dishes; I heard the patter of rain on the roof. *It's as if I am wide awake—but in such an uncomfortable way,* I thought.

We spoke very little during the meal, both of us lost in thought. When we'd finished, Pradeep said he wanted to go to bed early. I kissed him good night, and then went back to the living room to distract myself with a book. Our dog, Jimmy, pushed her cold nose against my hand, and I realized that I'd forgotten to feed her. I mixed up some leftover *dal,* rice, and *roti,* and carried her bowl outside. I sat beside her as she ate, watching the last rays of sun disappear behind the mountains.

That night, we were awoken to the sound of furious barking. Rushing out of the bedroom, we saw Jimmy standing on her hind legs at the front door, scratching to get outside. Her hackles were raised, the fur bristling down her back.

"There must be someone out there," I whispered to Pradeep, a chill of fear racing down my spine.

We peered out of the window. We saw nothing, but we both sensed a living presence close by. Just then, an agonized squeal split the air, followed by sudden silence. Jimmy stopped barking and listened intently—to what? After a few minutes, she padded over to us and flopped down beside our feet, heaving a deep sigh. The silence of the night closed around us once again.

We returned to bed, but sleep was elusive. I tossed and turned uneasily, unable to push away a growing feeling of dread. When the first rays of dawn lit the morning sky, we cautiously opened the door and went out to investigate. A light rain had fallen the previous night, and muddy streaks criss-crossed the patio.

I walked around to the side of our house. "Look over here," I said, suddenly. Just below our bedroom window were the paw-prints of a huge cat, the five pads distinctly outlined on the stones.

"It must have been a leopard!" Pradeep exclaimed. "Let's see what else we find."

We could see nothing more around the house, but when we stepped out of the gate we spotted the bloodied body of a stray dog lying in the ditch. Deep bite marks on the back of the neck confirmed that a leopard had been the killer.

"The poor dog must have made that horrible squealing sound," I said. "I guess the leopard got alarmed by Jimmy's barking, and ran off."

"It'll be back tonight," said Pradeep.

I shivered. The leopard's presence so close to our house seemed to hint of approaching danger. I glanced over at Pradeep and real-ized that he, too, had been unnerved by our nocturnal intruder. We walked slowly back into the house, saying nothing.

Pradeep had planned to spend some time at home to update the accounts and prepare the annual report of the health program. I was worried about his health, so I managed to convince him to stay home a little longer to relax and recover his strength. Since joining BMA over two years earlier, we had rarely had much time together. I thought back to our days in Rishikesh, when we would spend every Sunday exploring the countryside, visiting friends, or just relaxing at home. Every day, we'd had time for long chats and leisurely cups of tea. What had happened to us?

March is always a lovely month in the Garhwal mountains, and that spring seemed particularly beautiful. New life blossomed all around us and birdsong filled the air. Warm breezes wafted up from the valley, bringing the sweet scent of flowers. We took the children out for walks and picnics, and their spontaneous joy in the natural world was like a balm to our wounded spirits.

"I hope Papa never goes back to work," said Sonia, skipping ahead of us along the path. I wondered how much of our fear and uncertainty she'd been sensing. *Whatever happens, we must make certain that the children are not affected,* I thought.

Raman tugged urgently at my hand. "Look at that funny shell, Mama. It's walking," he exclaimed. At our feet, I saw a large snail inching its way across the path.

"That's a snail, and the shell is his house," I said. "Snails carry their houses with them wherever they go. Whenever they want to feel safe and snug, they just curl up inside their house."

"Safe and snug," whispered Raman, wonderingly. He squatted down and gently touched the snail's shell, the joy of discovery alight on his face.

Over the next few days, Pradeep put on a little weight and regained some lightness in his step. We shared some special moments of laughter and love, recapturing the magic of our early married days. The uneasy sense of foreboding that had been troubling us began to dissolve. *Perhaps there's nothing to worry about after all,* I thought.

But BMA and its demands were not far away. One of our health workers arrived at our home, asking Pradeep to make a field visit to Guptkashi. She explained that they'd been facing problems with the immunization program, and several people with significant illness were waiting for a consultation. Pradeep promised to come as soon as he could.

The next day, Pradeep and I worked on the final draft of the annual report. As I read through the typewritten pages I felt a flush of excitement. We actually had a functional health program! All five subcentres had clinics with two trained health workers, in addition to the clinic at Anjanisain. We'd developed training programs for health workers and for traditional birth attendants. Our health workers made village visits regularly and offered preventive services that included immunization for children and contraceptive options for women.

"Isn't it exciting?" I exclaimed, flipping through the pages. "I know that it's not a great health program yet—but it's up and running. And those health workers are so committed. I can't wait to see what this program will look like three or four years from now!"

Pradeep glanced at me, but said nothing. He took the typewritten pages, clipped them into a file folder, and stuffed it into his travel bag.

"I'd better decide what day to leave for Guptkashi," he said. We looked up at the calendar on the wall—it was the sixth of April, 1991.

The phone jangled. Pradeep jumped up, startled at the unexpected call. Suddenly alert, I watched intently as he picked up the receiver. Static crackled through the line. I could hear the caller shouting in short, gasping sentences. A look of stunned horror spread across Pradeep's face, and my breath caught in my throat. Time was suspended—the few minutes that Pradeep spent on the phone seemed endless.

When Pradeep hung up the phone, he whirled to face me. "Swami Manmathan—he's been murdered!"

"Wh-what?" I stammered. I could feel my legs beginning to tremble.

"I must go—right away. They've already sent the Jeep to fetch me." Pradeep rushed out of the room to throw some essentials into his travel bag. Not long afterward, we heard the roar of the Jeep's engine, and the blaring of its horn on the road below the house. Too distracted to say goodbye, Pradeep hurried out of the house and down the path.

In Anjanisain, a grim scene awaited him. Swami Manmathan had been sitting watching the news on television in the ashram kitchen. Dhanesh Balodi entered the room and shot him at point-blank range in the chest. Swamiji's body was sprawled on the floor, a thick river of blood congealing on the cold concrete around his still form. Pradeep and Cyril had to wrap up the body and carry it down to the road, where it was loaded into the Jeep and taken to Meerut for post-mortem examination.

Police inspectors visited the ashram in the turbulent days that followed, and reporters from regional and national newspapers came to interview Pradeep and Cyril about the horrifying event.

There was never any doubt as to the identity of the murderer. After the gunshot, several people had rushed toward the kitchen and seen Dhanesh emerging with his gun in hand. A few days after the murder, Dhanesh was arrested and put in jail in the town of Tehri.

Pradeep returned to Pauri. When Sonia and Raman heard the Jeep, they ran down the path to greet him, expecting his usual delighted response. But this time, he hardly acknowledged them, simply ruffling their hair and letting them tug him up the path. Gazing down at him, I felt shocked to see how gaunt and exhausted he looked.

That night, he awoke suddenly and sat bolt upright. Startled, I switched on the bedside lamp and turned to look at him. Sweat beaded his forehead, and his hands shook.

"What happened? What's the matter?" I asked.

"A nightmare . . . it was horrible. The body . . . all that blood."

I reached for his hand; it was cold as ice. "It must have been a gruesome sight. I can't imagine how awful it was for you."

We sat in silence for some time. Finally, I said, "Try not to think about it anymore. Dhanesh was arrested. He is in jail. You are safe now."

Pradeep did not reply. He turned off the light and lay down once more, his back toward me. I stared at the ceiling, thoughts swirling through my head. *Pradeep has been so shaken by these events. It must have been really terrible. What about our health workers? They must be feeling so insecure, maybe worried about the future of BMA.* I finally fell into a restless sleep.

The next afternoon when the children were having their nap, we took our tea outside and began to discuss the shocking event.

"I know that Swami Manmathan fired Dhanesh, after they had a bitter argument," I said. "But was that the only reason for the murder?"

Pradeep was silent for a few moments. Then he said, "There's all kinds of gossip going around. Some people are saying that Dhanesh had been paid by someone to kill Swami Manmathan. You know that Swami Manmathan had made many enemies over the years. There were people that hated him."

"I heard that several local politicians really resented Swami Manmathan. Maybe because he'd become pretty powerful in the area," I said.

"Yes, definitely there were some people who were suspicious of him, or maybe jealous. BMA just kept growing and growing. And everyone knew that BMA's money was coming from outside the country," Pradeep answered.

He spent several days at home, struggling to regain some equanimity. During that time, we reviewed everything that we knew about BMA and its mercurial founder, attempting to understand more about this disaster. We were well aware that BMA had some serious operating problems, some of which could be traced to the evolution of the organization. Funding for BMA's work had taken a huge jump in 1988, when Save the Children Fund invited Swami Manmathan and Cyril to submit a budget for a much larger program. I knew that large funding agencies such as Save the Children prefer to keep their administrative expenses as low as possible. Donors like to assume that when administrative costs are low, more of their money is going to "the people," where the need is greatest. This leads funding agencies to promote a few projects to which they commit large budgets, rather than having many smaller projects.

BMA had proven itself in the field, and so perhaps the Save the Children leaders assumed that it would be able to replicate that good work manyfold when its budget was increased. Yet we had seen the negative effects of the sudden influx of funds. The original vision of the work was getting lost, buried under a mountain of administrative detail.

Late one night when neither of us could sleep, we tried to analyze what was going wrong in the organization. "One of BMA's ongoing problems are those five subcentres," I said to Pradeep. "They're so far away from each other, it's really hard to coordinate the work. And people like you who have a leadership role have to be continuously travelling from one to another."

"It was part of Swami Manmathan's overall idea. He thought to plant seeds in different places in Garhwal," replied Pradeep. "Maybe it would have been all right if each subcentre had a strong leader. But BMA has a big problem—not enough people who have experience and can be leaders. When BMA got so much funding all of a sudden, many new people were hired. But some of them had no experience at all."

"There were some very bad hiring decisions," I said, grimly. "Think of Dhanesh himself. I heard that he already had a criminal record when he applied to work with BMA. And hadn't he been kicked out of the Indian army?"

"Yes, that's true," acknowledged Pradeep. "I am not sure how much Swami Manmathan knew about his background when he hired him."

"What do you think is going to happen in BMA?" I asked, my curiosity mingled with a pervasive sense of unease.

"I don't know," answered Pradeep slowly. "You know, I think that there are too many problems in this organization. These BMA projects—so many were planned in a big hurry. In some places, the village people were not very interested in the programs. So quite often we don't have good support from local people."

I knew that much of BMA's work was planned on a project-to-project basis, and that serious problems related to coordination and management were affecting the quality of the work. The idea of participatory development, in which village people themselves actively helped to shape development plans, was just not happening.

"Do you think that our health program is supported by the village people?" I asked.

"Mostly, it is," replied Pradeep. "But I never feel that I am getting ahead with our program—I seem to be constantly going from one crisis to another."

Pradeep's words certainly rang true. When we joined BMA three years previously, we were confronted with five established but scarcely functioning clinics in isolated locations, along with a substantial budget for their operation. It was our responsibility to make it all work. Pradeep was constantly travelling from one subcentre to another, setting up a reporting system for health data, establishing a drug supply system, and trying to upgrade the training of the health workers. There was no time to develop a clear vision for the health program.

Our health work was patterned on a standard WHO model of primary health care, which included treatment of common illnesses along with preventive health-care initiatives such as immunization, health education, and family planning. The WHO model recommends "participation of the people," but that is not always easy. Our brand of primary health care had been much more based on "provision of health care" than on a genuine process to incorporate the needs and wishes of village people into the health program.

We were also realizing that our health program suffered from cultural incompatibilities. Village people often found a biomedical view of the body incomprehensible, and they resisted our somewhat naive efforts to change their indigenous views of health and illness. Our young, unmarried nurses were reasonably trained, but they were under-used because village people wanted an older, mature woman, wise in the ways of the world.

"I know our health program has a lot of problems," I admitted. "But, Pradeep, I still feel optimistic. Think of how much we have learned in the past two-and-a-half years! We've got a good team of health workers now, and many of them are so dedicated and enthusiastic. They are gaining the trust of the village people. We'll be able to turn this into a really meaningful health program. I'm sure of it."

"I hope you are right," Pradeep said, with a sigh. He reached into his travel bag and pulled out a sheaf of papers—correspondence, field reports and accounts. "Why don't you try to sleep? I'm just going to catch up on some paperwork."

A few days later, just over a month after Swami Manmathan's death, another assassination shocked our world. On May 21, 1991, Rajiv Gandhi died instantly when a bomb hidden in a garland of flowers exploded. The female suicide bomber who had offered him the flowers was a member of the group known as the Liberation Tigers of Tamil Eelam (LTTE). This group was fighting for a separate homeland for Tamils in Sri Lanka, where bitter sectarian violence had been tearing apart the social fabric. When Rajiv Gandhi had been prime minister, he had sent the Indian army into Sri Lanka to quell the activities of the LTTE, earning the bitter hatred of that group. Though Gandhi had been voted out of office in 1989, fresh elections were to be held in late 1991, and the Congress party was expected to return to power.

The assassination of Rajiv Gandhi stunned and saddened me. I remembered his dreams for India, and the great wave of hope that had swept across the nation when he led the Congress party to power in 1984. He envisioned an India that would be strong and confident enough to step into the world as a major power, and he had been instrumental in liberalizing the rigid economic regulations that had prevented India from fully participating in the global economy. I hoped that his legacy would endure.

As soon as Pradeep had recovered a little, he began to plan his next field visit. Cyril had now taken on the leadership of BMA, but he was depending on Pradeep's experience and skills to help set the organization onto a firmer foundation. With Dhanesh in jail, the immediate danger to the senior staff of BMA had lessened. Unfortunately, BMA was not functioning as a cohesive unit, and the lack of coordinated leadership, combined with poorly trained staff, continued to hamper the evolution of the organization.

Pradeep was rarely home during the turbulent months that followed Swami Manmathan's death. Feeling lonely and worried, I invited my friend Pauline Rey to stay in Pauri during the hot season. Pauline, her Swiss husband, Marcel, and their two children lived in Rishikesh, and we'd become friends with them during our Sivananda Ashram days. Pauline is a talented artist. During her stay in Pauri, she created some beautiful soft toys, puppets with papier mache heads, and greeting cards made with pressed flowers. We obtained some funds from BMA's income-generation program to develop a small cottage industry to provide employment to women facing severe financial constraints. The *Kelona Udyog* (Toy Workshop) opened in May, with four local women as its first employees.

Guddi Devi was one of them, a thin woman whose face had the pinched look of chronic poverty. Her husband was an alcoholic, unemployed, and usually absent from the home. She and her three children lived in a small room in a rundown part of town, in the back of the home of her brother-in-law. She had a cow, but the animal provided only a pint of milk a day, not enough to sell. Her small income from the Toy Workshop provided her with the cash she needed to buy food and clothing, and to pay school fees.

Since Pauline would be returning to Rishikesh in September, I had to take on administrative responsibilities for the Workshop. Having neither business sense nor talent at crafts, I was quite unsuited to this role. I tried to keep track of the accounts, see that the women were paid on time, and monitor the quality of work. Even to my inexpert eyes, it was clear that Guddi Devi had little aptitude for her work. She was illiterate and had no sewing skills. Despite repeated training and constant guidance, she was still unable to produce the quality work that was needed. I felt frustrated and I know she did, too.

Guddi Devi had a five-year-old son named Ravi, who often came with her to the workshop. He and my son Raman played together, chatting away in the local dialect. Raman was a year younger, but already taller and heavier than Ravi. Raman's clothes were handed down to him. He particularly loved a Mickey Mouse T-shirt that had also been a favourite of my son's.

The monsoon rains began, and for days a torrential downpour inundated our Himalayan world. Power lines went down, phone connections were severed, and then the water pipes began to break, one after another. Water was literally everywhere—pouring from the sky, oozing through the walls, trickling beneath the windowsills—yet not when a tap was turned on! We began to see people complaining of diarrhea and dysentery, and before long, an epidemic of hepatitis broke out.

It was when Pradeep was home on one of his rare visits that Guddi Devi brought Ravi to see us, saying that he'd had low-grade fever and loss of appetite for several days. Now he was passing dark urine and light-coloured stools. He had early signs of jaundice and his liver was palpably enlarged. We gave Guddi Devi the standard advice on the care of a child with hepatitis, and reassured her that Ravi would be better before long. But Ravi did not improve. Two days later, when she brought him back for a recheck, he was apathetic and miserable. His liver was even larger, and he winced as I touched its border, well below the rib margin.

Ravi's condition continued to deteriorate. The next day, he was admitted into the government hospital, where intravenous fluids, ampicillin, and injections of neomycin and Vitamin K were given. A crowd of Guddi Devi's relatives gathered around the sick child in the hospital ward. Even Guddi Devi's husband was there, smelling of cheap rum.

I bent over the bed to examine Ravi again. He was wearing Raman's Mickey Mouse T-shirt, which hung in loose folds over his thin body. My fingers felt for the edge of his liver. A cold chill of horror raced up my spine as I realized that Ravi's liver was no longer palpable below the margin of his ribs. Such a rapid decrease in its size could mean only one thing—massive liver necrosis resulting from destruction of liver tissue by the hepatitis virus. I knew then that Ravi would not recover from this illness. Suddenly, the dank stench of the ward became overpowering: sweat, phenol disinfectant, and rum mingled with the peculiar musty smell of a child in liver failure. I told Guddi Devi that I'd be back in the morning, and then turned abruptly and left the room. Evening was falling and the cool air touched my face with the delicate softness of a caress. A hauntingly sweet fragrance hovered in the air. It was the scent of *Raat ki Rani* (Queen of the Night), the flower that releases its fragrance only after darkness falls. The dramatic contrast between the sordid horrors of the ward and the delicate beauty of the world outside touched me with an unbearable poignancy. This is life as it is perceived by the Hindu sages of old—the pairs of opposites: fear and joy, ugliness and beauty, agony and ecstasy. Behind beauty lurks horror; yet when horror reigns, beauty, too, may be found.

Ravi died at four o'clock that morning. The male family members wrapped the little body in a white cotton cloth and left the hospital just after dawn. They set off down the steep mountain path to the valley several kilometres away. There, with a minimum of ceremony, the body was immersed in the Ganga. The usual elaborate cremation and associated rituals of a Hindu death often do not apply to the death of a small child in Garhwal. Such deaths are too commonplace an occurrence; few rural families can afford the expense of funeral rites.

Later that morning, I went to find Guddi Devi. She was sitting in her mud-walled room, weeping, her head buried in her arms. We sat down quietly amongst the village women gathered around her, knowing that now all we could do was to share a little of her grief. One of the women handed us glasses of hot, sweet tea. How often I had shared tea with Guddi Devi, in the Toy Workshop and in my home. The tea-drinking symbolized the complex bonds that had formed between us: first, as employer and employee; then, as doctor and patient; later, as two friends. And now? Our bond was that of one mother for another, trying to share the deepest grief imaginable—the loss of a beloved child.

A few days after Ravi's death, an unusually heavy rainstorm caused a small landslip behind our house. The water supply pipes broke once again. We had to collect our water from a public hand-pump and then carry it up the steep path to our house. We had to keep our water use to about thirty litres per person per day, the bare minimum required to maintain health.

With water so strictly rationed, it became very difficult to maintain good food hygiene. One day in July, I began to feel nauseated and exhausted, and my urine turned dark. Even before I became jaundiced, I already knew that I had developed hepatitis. Sonia developed the same symptoms a day or two later. Raman seemed to be all right, but his energy was unusually low. Pradeep was away at the time, and communication was always difficult when he was at the field sites. I watched over Sonia anxiously, thinking of the tragic fate of little Ravi. Since hepatitis A is a viral disease, there is no specific antibiotic treatment for it.

To my great relief, Sonia recovered quickly and within a week she was back to her usual cheerful self. My own illness lingered for over a month and my health work in the villages ground to a halt. I had been hoping to spend some time in Agra with my sister-in-law in mid-July, as she was expecting her second baby, but I had to cancel these plans. Suchitra gave birth to a healthy baby boy, on July 20. I managed to connect to her by phone, never an easy matter from Pauri, to congratulate her.

Both Pradeep and Cyril continued to work hard to restore a sense of stability to BMA, Cyril working primarily in Anjanisain and Pradeep travelling to the field sites. It was exhausting work, and when Pradeep did come home for brief visits he looked strained and preoccupied. The news that Sonia and I had contracted hepatitis upset him considerably.

"I don't think we are safe," he said one day. "The political situation in Garhwal is unstable right now. BMA seems to be in a constant state of chaos. You and Sonia have been ill with a serious disease, and I didn't even know about it. What would've happened if either of you had developed liver failure?"

I tried to reassure him. "Sonia's fine now, and I'm just tired—that's natural after a bout of hepatitis. We'll be okay. The BMA teams really need you right now, to give them a sense of stability."

Pradeep had been ill with a bout of dysentery, and was still recovering. He looked thin and tired, and even Sonia and Raman could not elicit a smile from him. Over the next few days in Pauri, he spent most of his time poring over financial accounts and working on a report for Save the Children. He rarely read the spiritual books he'd once loved, and he had no time for his meditation practice. Sharing a morning cup of tea had always been a beloved ritual, a time to enjoy each other's company and share ideas and thoughts. But now even that precious time had been taken over by intense discussions about BMA's future.

"You're looking worn out," I said. "I feel like you've had to bear the whole burden of our BMA work ever since Swami Manmathan's murder. Why don't you let me do the next trip out to the field sites, while you relax and recover here?"

"Absolutely not!" Pradeep replied firmly. "You are still not completely well, and besides, the situation is still unsettled and dangerous. And I think it's just possible that things could become worse if you get involved right now."

"What do you mean?" I asked, indignantly.

"Part of the problem with BMA is that it gets foreign funding," Pradeep said. "Right now, the Bharatiya Janata Party (BJP) is getting more and more strong in Garhwal, and they are against any kind of foreign influence. If you become a high-profile figure in BMA at this time, those politicians won't like it. And that won't help to stabilize BMA at all. "

"But I have been living in this country for years and, after all, I am married to you—an Indian citizen! It's not fair!" I protested.

"Of course it's not fair, but that's just the way it is," replied Pradeep.

The BJP had been gaining popularity for several years, under the leadership of L. K. Advani, a politician who was often accused of vying for power by promoting pro-Hindu policies.

"Why do people support the BJP—doesn't that party promote Hindu fundamentalism?" I asked. "Hinduism has never been a fundamentalist faith. Its philosophies promote openness and tolerance."

"That's true," Pradeep agreed. "But before you are passing judgment on the BJP, you must think about how it started. Hindus have been feeling discrimination for many, many years. The Muslims during Moghul days destroyed thousands of Hindu temples in north India. And then Christians during British Raj days were constantly trying to convert Hindus to their own religion. During all those years, Hindus suffered loss of pride."

"I understand that. But still, why start discriminating against others?" I asked.

"Well, it is not right what Advani has been doing—playing the communal card just to get votes," said Pradeep. "But the BJP has done a lot to build up people's pride in Hindu culture. And this is a good thing, mostly. But unfortunately there are some people who become extremists, and that is very damaging. No doubt about it."

"What about our situation here in Garhwal, isn't there something we could do? If I could meet some of these BJP politicians, maybe they would realize that I am not a foreigner who is trying to undermine anything. I really want what's best for Garhwal," I said.

"Don't take it personally," said Pradeep. "I will tell you what is the problem. You are white and you are from the West. People here are wanting to make their own identity in their own way, without any outsider's help."

I felt frustrated and hurt by Pradeep's revelations. Why should people judge others simply based on external appearance, I wondered. Pondering this question, it dawned on me that as a white person growing up in a wealthy family in Canada, I had always occupied a position of privilege in the world. I'd enjoyed an excellent education, financial independence, and personal freedom.

Until now, I'd worn that cloak of privilege easily, protected from the pain of being judged unfairly based on skin colour, education, or social class. I'd never had to face the simple truth that life is not always fair.

After this conversation, I dropped the idea of making field visits, but I did manage to convince Pradeep to take a few days off to regain some strength. We tried not to talk about BMA, but, inevitably, our worries about the organization began to surface. A pervasive sense of unease threaded through our conversation, and we felt constantly on edge. Each night, I checked and double-checked the locks on the doors. I slept lightly, waking at the slightest sound.

A few days later, Pradeep left for another tour of the subcentres. After he'd gone, an atmosphere of uneasiness seemed to swirl around me like a fog, making me feel confused and anxious. The children seemed blissfully unaware of the situation, but even their laughter and chatter couldn't dispel the gloom that had settled around me.

Wanting desperately to distract myself, I decided to try my hand at a writing project. Many of our centres offered programs for adult women who wanted to learn to read. But good literacy material was hard to find—the primers intended for use by Indian schoolchildren seemed inappropriate for adult learners, particularly for village women in Garhwal. I decided to write a literacy primer with a compelling storyline, something that could speak to the realities of the lives of Garhwali women. Pauline agreed to do the illustrations.

"*Savitri, Ek Jivan Yatra*" is the story of a young woman growing up in a Garhwali village. The narrative weaves insights about health, education, and the environment into a plot that is filled with dramatic twists and turns. Pauline's illustrations faithfully reproduced the dress and jewellery of a Garhwali woman, and her sketches of village life were fresh and engaging.

Writing that little book provided a ray of light that shone through the clouds of doubt and worry that swirled around me. I felt calmer and began to dream again about the future. I imagined a time when BMA would be flourishing, and each of our health workers would be feeling happy and fulfilled. In my glass castle of dreams, Pradeep and I were young lovers again, with nothing on our minds except the delight of being together. All the worry and strain and conflict of the last few months would have vanished. Perhaps I was simply indulging in wishful thinking, or perhaps I really believed that the current crisis would resolve completely and that Pradeep would regain his enthusiasm for our work. Certainly, I was only dimly aware of the chasm that was developing between us, as our perception of the present and our hopes for the future began to diverge.

CHAPTER THIRTEEN:

In Search Of Birch

As the end of August approached, the rains began to ease a little. Our water supply was working again, and the electricity was less erratic. But Pradeep was still away almost all the time. I missed him terribly. I was also plagued with worries about him—his health and safety, but also a more ill-defined concern about what was happening between us. When he did come home, he seemed abstracted and distant. We'd begun to quarrel frequently, often over the most trivial matters. We rarely made love anymore. Even our morning teatime, such a precious ritual, had been invaded by our preoccupation with the problems in BMA. Because of my recent illness, I was still not strong enough to begin fieldwork again. I felt increasingly lonely, overwhelmed by the difficulties we were facing.

One day a letter arrived in Pauri with UK stamps. I recognized the handwriting immediately—it was from my Uncle Ken. He was a botanist who'd traveled the world to find different varieties of birch trees, a quest born out of his passion for the natural world. When he returned to his home in Devon, he planted the seeds he'd collected on his spacious property in the country. An arboretum took shape, filled with beautiful birch trees from all over the world. His wife, June, an artist, placed her sculptures and those of other artists amongst the trees. Thus, Stone Lane Gardens[7] was created, an environment of exceptional beauty.

The previous summer, I'd stopped in England after a visit to my family in Canada. I'd spent a few days with Uncle Ken and Auntie June. They lived in an ancient stone house with a thatched roof, surrounded by acres of green hills planted with birch and alder trees. Their home looked like a postcard depicting the beauty of the English countryside. When I'd begun to talk about my life in the Himalayas, a faraway look came into my favourite uncle's eyes.

"Did you know that there are species of birch and alder growing at high altitude in the Himalayas?" he asked. "Look at this—*Alnus nitida*. That's one of them!"

He pulled a dog-eared botany book off a nearby shelf, and flipped feverishly through the pages till he found the right section.

"Here is your most common Canadian species of alder, *Alnus rugosa*. I collected those seeds on my last visit to your family in Canada. And I've collected alder and birch seeds from many other countries. But in the Himalayas, there are some rare species."

"Then why don't you come and visit us?" I asked. "We could go off on a search for the elusive seed of *Alnus nitida*!"

Uncle Ken positively glowed. "What a marvelous idea!" he replied.

I slit open the thin blue envelope, unfolded the letter and quickly scanned the lines of familiar handwriting. Uncle Ken had not forgotten my invitation. He'd written to the Forest Research Institute in Dehradun, asking for information about birch and alder species in the Himalayas. One of their botanists had written to tell him these species could be found in several areas of Garhwal, particularly in remote areas of District Chamoli.

....

7   http://stonelanegardens.com/

Uncle Ken's letter to me read, *"I would be most interested in accepting your very generous offer to visit. It would be delightful to see you and the children again, and I particularly look forward to meeting your husband, Pradeep. I would plan my visit at the time when the seed will be on the trees—in October. I do hope that my visit would not inconvenience you."*

I reread the last line several times. It was certainly a strange time in our lives to be having a visitor—and yet, the thought of seeing Uncle Ken filled me with unexpected delight. When Pradeep returned home two days later, I showed him the letter and asked for his opinion.

"Of course you must invite him," he replied, immediately. "He is your beloved uncle. And I am thinking that we can arrange to hold a medical camp in our subcentre in Ghat. I've been planning that for some time. You know, Ghat is in District Chamoli. From there, we can find a local guide to take Uncle Ken into the mountains."

Thrilled, I wrote back to Uncle Ken, suggesting he come in the first week of October. The thought of his visit filled me with happy anticipation—it had been a long time since I'd looked forward to something.

In the weeks before his arrival, I had plenty to keep me occupied. We'd recently enrolled Sonia in the kindergarten class at St. Thomas School. The school was established by Christian missionaries more than fifty years earlier and was now run by Indian nuns. Our neighbours, the Zaidis, had a daughter of Sonia's age named Penaz. The two little girls were best friends, and they were both excited to start school. Wearing their smart brown-and-white uniforms, she and Penaz walked hand-in-hand down the winding path to the road, where they were picked up by a school bus.

I soon realized that kindergarten in India is very different from Canada. These five-year-old children were expected to plunge into serious studies. Their subjects included math, English, Hindi, handwriting, and general knowledge. For each subject, we had to buy an inexpensive soft-covered textbook and a notebook for homework. And what homework! Every day, I spent at least an hour-and-a-half working with Sonia on her studies. We lay in bed reciting multiplication tables and working on spelling. When Pradeep was not home to help her with Hindi, Sonia went for lessons with Mrs. Zaidi, who taught her and Penaz how to write the Devnagri script. Though I could speak and read Hindi, I had never learned how to write the language.

The study of general knowledge required these kindergarten tots to learn a remarkable variety of facts. They studied the names of trees, plants, and flowers; they rattled off the names of figures from Indian history; they memorized long lists of details about scientific discoveries. They also learned hundreds of obscure facts about world geography. One question read: Name a three-eyed reptile found only in New Zealand.

Answer: The tuatara.

"What? I don't believe it!" I gasped, highly skeptical about the existence of three-eyed reptiles. But, as I later discovered, there is indeed a creature called the tuatara that lives in New Zealand. The tuatara is the most ancient living reptile in the world, a species that is more than 200 million years old. Its third eye is found on the top of its head and is called the parietal eye. Though this eye contains a lens, cornea, and retina, its function is obscure because it is only visible on the hatchling tuatara and becomes covered with scales in the adult reptile.

The tuatara is certainly a fascinating creature, but I was doubtful about the usefulness of this knowledge for five-year-old children living in Pauri Garhwal, India!

By the end of September, I had fully recovered from my bout of hepatitis and I felt full of energy once again. The weather was beautiful, with clear skies and warm breezes. Best of all, the problems besetting BMA seemed to be calming down. Dhanesh Balodi remained in jail, the health program was running better, and Pradeep was able to spend more time at home. Uncle Ken was due to arrive for his visit the following week, and we were all excited to greet our first overseas guest.

Teeka Ram met Uncle Ken's flight from London and accompanied him to Pauri, travelling first by train and then by Jeep. I was sitting on our verandah when I heard the sound of the vehicle. Jumping to my feet, I saw the familiar figure of my uncle emerging from the Jeep. Carrying an enormous backpack, he began to climb the winding path to my house, his bald head fringed with white hair framed by the blue cloth of his pack. I was relieved to see that he seemed completely unfazed by his arrival into the chaos of India. He gave us warm hugs, a delighted smile on his face. Tea appeared, such an essential for a beloved relative from England.

I realized that we'd run out of biscuits, so I walked down to the corner shop, leaving Uncle Ken and Pradeep to get acquainted. I had a quiver of misgiving as I left them, wondering if Pradeep would take this opportunity to air his views on the evils of the British Raj. Most Indians seem to look back on that time with a philosophical air, saying, "Well, we got cricket from the British, so it wasn't all bad." However, many intellectuals and scholars still bear some resentment about those days of oppression and humiliation. Pradeep himself held strong anti-British views, which had occasionally resulted in heated arguments between us.

On my way back, I looked up at Pradeep and Uncle Ken sitting on the verandah, and smiled at the marked contrast between these two men I loved. Pradeep was dressed in his usual loose-fitting *kurta*, the traditional Indian garment that he wore over a pair of pants. As always, he looked slim and trim, his wavy black hair neatly combed and his pants nicely pressed. He was talking in an animated way, leaning forward with an intent expression on his face and gesticulating with his hands. I was too far away to hear his words, but I guessed it must be some point of philosophy—the only subject that would spark so much enthusiasm from Pradeep.

Uncle Ken was sitting back in his chair, a cup of tea in hand. He was dressed in rumpled corduroy trousers, an old tweed jacket with leather patches on the elbows, and sturdy walking boots. A fringe of untidy white hair circled his balding head. I felt a sudden rush of love for him, an almost visceral sense of connection.

Over the next few days, I realized that Pradeep and Uncle Ken were getting along very well. Pradeep's intuitive grasp of human nature is profound, and he'd immediately recognized the transparent soul of my favourite uncle. I was delighted to see Pradeep beginning to talk about his favourite subject—the deeper meanings of life. His own spiritual quest, so passionately pursued in Sivananda Ashram, had been cast aside in BMA. The daily crises of our lives in Pauri left no space for quiet contemplation.

A few days after Uncle Ken's arrival, we all set off on our expedition to District Chamoli. Sonia had already become fast friends with her Great Uncle Ken, and she kept up a running commentary throughout the trip. Raman was more shy, but soon began to quietly present Uncle Ken with offerings from the natural world—a snail, a flower, a coloured stone.

When we reached the small town of Ghat, Pradeep made inquiries about a local guide to go with Uncle Ken in search of birch. The next morning, a lean, middle-aged man dressed in traditional Garhwali dress appeared. Bharat Singh knew the area very well and seemed quite prepared to accompany my uncle. He did not know a single word of English, nor did Uncle Ken know any Hindi. However, neither seemed at all concerned about the language barrier. The next morning, they shouldered their packs and set off for the high mountain pastures where Bharat Singh thought they could find birch and alder.

Soon after they'd left, Leela arrived in the BMA Jeep, laden with boxes of supplies for the medical camp. We reviewed the arrangements for the camp, and, as usual, Leela had all the organizational details in place. We'd be holding the camp in a local school building, and we spent the rest of afternoon getting set up.

Over the next two days, Pradeep and I saw about 150 patients. Leela and a health worker from the subcentre managed the flow of patients, did dressings and immunizations, and dispensed medications. The other health worker from the subcentre assisted me with communication. The dialect spoken in this remote part of Garhwal had significant differences from standard Hindi, including many words I did not understand.

A woman from a village on the other side of the mountain brought her nine-year-old child for consultation. He had developed lumps on the right side of his neck several months earlier, and recently one had started to ooze slightly. The boy also had a poor appetite and a low-grade fever. The lumps were rubbery enlarged lymph nodes typical of scrofula, in which the tuberculosis bacterium infects the nodes of the neck. I took the mother to a separate room to talk to her about the diagnosis. In Garhwal, patients suffering from TB are often reluctant to seek treatment because of the stigma associated with the disease. I encouraged her to go to the District TB hospital where she could get free medications for her son, and reassured her that he would recover completely. The health worker assisting me wrote down the woman's name and promised she would follow up and make sure the child got the needed treatment.

Some of the patients we saw required specialized treatment that we could not provide. A child of three had been badly burned after a fall into an open fire as a toddler. She now had extensive scarring that had caused contractures of her right elbow and knee, significantly limiting the movement of her right arm and leg. Pradeep told the mother that surgery could be helpful to improve the child's mobility, and wrote a referral letter to a colleague, a plastic surgeon practicing in the city of Dehradun. Over the years,

Pradeep had established a vast referral network made up of classmates from his medical college. All these physicians were willing to see patients that we referred at low cost. I hoped that this family would make the trip to Dehradun to see the plastic surgeon, but I was not sure if that little girl child would be valued enough for this to happen.

On the morning of our third day in Ghat, Uncle Ken returned, proudly waving his precious seed bags. He had found not only the elusive *Alnus nitida*, but also the Himalayan birch. We all gathered in the courtyard, eager to hear about their adventures. He and Bharat Singh had journeyed for more than two days before finding their first birch tree. They'd spent their nights in the stone huts of shepherds who drive their flocks into the high pastures during summer.

"It was an absolutely unforgettable experience," said Uncle Ken, his eyes sparkling with enthusiasm. When Bharat Singh got up to leave, Uncle Ken warmly embraced him.

Uncle Ken stayed at our house in Pauri another week. One afternoon, he and I took a walk along the road behind our house, reaching a high point that offered a splendid vista of the Himalayas. We sat on an old stone bench on a grassy patch beside the road.

"Remember that wonderful trip we took to search for our family roots?" I asked. Some years previous, we'd travelled together to the north of England where our ancestors had lived. Both of us had heard many stories of the "olden days" in England, before the family lost its fortune. I knew about "Elliscales," the family home, and the land surrounding it. I knew about the tin mines, and the shipyard, and the three-masted schooners that were built in that shipyard.

But on that trip, we also discovered a darker history. Near our ancestral home was another large house, "Dowdales." We learned from the town registry records that my great-grandfather's cousin

George had built the house, but had only lived in it for a year or two. At the age of thirty-two, he shot himself.

"I'd never even heard of this uncle," I said.

"In a way, I'm not surprised," said Uncle Ken. "You know, suicide was a terrible thing in those days—a blot on the family's name. I suspect it was covered up."

A wave of sadness washed over me when I thought of the young man whose name had been erased from the oral history of our family because of the manner of his death.

"It's all through our family, isn't it?" I said. "Depression, I mean."

"Oh, yes," replied Uncle Ken. "There are many tragic stories."

I thought of my own father, who had struggled for years with bouts of crippling depression. I vividly remember him coming home from work, his footsteps slow and heavy. Hardly acknowledging us, he would trudge down the hall to his bedroom and close the door behind him. There he would lie, immobile, locked in his private world of pain. Sometimes, a whole weekend would pass in which we'd hardly see him. But on Monday morning, he would force himself to get up and go to work—an act of great courage and determination. Like so many people of British extraction, he had a horror of self-exposure and refused to seek help. When my mother begged him to see a doctor, he responded grimly, "Nothing can help when you are losing your marbles."

My father's bouts of "marble trouble" lasted for years, casting a dark shadow on our lives. I thought of all the veiled references my grandmother had made to various family members over the past generations who'd struggled with depression. They'd suffered greatly, yet the stories of their battles with serious illness were no more than a shameful family secret.

Uncle Ken and I walked back home, both of us preoccupied with our own thoughts. What would it be like to suffer from a serious depression, severe enough to end in suicide? Trying to shake myself free of these dark thoughts, I asked my uncle what else he might like to do before he had to leave.

"Well, the most wonderful thing would be to take a long walk in the jungle. Pauri is at an altitude of about 6,000 feet, and I suspect there will be a simply superb variety of trees in the forest around here," he replied.

Pradeep was able to find us a local guide, Rana Singh. We planned an expedition to Kirsu, a secluded beauty spot located in a dense tract of unspoiled forest about ten kilometres from Pauri. A small bungalow nestles in a clearing, and from this spot, magnificent views of the mountains can be seen. Pauri was an administrative centre for the British during the days of the Raj, and I could imagine British officials coming to this little bungalow for a restful weekend.

Rana Singh led us along a trail into the forest, where we entered a magical world. The unspoilt Himalayan jungle is astonishing in its variety and richness of plant and animal life. I had my field guide to the birds of India and a pair of binoculars, and I pointed out babblers, finches, and a Himalayan thrush.

But Uncle Ken's primary interest was not birds. He pulled a notebook and pencil out of his pocket and began to scribble down the names of the tree species we saw—*sal*, *neem*, horse chestnut, silver oak, and teak.

"Good gracious, look at this splendid specimen!" he exclaimed, stopping in front of a Himalayan rhododendron, which is a full-sized tree rather than the bushy plant that one finds in Europe and North America.

Rana Singh said, "In the springtime when these *buraans* trees are blossoming, we village people pluck the red flowers to make juice. And look at something else, over here."

He walked a few steps beyond the rhododendron tree. "See this," he said, peeling a little bit of lichen off a large rock. "If you put this into a pot of *dal,* it will cook much more quickly, even at high altitudes."

A few minutes later, he pointed to a clump of plants with broad, yellowish-green leaves. "That is wild turmeric plant," he said. "We Garhwalis use this plant to make medicine. You grind it into paste and apply to bruises and sprains—it is good for pain and swelling. We also use it to clean wounds."

I had often heard about the use of this plant from Garhwali patients, and Pradeep had told me that scientific studies have shown that turmeric does have antiseptic properties.

Just then, we heard a faint but distinct sound of barking.

"Is that a dog?" I asked in surprise.

"No, no!" replied Rana Singh. "It is our little barking deer, which is very common in this part of Garhwal. It makes that sound when it is alarmed, to warn its friends of danger. There must be a tiger about." He cast a sideways glance at us, and I felt a distinct suspicion that he was trying to test our nerves.

Uncle Ken didn't turn a hair. He was examining some delicate white flowers that appeared to be growing off the trunk of the tree.

"Look, this is an orchid," he said. "What a lovely specimen! I didn't expect to see them in this part of the mountains. They typically grow in the northeastern part of the Himalayan range." He snapped some close-up photos of the flowers with their epiphytic roots curled around the branches and trunk of the tree.

After our marvelous hike was over, the Jeep driver dropped Uncle Ken and me at the bottom of the path to our house. Looking up, I could see Pradeep with Raman on his shoulders waving to us from our patio. Sonia was tugging at his hand, and I guessed she was urging him to walk down to meet us. To my delight, I noticed that Pradeep had a happy smile on his face. It had been so long since I had seen him looking relaxed.

A day or two later, Pradeep and I took Uncle Ken to the village of Khandusain where one of our subcentres was located, to show him some of the work we were doing. On the way to the centre, we stopped the vehicle at a high point where a whole range of mighty Himalayan peaks glistened in the distance.

"How marvelous!" said Uncle Ken, scrambling out of the Jeep. But to our astonishment, he dashed over to the opposite side of the road and began to inspect the grassy bank closely.

"What an unusual variety of primrose!" he muttered, inspecting the tiny flowers dotting the bank. For Uncle Ken, the living world of plants and animals held infinitely more fascination than the most magnificent mountain range.

When we reached the centre, our workers spilled out of the building to greet this foreign visitor. Cups of tea arrived almost immediately. Uncle Ken sat casually on the stone wall surrounding the property and sipped his tea with relish. As we sat there chatting with the workers, a cow came ambling along the road. Stray cows are a common sight all over India, and this particular one took an interest in Uncle Ken. She stopped beside him, and he reached out to gently scratch her forehead. Soon, she began to rest her muzzle on Uncle Ken's shoulder, obviously enjoying the sensation. A little while later, another cow came walking down the road and this one also stopped, clearly curious about what was happening. Uncle Ken began to stroke her muzzle, as well.

"I think they like a little attention," he said, smiling.

Uncle Ken left a few days later to travel to the state of Himachal Pradesh, where he planned to look for other populations of birch and alder. I longed to go with him, to enjoy the next phase of his "search for birch." But family responsibilities kept me at home, and so we sent Teeka with him again. On this trip, Uncle Ken didn't find as much seed, but he took many photographs of the birch and alder habitat. The precious seeds that he collected in Garhwal are now full-grown trees, taking their place alongside similar trees from all over the world in Stone Lane Gardens in Devon.

My uncle's visit was a delightful interlude in our lives, a time of family togetherness and joy in the beauty of nature. But storm clouds were gathering in our world, and the peace we'd enjoyed during those weeks would soon be violently swept away.

CHAPTER FOURTEEN:

Earthquake

The magic of Uncle Ken's visit lingered after his departure. The conflict between Pradeep and myself had eased, and we were beginning to recapture our delight in each other. We enjoyed lovely walks in the forest while we talked about everything from Raman and Sonia's latest escapades to the most rarified points of philosophy.

But this peaceful interlude was not destined to last long. On the night of October 20, 1991, Pradeep and I were shaken suddenly out of sleep. Our bed rocked alarmingly.

"Earthquake! We must get outside!" shouted Pradeep. We flung off our covers and dashed out of the house. When we got outside, we suddenly realized we had forgotten our children. A very bad moment in parenting! We ran back inside and plucked them from their beds, wondering if the house was going to collapse around us. The sensation of the ground moving terrified us.

All our neighbours were outside, as well, huddled in groups and talking anxiously. Earth tremors are quite common in Garhwal, a geologically unstable area. But this event was far more severe, and the fear and uncertainty were palpable. When the shaking subsided, we walked tentatively back inside and inspected our house for damage. Other than a large crack in the living room wall, it seemed structurally intact. We eventually got back to bed, but sleep was elusive.

Early the next morning, we received a phone call from Save the Children Fund in Delhi.

"Are you all right?" said an anxious female voice. When we reassured her that we were fine, she told us that the earthquake had been a major one, its epicentre in Uttarkashi about 180 kilometres to the west of us. Reports were coming in telling of entire villages that had been flattened, bridges destroyed, and roads badly damaged. It was feared that the death toll would be high. The Indian army was about to begin rescue operations.

Pradeep managed to phone Anjanisain and contact Cyril. Fortunately, everyone was all right and the ashram had not been damaged. Pradeep and Cyril talked about what BMA could do to participate in the relief efforts. Recently, a dynamic young Garhwali man named Hem Gairola had joined BMA, and he was appointed to lead a team to Uttarkashi. Pradeep would join them a day later with a medical team, after outfitting the ambulance with more supplies.

The rest of the morning was spent in feverish preparation. Pradeep wrote lists of supplies, medications, and equipment. The latest radio reports stated that over 1,500 people had died in the earthquake, and tens of thousands were rendered homeless. Both Indian and international agencies were participating in relief efforts. Pradeep planned to meet District Magistrate for Uttarkashi District, the senior administrative officer in the Indian government for that area, in order to coordinate BMA's program with other relief efforts that had been launched.

Pradeep spent a week at the earthquake site, returning home utterly exhausted. He described the medical work that he'd begun at the BMA camp in the village of Bhatwari. A team of our health workers had been assisting in rescue, first aid, and transport of injured people to the Uttarkashi hospital. The next step would be field visits to more remote villages to assess the evolving health needs of people recovering from the disaster.

"Please let me go with the next team," I said. "I'm fully recovered from the hepatitis. And Uttarkashi is far from Anjanisain and all its problems. Girish says he'll come with me, and I'm sure he'll be helpful at base camp."

Pradeep reluctantly agreed, realizing how badly he needed time to rest. Excited at the prospect of getting back to work at last, I made plans to accompany a second medical team to the disaster site. Ten days after the quake, I arrived in Uttarkashi in our ambulance that had been refitted with fresh supplies. My first impressions included a steel bridge twisted beyond recognition, a whole village transformed into rubble, a mountain split by gaping clefts.

Our organization had established a base camp on a farmer's field near the site of a devastated village. Reaching the camp, I was greeted with great emotion by members of the medical team. The crisis of the earthquake had created a special bonding among our organization members. Team members who usually didn't get along were suddenly close companions; others who had previously lacked drive were inspired to work tirelessly.

Rescue and medical care of the injured had been the priority of BMA's relief program initially; now, construction of temporary shelters was the most pressing need. Floods of supplies were pouring into the base camp. Our principal funding agency, Save the Children, was generous in its support and flexible in helping us to meet the needs of the relief program.

By this time, almost two weeks after the earthquake, a full-scale relief effort was in progress. The government of India, the major implementing agency, provided medical services, emergency shelter supplies, and financial compensation to earthquake victims. International relief agencies were also providing a range of services. Finally, about twenty NGOs, including BMA, were actively involved in relief efforts at the village level. With so many diverse groups at work, the relief efforts were not always well coordinated. The District Magistrate of Uttarkashi, a dynamic and brilliant young man, made a great effort to integrate services.

The medical program that Pradeep had established at the base camp was running smoothly. To assess the health situation further afield, I decided to visit a newly established outpost relief camp established near some high-altitude villages. Accompanying me were our health workerm Savitri, a *dai* named Ujjala Devi, and two young men involved in the shelter-building program. Two mules were laden with supplies, including polythene sheets for shelters, lightweight tents, medical supplies, and food for the workers.

As we wound our way up the narrow path, we could see the Bhagirathi River coursing along the valley floor far below. The trail was very steep, twisting up the face of the mountain in the seemingly endless switchbacks. I was still weak after my bout of hepatitis, and I had to pause periodically to catch my breath. A donkey passed us carrying a load of supplies to the affected villages. Ujjala Devi stopped the driver and asked him to put my backpack on the donkey's back. He readily agreed to this and we began to lash the pack onto the load the animal already carried. But nobody had consulted the donkey in this matter! He suddenly bucked, and my backpack sailed off his back, bounced on the rocky trail, and then began to roll off the cliff. As quick as lightning, Ujjala Devi flung herself over the edge of the cliff, grasping a sturdy bush with one hand to steady herself and managing to catch the backpack with the other hand.

I was horrified at this rash action, and as we helped her to safety I gasped, "Why did you do that?" She replied modestly, "Well, I didn't want you to lose your things, Madam!"

We reached the village where we had our outpost camp by late afternoon. Here, forty-five people had died during the earthquake, out of a population of 260. Most of the houses were damaged beyond repair, and the villagers were tearing apart the wreckage of their homes to salvage building materials for shelters. Our workers were assisting villagers to construct temporary shelters using salvaged wooden beams, tin sheets, and polythene.

The initial medical relief work, ten days earlier, had involved primary treatment of injuries and evacuation of the seriously injured to the district hospital in Uttarkashi. There, government and army surgical teams were working day and night to cope with the flood of injuries. Now the medical work was focussing on the followup care of these injuries, treatment of acute respiratory infections, and coping with an outbreak of scabies. On the preventive side, water supplies were being treated and an immunization campaign planned.

After a brief rest at the campsite, I set off on "medical rounds" with Savitri and Ujjala Devi. In the ruins of a house nearby, we visited an old woman with a broken pelvis and a fractured forearm. Her cast looked fine and she was being nursed with great care by her daughter-in-law. The old woman's husband stirred up the fire and put the kettle on. When we'd all been served tea, he told us the frightful tale of the night of the earthquake. The back room of the house had collapsed completely, killing his younger son and two grandchildren.

"Why was I spared?" said the old man, his voice breaking. "I have lived my life. But those little ones, and my son . . ."

As we were finishing our tea, a woman living nearby came to show us her baby. The child was just ten days old. He'd been born at eight o'clock on the evening of that fateful night. Although the room where he'd been sleeping had collapsed, he miraculously suffered only a fractured collarbone.

"What's his name?" I asked, examining the collarbone. The mother looked away shyly, hiding a hint of a smile.

"Bookamp Singh," she whispered. We all giggled. *Bookamp* means "earthquake" in Hindi—certainly an appropriate name for a lucky little baby!

By the time we'd seen the last patient, it was late afternoon. We hurried through the ruins of the village, followed the path down the mountain, and reached the BMA campsite just after dark. Several of our workers were gathered around a crackling fire, their hands outstretched toward the blaze. The aroma of *rotis* and *dal* floated toward us, and I suddenly realized how hungry I was.

"Madam-ji, *idhar aiye! Batiye!*" called Indu, one of our health workers, beckoning me to sit beside her on a log.

Girish brought me a plate of food, and I tucked into the meal with relish. Indu and I talked about our day's work. She told me that she'd been checking the medical logbook from one of the outpost camps, and had found that the incidence of acute respiratory infections in small children had been rising alarmingly over the past two weeks. With winter fast approaching, we also worried about the possibility of a measles outbreak, which could have terrible consequences for overcrowded, undernourished children. An emergency immunization plan was being organized jointly by the government health services and our health services, using vaccines and equipment from government supply, our outpost camp infrastructure and personnel from both health services. Indu had already started to plan how the teams would cover the designated area.

How capable and competent she is, I thought. *With health workers like her on our team, I feel as if we are just on the threshold of creating a health program that is really excellent.* I finished the last bite of *roti* and potato, and sat silently, lost in thought.

"*Chai, Madam?*" Girish asked, carrying a huge kettle that had just come off the fire. I sipped the tea gratefully, listening to the chatter of the people around me. The cadence of the voices rose and fell, threaded with a special animation I had never heard before. I closed my eyes, enjoying the sound of the voices without trying to listen to any specific conversation. Being a part of this team filled me with joy—facing the hardships of work in these ruined villages, followed by these simple delights of the warmth of the fire and the taste of fresh *roti*. I looked around the circle, noticing the light of the flames dancing on the faces of my companions. *I love each one of them, in their own way*, I thought.

A snatch of conversation suddenly caught my attention. ". . . *baag mara gaya* . . ." *Baag*? A leopard? I suddenly sat bolt upright and listened carefully. One of our workers said that a leopard was prowling the area. I remembered the stories of Jim Corbett, the famous hunter who had tracked down so many man-eating leopards and tigers in Garhwal. He'd written that after a natural disaster, a leopard would occasionally feast on a human corpse, and thus acquire a taste for human flesh. That leopard might then become a man-eater, actively seeking out living victims and unleashing a reign of terror in Garhwali villages.

In this village, not a single house remained intact, and the villagers were living in tents or makeshift shelters, virtually unprotected. As I crawled into the tent I shared with the three nurses on the team, uncomfortable thoughts of feline predators occupied my mind. I decided on one precaution—I would sleep with my head inside my sleeping bag. If a roving leopard could see my face, I reasoned, he might well be tempted to try some Canadian cuisine!

I slept uneasily until about four in the morning, when I was jolted awake by someone roughly shaking my sleeping bag. Confused and startled, I opened my eyes and fumbled for my torch. The pale beam of light faintly illuminated the interior of the tent. I could see nobody except for the huddled forms of the two nurses, who were both sleeping soundly. I sat quietly, every sense alert. When the shaking suddenly began again, I realized that it was an aftershock of the earthquake. Pradeep had told me that dozens of aftershocks had occurred since the time of the quake.

Somewhat relieved, I lay back down and managed to slip back into sleep.

About four weeks after my first visit, I made another trip to the earthquake-affected area. Winter had begun to close in, and icy winds swooped down the valley from the mountains beyond. The focus of BMA's work was now on shelter for the winter. In the higher villages beyond Uttarkashi, snowfall would be expected in January. The teams worked directly with village people, helping them decide on the best options for emergency shelter, obtaining materials, and assisting the village people in construction. Though conditions were difficult, nobody complained. Once again, I saw how well the BMA teams could function.

Many of the village people who'd faced disaster showed extraordinary courage. I thought of some of the people I'd met during my two visits—an old man who'd lost most of his family, going back to his fields to sow his potato crop; a woman caring for her mother-in-law who'd fractured her pelvis; teenage girls helping to organize daycare for the young children of the village. *How awe-inspiring it's been to see the response of the human spirit to great adversity.*

On the last night of my visit, I joined the other workers around the campfire. Sitting nearby was Hem Gairola, who had been leading the work ever since the earthquake struck.

"You've done an amazing job, all of you," I said, looking at the faces around the fire. "I am so proud of the work that's happening. Every one of you has done far more than I could've ever imagined."

"Madam, we are feeling so much of energy. Somehow, when you see people suffering like this, you want to do *seva* to help them," responded Indu.

I turned to Hem. "BMA has been getting so much great public-ity for its work after the earthquake. So many newspaper articles, even a mention on the television news! Don't you think this will have a good effect? Maybe some of the people who were against BMA will be more supportive."

Hem looked at me skeptically. "Do you really think so?" he said.

"Well, of course I do! I think that this is the start of a whole new phase of BMA's evolution. A very positive and exciting phase."

Hem was silent for several long minutes. Finally, he said, "And what about the murder?"

"The murder? Well, it was terrible of course, but it's behind us at last. In the past six months, we've managed to get BMA back on its feet. We must put aside that dark past, and focus on the future."

"Do you think it is so easy to put aside the past?" Hem said, sarcasm edging his voice. "Let me tell you something. Dhanesh Balodi was released from jail last week. He's free. And we'll be seeing him again before long."

I gasped in horror. "But how could that be? Everyone knows he committed the crime."

"He was released on bail," said Hem. "He has supporters, you know."

I stared at Hem, speechless. My stomach knotted with fear. The people around me huddled closer to the fire, and silence fell.

An icy wind nipped at my face, chilling me to the bone.

CHAPTER FIFTEEN:

Remembering Gaumukh

The growl of the BMA Jeep announced Pradeep's arrival early one morning several months after the earthquake. We were completing a review of the health program, and he was just returning from a visit to Anjanisain. Sonia and Raman heard the Jeep even before I did, and they looked up at me with delight in their eyes. We rushed out to the patio, and from this vantage point we could see Pradeep far below, pulling a heavy bag out of the back seat of the Jeep. As I watched him walk up the path to the house, I felt a faint chill of dismay. I couldn't see his face, but something about the set of his body disturbed me. His shoulders drooped slightly, and the spring in his step was gone. He seemed to be dragging himself up the slope.

Sonia and Raman tore down the path, shouting, "PAPA! PAPA!" He looked up and held out his arms for a hug.

We sat on the verandah sipping tea and eating Teeka's excellent *aloo parathas.* Pradeep said very little, eating his *paratha* mechanically.

"What is the matter? You look so stressed," I finally said.

"Dhanesh Balodi. He's out of jail, I guess you know that," Pradeep said, "Yesterday in Anjanisain, I met him."

"What?" I gasped. My fingernails dug into my palms.

"I was standing outside the guest house. I looked down the hill toward the valley. I saw him cross the road and start up the path to the ashram. I knew it was him, even at that distance."

"Then what?" I whispered.

"He saw me. He was getting closer and closer. I wanted to run, but I felt like I was glued to the spot. I couldn't move," Pradeep began to speak rapidly, his words tumbling over one another. "When he got closer to me, he took out a long knife. He shook it in front of me and said that he was going to kill me, and Cyril, too. Then he said that he was planning to destroy BMA completely."

I stared at Pradeep, my heart pounding. "What did you say?" I finally asked.

"Nothing. I couldn't say anything, I was so filled with fear. But then I did have a strange experience—I guess you could say a spiritual experience. I felt like I was being protected by some invisible barrier. My fear left me completely and I was just standing there, completely calm. Then Dhanesh turned around and walked away."

"How strange," I murmured.

"It was very strange. Nothing like that has ever happened to me before."

Pradeep said nothing more about the incident. After he'd finished eating, he got up abruptly and went inside, ignoring the children's pleas to play with him. He lay down on the bed, staring silently at the ceiling. I could tell that the trauma of recent events had taken a terrible toll. He had trouble sleeping that night, and was bothered by nightmares and bouts of severe anxiety.

The next evening, he said quietly, "I want to quit. The situation is becoming more dangerous by the day, and it's stupid to go on taking chances like this. We need to get out."

Stunned, I said, "How can you say that? You know that BMA is really vulnerable right now. There are some horrible people who are just waiting for something to happen. If the leadership of BMA begins to crumble, they'll move in. How can we quit now?"

Pradeep replied, "There always was something wrong about BMA—you and I both knew it. This Dhanesh problem just didn't come out of nowhere. Swami Manmathan made a lot of enemies, and that bad karma is still affecting BMA."

"But this is our work of nearly four years! We've poured so much into it, and things are finally coming together. Think of all our health workers—they are looking to us for leadership. We can't just leave!" A tide of rage washed over me. That rage was directed toward Dhanesh, the murderer who threatened my husband and my work, but also toward Pradeep, who was backing down when I thought now was the time to stand and face the enemy.

Pradeep tried to reason with me. "You don't understand what danger we are in," he said. "The regular system of law and order has broken down in Anjanisain. Right now, there is only a form of tribal law in those villages. That tribal law will not help us— too many local politicians hated Swami Manmathan. And don't forget, Dhanesh himself is from one of the villages. Do you think his family will betray him?"

I was silent for some time, realizing the truth of what he was saying. Serious death threats against both Cyril and Pradeep had been made, and yet the local police did nothing. It became increasingly clear that the police had either been bought off or were in some way sympathetic to the murderer's cause.

Dhanesh continued to make threats against BMA and its senior staff. Days and weeks passed, but the murderer was still at large. My hopes that Dhanesh would be arrested gradually began to fade, and I realized that nobody would dare to arrest the murderer. We could expect nothing from the formal system of law in Garhwal.

Even though I'd begun to realize the gravity of our situation, I was still unwilling to consider leaving BMA. I wrote in my journal, *No matter what, I can never leave Garhwal. Here I feel truly alive, like I've never felt before. I feel like I'm on a quest, a quest for new understanding about life. Of course, it's been very difficult at times— but why would such a journey be easy? We simply must continue.*

Pradeep's nerves were strained to the breaking point, and he became increasingly angry about my determination to stay. Before long, we were embroiled in the most serious conflict we'd ever faced. We'd had disagreements and arguments in the past, but we'd always managed to work through them. But this conflict over our future with BMA was different. We were both becoming more and more entrenched in our own positions—Pradeep wanting to leave and I wanting to continue. The atmosphere in our home was charged with tension. Both of us knew that the children were troubled by our conflict, and we tried to avoid arguing in front of them. But as time went on, the divide between us continued to deepen.

When Pradeep decided to go on a long-overdue field visit to the Guptkashi subcentre, I felt a sense of relief. Guptkashi was a peaceful place that had been untouched by the turmoil and violence of the past months, and Pradeep would be safe there. But mostly, I was relieved that I didn't have to think about leaving BMA, at least for the time being.

After Pradeep left, the weather turned bitterly cold. One morning, we woke to find a light snow dusting the ground and frost etching the leaves of the trees.

"How pretty it is, Mama!" exclaimed Sonia, standing on tiptoes to peer out of the living room window.

After a hot breakfast of porridge and toast, I helped Sonia get ready for school, dressing her in many layers of clothing. Later that morning, Raman and I bundled up and went outside to enjoy the winter sun. I sat on a wicker chair on the verandah reading while Raman played with his collection of toy cars. Jimmy lay by his side, her thick fur making her impervious to the cold. As the pale sun warmed the land, the frost dripped off the trees and the snow melted from the patio stones.

The postman came, delivering two letters for me—a long blue airmail envelope with Canadian stamps, and a card with an Indian return address. I opened the card first, a note from my friend Ginny Srivastava, inviting me to a conference for widowed women, to be held in the city of Jaipur. Ginny had been helping widows create grassroots organizations, enabling them to mobilize the power of these groups to fight for their rights.

I thought of the women whose development work I most admired—Ginny Srivastava and Vandana Shiva, an internationally renowned social activist. I longed to be like Ginny, who could perceive the strengths of the poorest women and help them to discover their own power. I longed to be like Vandana Shiva, who could analyze the complex web of global policy that traps women in cycles of poverty. This work seemed so important, so relevant.

But I realized that I could never be like either of them. When I looked at Garhwali women, all I saw were stories—stories of the heart. I could perceive the women's pain, their joy, their frustration, their longing. But what use was that? It seemed such a nebulous talent. I sat with my chin cupped in my palm, gazing out over the valley. Far below me I could see a village. Wisps of smoke from cooking fires lazily drifted upward. I heard the faint barking of a dog and the pounding of a pestle. Beyond the village lay terraced fields. I could see the miniscule figure of a man ploughing his field with his buffaloes, getting the soil ready for the winter crop of wheat. The landscape soothed me and calmed the uneasy voices in my mind.

I turned back to the book I was reading—*The Little Prince*, by Antoine de Saint-Exupery. The story, seemingly so simple, has layers of meaning that speak to me every time I read it. A sentence suddenly jumped out at me: "It is only with the heart that we see rightly."

My ability to perceive the women's pain and joy, to feel their stories—Is that what Saint-Exupery meant by seeing with the heart?

The discordant jangling of the phone startled me out of my reverie. I leaped up to answer it, my heart pounding. *Something terrible has happened to Pradeep! Phone calls in Pauri always bring bad news.* Relief washed through me when I heard Pradeep's voice on the line, sounding calm and collected. He said that the Guptkashi visit had gone well, and that he was planning to visit the field site at Ghat before returning home.

He sounds almost cheerful. Maybe he's come to his senses and realizes that we can't leave BMA and all the work we've done, I thought hopefully.

Suddenly, I heard Jimmy barking, an urgent intense bark that caught my attention immediately. Dropping the receiver, I rushed out of the house. Raman had somehow climbed the brick wall surrounding the patio, and was perched precariously on top. Below him was a drop of at least twenty metres. I dashed toward him, my feet slipping on a patch of melted snow. As I snatched him into my arms, I knocked one knee heavily against the wall. It crumbled under the impact, and a whole section tumbled over the edge.

Gasping for breath, I stumbled back to the verandah and collapsed onto the chair. Raman wriggled free of my grip and hugged Jimmy, who'd bounded to his side. I stared at the broken section of the wall gaping before me, and felt a strange rush of fear. My hands started to shake, and my blood turned to ice in my veins. I tried to calm down, telling myself that this feeling was just an after-effect of a narrow escape. But the fear felt deeper, more visceral than that.

That night I dreamed of the broken wall, its crumbling bricks falling away until nothing at all was left. I awoke suddenly, feeling a sense of panic. The broken wall had taken on an ominous significance in my mind—a breach of our defense, a violation of our sanctuary.

Eventually, I fell into an uneasy sleep. The next morning, I was still edgy, unable to shake a dark feeling of foreboding. About mid-afternoon, I heard the gate creak open and footsteps pound up the stairs to the patio. I waited for a knock, but none came. My heart thumping with sudden fear, I opened the door a crack and looked cautiously outside. A tall young man with tousled blond hair was standing with his back to me, taking photographs of the distant mountain range.

When he heard the door open, he turned around and said cheerfully, "Oh, you must be Karen! Hi, I'm Rick. I'm from New York City."

I must have looked rather startled, because he said, "I've been visiting with Cyril for the last couple of days. He told me to come and see you—a fellow North American. So here I am."

"Ok, well, come on in," I said, gesturing toward the door.

My unexpected guest followed me into the house, and settled himself easily on our sofa. He slung a grubby backpack onto the chair opposite. A tangle of cables sagged out of the pack, which had a broken zipper. I soon learned that he was an amateur photographer and had been travelling around Garhwal.

"Gorgeous scenery. It's even better than Nepal—and minus the tourists, which is a big bonus," he said, conversationally. "So tell me about your work. What are you doing up in this neck of the woods?"

I told him a bit about how Pradeep and I had come to Garhwal, and our vision for the health program. As I talked about the women who worked with us, I felt the tension and anxiety of the past few days washing away. Instead, I felt a familiar rush of emotion—a delicious sense of engagement and enthusiasm. Rick leaned forward a little, studying my face.

"These women are really special," I said. "We have more than just a work relationship. I find it so exciting to see them share their dreams for the future. Many of them are getting their first real chance to create their own path in life."

Teeka brought out tea and biscuits, and the conversation turned to more general topics. I asked Rick about his travels, and his life in New York. We chatted about hiking in the Adirondack Mountains, a place we both knew well.

Then Rick suddenly remarked, "Hey, I heard from Cyril that the head guy of your organization was murdered last year."

"Yeah, that's right," I said. "But that's not the worst of it. Right now, his murderer is still on the loose, and he's threatening to kill Cyril and my husband."

"Holy shit," said Rick, staring at me.

I didn't feel like discussing the current situation with a stranger. To change the subject, I pulled out some photo albums and began to show him images of the women we worked with.

"This is Savitri, she's one of our best health workers. She's amazing, really," I said. "You can't imagine how much she's learned, and she's become so confident and well respected. And here is Leela. She's from Kerala in South India, but she's learned Hindi and is one of those super-organized types who really get things done. I quite often go on trips to the villages with the two of them. You can learn so much about health when you actually go to the villages."

"Oh, yeah? Cool," said Rick casually, glancing at the photos. He leaned back, crossing his arms behind his head and stretching his long legs out in front of him.

I gazed at him for a few moments. He looked rather unkempt, with his tattered jeans and faded green T-shirt, yet something about him suggested a life of privilege. Perhaps it was his easy self-confidence, a trait I was beginning to find irritating. I turned back to the photos.

"Now this is a young woman named Champa," I continued. "She was widowed at age nineteen—really tragic. Widows in Garhwal usually don't get a chance to remarry. Families are pretty traditional and they disapprove of it. So it's tough for someone like her. We're training her as a health worker, but I'm not so sure about her yet. She's a bit silly and airheaded—you probably know the type."

I suddenly noticed that I'd lost my guest's attention. He was gazing at the crack on our living room wall.

"How'd that get there?" he asked.

"Oh, it happened during the earthquake a few months ago," I replied. "Here, look at these pix." I flipped to the collection of photos I had from the earthquake, showing him images of a twisted steel bridge, gaping chasms in the earth, and ruined stone houses.

"Holy shit," Rick said again.

I felt a prickle of annoyance at his reaction. I closed the photo album and replaced it on the shelf.

"So where are you headed after this?" I asked rather pointedly.

"Oh, I'm going back to Delhi and then flying home in a few days," he replied. A brief silence fell. Then he suddenly said, "Hey, listen. Don't mind my saying this, but if I were you, I'd get the hell out of this place."

What an arrogant jerk, I thought, anger surging through my body. *What gives him the right to say something like that?*

Just then, the room darkened perceptibly, and we heard a low rumble of thunder in the distance. Rick looked at his watch, and said, "I'd guess I'd better get going."

It was four o'clock in the afternoon. Rick was headed to Kotdwar, a three-hour drive along treacherous mountain roads. According to the rules of hospitality in Garhwal, I should have insisted that he spend the night and begin his journey the following morning.

But I couldn't bring myself to offer the invitation. Feeling unaccountably irritated, I wanted to see the last of him.

Thunder rumbled again, closer this time, followed by a streak of lightning that lit up the room. We heard a heavy thrumming on the roof as rain began to pour.

"Gotta get this show on the road," said Rick, stuffing his camera into his bulging backpack and slinging it over his shoulder. "Take care, OK?"

I watched him stride down the path to the road where his Jeep was parked. A flash of lightning briefly lit up his silhouette, and then his figure disappeared into the gathering dusk.

Teeka came out of the kitchen, and asked me what our foreign guest might like for supper. When I told him that I hadn't invited him to stay, Teeka's face registered disbelief at this violation of mountain hospitality. I brushed aside his unspoken question, saying, "Oh, he wanted to go, Teeka. No use asking him to stay. People from North America do whatever they want to do, and say whatever they want to say."

I turned sharply on my heel and walked to my tiny office at the back of the house, banging the door behind me. Settling down at my desk, I pulled out a bulging folder and began to sort through a sheaf of documents about our health program. The following week, I was scheduled to travel to the subcentre of Gairsain, at the eastern border of Garhwal in District Chamoli. I planned to spend time in the subcentre clinic, checking medical supplies and collating data about clinic visits and village programs. Our two health workers were arranging a time when I could see several patients with complex medical problems. After that, we had a three-day *dai* training program scheduled, with eighteen women registered.

I think this time the program will be way better. That first dai training in Anjanisain was really embarrassing—I made such a fool of myself. But this time, it'll go better. I'm sure of it.

I made pancakes for Sonia and Raman that evening, and then we all cuddled up in bed together. Sonia told us a complicated "made-up" story about a frightened donkey that was magically transformed into a fire-breathing dragon. Listening to this intriguing narrative, I felt myself relax for the first time in days. We fell asleep peacefully to the sound of rain pattering on the roof.

Some hours later, the storm began again. Thunder boomed across the valley, and lightning illuminated the room in sudden flashes. I lay awake, staring at the ceiling, watching a patch of damp slowly spread across the cracked plaster. Finally I turned on the light and tried to review my notes about the *dai* training program, but I couldn't concentrate. With a sigh of frustration, I rolled out of bed and tiptoed to the kitchen, where I heated up some milk. Cradling the cup in my hand, I sat in the darkened living room, gazing out at the shadowed valley beyond.

Could Rick be right? Have I lost perspective completely about my work? I know that I'm passionate about the work—but when does passion become obsession?

I picked up the letter I'd received that morning from John Last, a dear friend and mentor, who is a world-renowned figure in the field of public health. I'd met him in 1987 at a conference in Halifax. At one of the dinners, I found myself sitting at the same table as John and his wife, Wendy. John had asked me about my work and I told him what Pradeep and I were doing in India. Wendy had wanted to know about Pradeep and Sonia, and like a typical proud mother, I pulled some photos of Sonia out of my purse. By the end of that dinner, I had felt as though I had known John and Wendy for years. He and Wendy extended an invitation to meet them at their home in Ottawa on my next visit to Canada. How extraordinary, I thought, that someone as famous as John Last would be so easy to talk to.

John became my beloved mentor, a man who was always willing to listen to my ideas and give me well-reasoned advice. A few weeks earlier, I'd written to John to describe the chaos that was threatening to engulf our little world.

"If the situation is becoming dangerous, you must leave Pauri," he wrote. "You've learned a great deal in India and perhaps now is the time for you to consolidate your knowledge. You could come back to Canada and pursue some further studies in international health, perhaps by getting a masters in public health. After that, many opportunities might come your way. Your experience with women in Garhwal combined with a masters in public health would make you an excellent candidate for a job with a multilateral agency."

I knew that John's words illuminated a possible path ahead, at a time when our world was plunging into darkness. *But, John, how can I give up now? Don't you know how important this work is to me? Do you really think I'd be happy anywhere else?*

Jimmy came padding along to see why I was sitting up at night. She pushed her snout into my lap and looked up questioningly at me. Grateful for her soothing presence, I stroked her gently and soon my eyes began to feel heavy. I returned to bed, where I fell into a dreamless sleep.

A few days later, I was sitting on our verandah re-reading John's letter. I lingered over the last lines, comforted by the familiar tone of his words. Folding up the paper, I gazed out over the beautiful vista before me. Spring was coming to the mountains. Fresh green leaves adorned the trees in the valley below, and the flowers of the yellow laburnum tree were beginning to blossom. A hawk spiraled lazily upward on a rising column of hot air. Far beyond the valley, I could see a vast range of Himalayan peaks striding off into the distance.

My peaceful reverie was interrupted by the guttural roar of a motorcycle, which spluttered to a stop on the road below our house. A stocky, bearded man dismounted and began to stride up the path. I recognized him as one of the field staff in the organization for which my husband and I worked. I didn't know him well, but I'd heard that he was quite a tough character.

He greeted me with a brief "*Namaste*" and then abruptly asked to speak to my husband. When I told him that Pradeep was not expected back for several days, he frowned and gave an impatient sigh. I offered him a cup of tea, slightly puzzled by his brusque manner. He sank heavily into the wicker chair beside me.

We exchanged a few remarks about each other's health and families, but he seemed strangely reluctant to talk. An uneasy silence fell, broken only by the sound of his fingers drumming against the arm of the chair. After the tea arrived, he suddenly began to talk, the words spilling out of him in a succession of rapid-fire bursts.

"Madam, we are facing a major crisis," he said. "It's serious. Dangerous. Do you know what is going on? What's happening?"

"I did hear that Dhanesh Balodi has been released on bail," I replied. "But do you think he is still a threat to us?"

"Dhanesh Balodi wants to destroy our whole organization. And believe me, he will stop at nothing. Do you know that before he murdered Swami Manmathan he had already killed seven other people? Did you know he had been trained as a commando in the Indian army, and was kicked out because of his violent behaviour?"

"I have heard that, but I didn't know if it was really true." I said, a cold coil of fear twisting my gut. "Why he was let out on bail? Everyone knows that he killed Swami Manmathan—he even boasts of it himself."

"He has a whole network of thugs who work with him. The police know how dangerous he is, even when he is in jail. And you know, there are powerful people around Anjanisain who are jealous of the organization. Swami Manmathan never cared about pleasing local politicians, and he made a lot of enemies."

I was silent for a long time. Finally, I asked, "So, what do you think will happen?"

"Dhanesh is going to cause more trouble, I am sure of it. There is not one of us who is safe from him."

Frustration and rage boiled within me at the thought of being held hostage by this evil man. Turning to look directly at the man beside me, I asked, "Surely, there must be some answer to this? Some action we could take?"

He returned my gaze steadily. "Yes, there is something we can do. That's why I came today to talk to your husband. There is a man in one of the villages near Anjanisain who hates Dhanesh Balodi. He has a personal score to settle with him. If he gets the right encouragement, he would kill Dhanesh. And by encouragement, I mean money, from all of us."

My mind whirled, filled with fear and horror. Could this really be happening? I stood up abruptly and said, "I'll tell my husband you were here." With shaking hands, I picked up the teacups and plates and retreated into the house. I leaned against the door, my heart pounding. The gate creaked. My unwelcome visitor had left.

Late that night I lay awake, pondering that horrifying conversation. As the hours wore on, images from the past three years rose unbidden in my mind—Swami Manmathan's angry gestures, our field workers locked in bitter arguments, a village woman's veiled warning. I realized with painful clarity that I had been deceiving myself for months, refusing to acknowledge the conflict and chaos that were overtaking us. I'd created a delicate glass castle of illusion about our life in the Himalayas. The translucent outer walls allowed so much to pass through—anger, argument, deception. Inside my castle, the mirrors on the walls reflected images of a well-stocked rural clinic, a young nurse flushed with delight, a smiling village woman.

But my visitor today had assaulted that delicate illusory castle, and it now lay in shattered shards around me. The ugliness and danger of our current situation had finally become real to me, and cold fear coursed through my veins. I was horrified at the thought of being party to an organized killing. Yet there was another emotion mixed with the horror, one that I could not identify at first. Suddenly, I realized that a part of me was seething with excitement. To have Dhanesh killed! Perhaps it could be justified morally, in some way—surely it was a sort of self-defense? An evil act for the greater good?

I slept very little that night. Early the next morning, I got the children dressed and ready for a journey. We were making preparations to leave for the meeting in Anjanisain, where the crisis would be discussed with all the senior staff and team leaders from the subcentres. But before I set off for Anjanisain, I would be going to Rishikesh. Pradeep and I had decided to leave Sonia and Raman for a few days with Pauline and her family. The situation was becoming more and more unstable, and we wanted our young children out of the tense atmosphere.

We travelled to Rishikesh by Jeep, and Sonia and Raman seemed quite happy about the plan to spend some time with Pauline. They cheerfully waved goodbye to me as I set off on the next leg of the trip. On the journey from Rishikesh to Anjanisain, I gazed out of the window at the landscape I had traveled so many times before. *Everything looks different now*, I mused. On my first trip through these hills years earlier, Pradeep had told me about the myths and stories associated with each hill, valley, and river we passed. The little villages clinging to the hillsides looked so picturesque. We'd stopped to admire an ancient Shiva temple by the side of a bubbling stream, where village people came to worship. I remember thinking how privileged we were to live in such a sacred landscape.

Later, when Pradeep and I first joined BMA, my perception of Garhwal began to change. I noticed the deforestation of the land, the drudgery of women's lives, and the desperation of unemployed men. The villages were no longer picturesque—rather, I saw poverty and privation. When I spoke with village women, I began to notice their hollow cheeks and work-worn hands.

And now once again, my perception had changed. Though the winter sky was cloudless, it seemed as if darkness had spread over the land. Remnants of forest straggled over the barren hills, like a ragged cloak pulled across a wasted body. Rain had fallen the night before, and the road was gaping with potholes and slippery with mud. The waning sun dipped behind the mountains, casting menacing shadows across the valley. We drove through a road-side village, and I noticed the windows of the houses—shuttered against the cold, closed from view. Everything was strangely quiet, as if the village itself had turned its back on me.

I met Pradeep in Anjanisain. He told me he had been conferring with Hem and Cyril, and they'd decided to hold an open meeting to discuss the crisis, with all the BMA team leaders. The meeting would be held the next day, and already I could see people arriving from different parts of Garhwal.

The next morning, we gathered in the large meeting hall. Many of our senior health workers were there, including Leela, Unita, and Savitri. But now, each person in the room looked tense and strained. It seemed that the fragile system of law and order in Anjanisain had broken down completely. Local police would do nothing to protect BMA.

"Who is the final authority for matters like this?" I asked. "There must be somebody else we can appeal to."

"It's the District Magistrate of Tehri Garhwal," replied Cyril. "He is really the person responsible for law and order throughout this district. But he's a very different person from the District Magistrate of Uttarkashi. We've tried to contact him many times about the Dhanesh situation. But he simply won't respond."

Just then, one of the team leaders said, "I have an idea! Suppose we organize a mass demonstration in front of the District

Magistrate's office in Tehri? We could plan it for April 6, which is Swamiji's death anniversary."

"We can invite the press and get some publicity. The DM might be embarrassed enough to actually do something for us. We could force him to arrest Dhanesh," said one of the health workers.

Suddenly, sparks of energy ignited our group. As we tossed ideas back and forth, a rough plan began to emerge. Workers at each subcentre would advertise the upcoming event and ask for support from the village people. We would try to get as many people as possible to attend the event. Reporters from Dehradun and even Delhi would be invited. BMA's name had been in the news many times recently because of the good work done at the time of the earthquake. We could capitalize on this now.

By the time the meeting adjourned, we had a clear plan in place. The team leaders would return to the subcentres and begin to spread the word about the demonstration. Since it was already mid-March, all the organization would have to happen within the next two weeks. I promised to speak to the women working in the Toy Workshop in Pauri, and both Pradeep and I would help with publicizing the event at the Khandusain subcentre. I left Anjanisain feeling hopeful and energized.

How exciting it would be if we could mobilize the power of non-violent resistance! I just know that the women of the villages where we work will attend the demonstration, as a show of solidarity with our organization.

In the Toy Workshop, Guddi Devi was one of the first to volunteer. It would not be easy for her to attend—she would have to take her two young daughters to her mother's village thirty kilometres away, because she'd be away for three days. But she was determined to be there.

The demonstration was a moving experience for us. Eight hundred village women attended, leaving their homes, farms, and families to show us their support. Other voluntary agencies working in the area and many prominent local activists also came. A memorandum was presented to the District Magistrate outlining the current situation and urging him to take action. The demonstration was a remarkable example of the power of women's non-violent action and it received national coverage in the news. Within two weeks, state government police raided a village near Anjanisain and arrested Dhanesh. The problem was over, at least for the time being. I felt a sense of gratitude to those village women whose strength inspired us all.

I said to Pradeep, "Now we must really get down to hard work, and prove that BMA's evil was a thing of the past."

But Pradeep had other ideas. He said to me, "No! Don't you see? It's time to quit! We've shown that we have courage and we can fight. We may have won this battle, but we can't win the war. We need to get out right now."

I stared at him in disbelief. Then I replied, angrily, "I don't want to leave. We can't just give up on everything we've started. We've got to see it through."

Pradeep glared back at me. "You are being really foolish. I can guarantee you that Dhanesh will be released from jail within a few months. Maybe even weeks. The whole problem will start again. You're putting our whole family in danger."

A bitter tide of anger rose within me. "So we just leave? Then what happens to everyone else in BMA? Aren't they in danger, too?"

"Don't you see—we have become easy targets," said Pradeep. "You're a foreigner, and I am too well known to BMA's enemies. It would be much better if we hand over our health work to someone else. I've already been speaking to a doctor who's willing to take over from us."

"What?" I gasped. "I can't believe it!"

A tense silence fell. Finally, I rushed out of the room, hot tears stinging my eyes.

Over the next few days, Pradeep and I hardly spoke. Silence settled between us, heavy and cold.

We lay in bed, staring up at the ceiling. "I still can't believe that you're willing to give up on all our work," I said, stubbornly.

A long silence followed. Then Pradeep finally said, "I'm not backing down on this. You must choose between BMA and our marriage."

"What?" I hissed furiously. "I thought you always said that marriage was for life. That you'd never consider separating. That we'd always work things out. What happened to those ideas?"

"I could never imagine anything like this happening," Pradeep replied, angrily. "And I could never imagine that you'd be willing to risk our lives for the sake of work."

Days passed, and we hardly exchanged a word. One afternoon, after yet another bitter argument, I turned angrily away from Pradeep and left the house, slamming the door behind me. As soon as I stepped onto the patio, I noticed that another segment of the boundary wall had collapsed.

Falling apart—just like our marriage. Just like our lives.

The rain from the day before had washed the air clean of dust, and a soft breeze was sweeping up from the valley below. Evening was falling, and the sky was deepening into hues of mauve, dusky pink, and purple. Delicate wisps of cloud draped the mighty range of Himalayan peaks, casting dancing shadows onto the snowy slopes.

Gazing at the play of light and colour on the mountains, I could feel anger and tension ebbing out of my body. I sank down onto the verandah steps, feeling the breeze cool my hot cheeks. After some time, I heard the door creak open. Pradeep came outside and sat down beside me. He said quietly, "Do you remember when we made those vows to each other after we got married? Standing by the glacier at Gaumukh? We said we'd choose our paths together, and so far we have done that."

"Yes, so far we have," I murmured.

Pradeep continued, "But we also talked about the possibility of a serious disagreement. Remember? We said that a time might come when one of us might not be able to continue on a certain path. This is that moment. I just can't go on in BMA."

I was silent for many minutes. Finally, I made my choice, realizing that it was time to honour the vow we had made. Within a few days, we handed in our resignations to BMA.

CHAPTER SIXTEEN:

A Canadian Interlude

"So we've quit BMA. Now what do we do?" I asked Pradeep a few days later. My voice had a brittle edge—the jagged shards of conflict still cut.

"You are completely free to decide," he replied, tersely. "Just as long as we get out of here."

"I need a break from all this madness. I want to go back home—to Canada." Suddenly, tears welled up in my eyes. *So much for thinking that Garhwal is my true home.*

Getting up abruptly, I walked outside and dropped heavily onto one of the wicker chairs on the patio. My chest felt tight and uncomfortable, as if I couldn't breathe properly, and my heart thudded against my ribs. I twisted a lock of hair around my forefinger, in a habitual gesture of worry.

Slowly, I began to notice my surroundings. The monsoon was nearly over, but the air still retained a soft moisture. The rains had coaxed the parched valley back into life, and the fields shimmered with the tender green of new growth. Beyond, the mighty range of Himalayan peaks stood guard over the land. I felt the tension in my muscles slowly dissolve.

Pradeep joined me a few minutes later, and we sat in silence for some time. Finally, I began to talk, telling him hesitantly about John Last's suggestion that I pursue further studies in international public health. Pradeep was encouraging, saying that he would be happy to go wherever my studies might take me, and that he would like nothing more than to have time for his own spiritual practice and reflection.

So in October of 1992, I returned to Canada with the two children. Meanwhile, Pradeep made arrangements to hand over the leadership of the BMA health program to the doctor he had recently recruited, Dr. Sachin Srivastava. Pradeep was very happy to find Sachin, who had considerable experience in the NGO sector and seemed ready for the challenge of BMA.

In Canada, the children and I initially stayed with my parents while I looked for a job and a place for us to live. I also began to explore the possibilities of graduate study for the following year. I considered doing a master's in public health, or perhaps a degree in epidemiology. At McMaster University in Hamilton, Ontario, I met a former professor of mine who had spent many years in India. I described my interest in learning about ways that people in a different cultural context think about their own bodies in sickness and in health. If I had a method for exploring these understandings, I felt that I could design a more culturally appropriate health program.

My professor said, "If that's what you wish to learn, then you must study medical anthropology."

He offered to introduce me to Ed Glanville, a professor in the department of anthropology. Ed and I had an instant rapport, and after talking with him, I realized it was indeed anthropology that caught my interest. To be considered for a master's degree, I would have to complete some prerequisites, so I enrolled in two foundation courses in anthropology for the winter semester.

Meanwhile, I'd found a job filling in for a doctor on an extended leave, and I'd also rented a small furnished house belonging to an elderly woman who was planning to go on an extended visit to New Zealand. The day before Pradeep arrived, I spent hours getting the house ready for our little family.

As I drove to the airport to pick him up, I felt uneasy. Memories of all those bitter conflicts from the past few months swirled in my mind and I began to worry. *How can we move on from all of that? Can we ever mend those wounds in our relationship?* But when I saw him come through the arrivals gate at the airport, I felt an immediate rush of joy. As we hugged each other, I felt my worries begin to fade.

"Wait till you see our house, I bet you'll love it," I said, as we sped along the highway to Hamilton.

As soon as our car crunched onto the gravel driveway, my Mum opened the front door and welcomed us inside. Sonia flung her arms around Pradeep's legs, screaming with excitement.

"Papa! Papa! Why did it take you so long to get here?"

Raman stood back a little, his eyes wide with wonder. Pradeep reached out his arms to enfold them both in an embrace.

Sonia tugged Pradeep's hand urgently.

"Come and see our nice, cozy house," she said. Bubbling with excitement, she pulled him from room to room, explaining every feature of our new abode. The main floor had three rooms—a tiny front bedroom, a living room, and a kitchen. Narrow winding stairs led up to the second floor that had two bedrooms and a bathroom.

"This will be your bedroom, because it has one big bed," said Sonia, flinging open one door. "And this one is for me and Raman, because it has two small beds. And you can see, I've already fixed it up for us." She proudly showed us a series of her drawings taped to the back of the door.

Mum called up from the bottom of the stairs, "I'm going now—enjoy some family time! There's dinner on the stove. Come up and see us tomorrow, won't you?"

Later that evening after the children were settled in bed, I carried a tray with cups of tea and homemade cookies into the living room. Not more than ten feet square, the room was crowded with old-fashioned furniture—an overstuffed sofa covered with a pink-and-white crocheted blanket, two armchairs whose seats were upholstered with faded tapestry, a heavy maple coffee table with matching end tables. We sank down onto the sofa, cups of tea in our hands. On the wall opposite hung a plate commemorating the Queen's twenty-fifth Jubilee, and another one of Expo '67, the world exhibition held in Montréal. Heated air rose through an iron grate in the floor and swirled around the room, embracing us in welcoming warmth. On the mantelpiece was an Inuit soapstone carving of a seal, and beside it was a wooden carving of an old man sitting in a rocking chair. The lamp beside us cast soft shadows across the room.

"It's like a safe haven, isn't it?" I breathed.

Pradeep sighed deeply and nodded. After some time, he said, "I'm so glad to be out of that horrible situation in BMA. I thought you'd never agree to leave."

Studying his face, I realized that he was still struggling with both anger and hurt over my stubborn refusal to quit.

"I think I was so attached to our work that I lost all perspective," I said. "I kept trying to deny the danger we were in."

"Sometimes, it seemed like all that you cared about was the work," Pradeep replied, with a sudden note of bitterness in his voice.

"It must have seemed like that," I murmured, feeling a stab of pain and guilt at his words.

We sat in silence for some minutes. Then Pradeep said, thoughtfully, "We've traveled so far from where we began, haven't we? So much exploration and learning. And suffering also."

"It turned out so differently from what I ever imagined or expected," I said, with a sigh. "I just keep thinking about what Bill always used to say. We get too attached to our expectations, and that's what causes much of our suffering."

"Yes, I think Bill was very right about that. But of course, it's not easy to remember that bit of philosophy when you are doing something you really care about," replied Pradeep.

He moved closer to me and put his arm around my shoulders. I cuddled up to him, feeling hot tears prick my eyelids. The turbulent events of the last few months were becoming blurred in my mind, as if I had woken up from a terrible nightmare.

We spent that night in each other's arms. The strain and tension of the preceding months began to dissolve, and we rekindled the love we'd shared for so many years.

"Do you think we'll ever return to Garhwal?" I asked, as we lay hand-in-hand in bed.

"Oh yes, definitely we will," replied Pradeep. "Things went wrong at BMA, but we don't need to give up—we'll go back to Garhwal and try again in a different way. But now all I want to do is rest and recover."

Our little house was just ten minutes away from my parents' home. Sonia and Raman soon got into the habit of spending Friday nights at their grandparents' house, where they would be treated to story time, bedtime songs, and Saturday morning homemade waffles. We enrolled the children in a local public school, Sonia in Grade One and Raman in Junior Kindergarten. Pradeep walked them to school in the morning and picked them up in the afternoon. In the evenings after I returned from the clinic, the four of us often cuddled up together on the sofa and watched *Star Trek* episodes on television. Pradeep was fascinated by this series, with its philosophical questions about the nature of the universe and the place of human beings within it.

He also began his spiritual practice once again, which he'd neglected during those turbulent years at BMA. His exploration in meditation broadened to include a study of Kundalini, a branch of yoga that focuses on enhancing the flow of energy within the body. Kundalini practitioners speak of seven energy centres, or *chakras*, which can be perceived during meditation as a column of energy rising from the base of the spine.

With the vast resources of the McMaster University library at his disposal, Pradeep began to read widely in the fields of Western psychology and neurosciences. His aim was to put his own spiritual experience and practice into a Western intellectual framework. Could the profound experiences of those Hindu sages of old be put into a language comprehensible to the pragmatic modern reader? Could Kundalini experiences be explained in the language of neuroscience?

Meanwhile, I was thrilled by the anthropology courses I was studying. In class, I often felt like leaping to my feet and shouting, "Of course! I understand that completely."

After my experiences as a doctor in rural Canada and India, my mind was like fertile soil waiting for the seeds of new ideas.

The anthropologists' innate curiosity about the human condition captivated me. They recognize a moral obligation to take other cultures seriously—to think of cultures as coherent systems that are best understood within their own context. I began to imagine culture as a stunning piece of fabric whose beauty comes from both the design and the varied colours of the threads. As you study the fabric, you notice the dominant patterns and colours immediately. With time, you begin to appreciate the intricacy of the designs and the subtle meanings that they convey. But it may take years before you begin to realize that each thread contributes to the beauty of the whole fabric.

When I first began to work with the Garhwali people, I'd understood little about their intricate patterns of life. As time went on, I gradually began to learn about the culture from the intimate perspective of the village *dais*—women like Aarti Devi and Sushila Devi. I'd realized that our program would never be relevant unless its design incorporated an understanding of health from the point of view of the village people. When the crisis in BMA blew up, I'd only just begun to use those insights to make changes in our health work.

The anthropologist's commitment to try to understand cultures "from the inside out" gave me a fresh perspective on my medical work in both Garhwal and Canada. In Garhwal, this perspective could help shape a health program that would take into account the village people's concepts of health. In Canada, this approach could illuminate the patients' perception of their illnesses, allowing me to respond in more effective and compassionate ways.

Another revelation from anthropology was equally fascinating. The anthropologist argues that our view of reality is profoundly shaped—or "constructed"—by our underlying assumptions about the world. I thought of all the hours Pradeep and I had spent, particularly during the early years together, arguing over our radically different perspectives of the world. Both of us began to realize that many of our assumptions were based on our cultural conditioning rather than on a carefully considered value.

During those early days in India, I also realized that my own way of interpreting the world had been shaped by the dominant Western patterns of scientific and rational thought. I remembered how frustrated I would become when faced with situations that were not explainable in rational terms. I thought back to that moment during the *Kumbh Mela* festival, when the devotees were suspended in a trance of divine bliss. Perhaps in learning to view the world through rational and scientific eyes, I had lost the ability to experience the world in other ways.

Summer came, and I took a break from my studies. It was a time to delight in family life, and each day unrolled with easy grace. Sonia and Raman signed up for T-ball, a sport that has been specially adapted for young children. The ball is placed on a wooden tee, rather like a gigantic golf tee, and the child then bats the ball. Except for the use of this tee, the rest of the game is just like baseball.

Sonia took to the game at once, concentrating intensely and hitting the ball with all her might. Raman, on the other hand, didn't quite see the point of T-ball and was much less engaged. His coach soon realized this and Raman was usually assigned to the far regions of the outfield. He was quite content out there, spending his time happily investigating the grass under his feet and searching for ants or beetles.

On one memorable occasion, a player on the opposing team hit the ball with terrific force. It came sailing through the air towards Raman's territory in the far outfield.

"RAYMOND! GET YOUR ASS IN GEAR! CATCH THAT BALL!" yelled one of the mothers of a child on our team.

Raman looked up, startled out of his reverie. He scrambled to his feet, hastily put his baseball glove onto his hand (he'd been balancing it on his head), and ran after the ball.

Pradeep and I glanced over at the woman who had shouted at Raman. Her face was taut with emotion and her fists were clenched. We tried not to giggle. It was clear that for some parents at least, T-ball was much more than just a pleasant children's pastime!

When September came, I began my master's degree in anthropology. It was strange to be back at university years after graduating from medical school, but it was exciting to be studying something as intellectually stimulating as medical anthropology. I soon fell into the student's routine of attending classes, researching, and writing papers. Every assignment I wrote related in some way to our work in India.

My studies of anthropology provided perspectives about illness that were illuminating to me as a physician. Most of our medical training encourages us to think of the body as a machine, an intricately organized set of parts. When a part breaks down, the machine doesn't work—the person falls sick. Our job as physicians is to fix the machine. Sometimes, the patient's symptoms relate directly to the malfunction of a particular organ. In this situation, health practitioners are often able to diagnose the problem through listening to the history, a physical examination, and appropriate medical tests.

Yet sometimes patients complain about symptoms that have little or no direct relationship to the physical body. The patient may be suffering from unexplained pain, heart palpitations, low mood, or fatigue. After ruling out physical causes for the symptoms, doctors usually term these illnesses "psychosomatic," physical manifestations of mental distress. Since treatment of psychosomatic illness is not straightforward, physicians who are only comfortable within a biomedical model can feel frustrated. Many physicians speak disparagingly of such patients, almost as if the patient were to blame for his or her problem.

One evening I asked Pradeep how such patients would be treated in India.

"Well, I think our medical doctors wouldn't have good treatments, either. You know, we were trained in the same Western model of medicine as you were. But often doctors in India will realize that they can't treat these illnesses and they will tell the patient to go and see another type of practitioner – maybe an Ayurvedic doctor, or a homeopath, or someone else. We have so many types of practitioners in India."

India's pluralistic approach to healthcare had always interested me. People would choose which practitioner to consult in pragmatic ways, trying several systems of medicine if one approach was not effective.

I continued to read about psychosomatic illness in the anthropological literature, and discovered a fascinating perspective by Arthur Kleinman, a psychiatrist and anthropologist who worked for years in China. He studied people complaining of the condition of "neurasthenia," a collection of vaguely described symptoms that do not fit any specific biomedical diagnosis. Most of these people had experienced severe social oppression during the Cultural Revolution. Through dozens of interviews with these patients, Kleinman began to tease apart the multilayered cultural meanings of their symptoms. Their dizziness related to their perception of a world out of balance; their heart palpitations to the fear they'd embodied for so long; their fatigue to an exhaustion that was soul-deep.

I realized that when people suffering from neurasthenia speak about their symptoms, they are using the language of the body as a tool of communication. *So, speaking through the body becomes a way in which to express emotion that cannot be spoken aloud, emotion that is instantly recognized by other survivors. And the language of the body is very different from the language of medical diagnosis. The language of the body is ambiguous, fluid, metaphorical. But the language of medical diagnosis is concrete, hard-edged and specific. No wonder doctors have trouble understanding psychosomatic illness!*

Doctors who only speak the language of medical diagnosis describe are at a loss to describe conditions that don't relate directly to the malfunction of a body part, calling these conditions "medically unexplained symptoms," or psychosomatic illness. This poverty of language can lead to a misunderstanding of the subtle meanings of an illness. Even worse, if the doctor denies the reality of the condition, it can lead to a rupture in the communication between doctor and patient, and a loss of trust.

Thinking about my own years of medical practice, I remembered my own confusion when faced with patients complaining of psychosomatic illness. *Perhaps if I search for the origins of symptoms in the patients' social world, I could discover a path to a richer exploration of their illnesses. I could begin to understand the language of the body as a form of communication – subtle yet revealing.*

These insights thrilled me, giving me an entirely new perspective on medical practice. I realized the ideas of anthropology could be useful not only in my work in India, but also for medical practice in Canada. *Imagine if medical students could be taught some of these ideas – how refreshing that would be!*

The first semester of my master's degree was nearly over and the Christmas break was approaching. I worked hard to complete the last assignments for my courses, so that I could enjoy the holidays with my family.

Sonia and Raman had been looking forward with great enthusiasm to Christmas in Canada. Home-made paper decorations festooned the house, and Christmas lights twinkled in the front window. The bedtime stories that I read to the children had a festive theme, and after I'd turned out the lights I could hear much giggling and whispering about plans for the great day.

But just a week before Christmas, Sonia came home from school looking woebegone. When I asked her what the matter was, she replied, "Someone at school told me that there is no such thing as Santa Claus. Is that really true?"

I stumbled through an explanation about Santa not actually being a real person, but that he was part of a special story that was all about loving and giving.

Sonia was silent for some time. Finally, she said, with a deep sigh, "I guess I understand. But don't you think it's sad? It means that there is no magic in the world."

Despite my daughter's disillusionment, Christmas in Canada seemed quite magical to me. A few days before December 25, we awoke to a world blanketed in sparkling white snow. A white Christmas! Each day of the holidays held a special joy for me, a time of family togetherness. My brother, Len, introduced Sonia and Raman to the joys of tobogganing, sending them flying down snowy hills. That day, we came home to find my Dad and Pradeep engaged in an intense conversation about world politics. What an intriguing sight! Watching them, my Mum and I shared a giggle. Two more different men could hardly be imagined, yet they had formed a bond.

When the holidays were over, I began the second semester of my master's program. One of my courses was in interpretive anthropology. Instead of considering a culture as something to be observed, the task of the interpretive anthropologist is to learn about the ways people understand their world. I wanted to learn more about the ways emotions are expressed through the physical body, and how the culture in which we live shapes the expression of those emotions.

I explored the writings of anthropologists who studied the cultural meaning of symptoms in various contexts. Byron Good, working in Iran, noticed that the many women who attended outpatient clinics were complaining of "heart distress," a vague constellation of symptoms centred around the heart. Yet medical testing of these women rarely revealed any pathological abnormality in the cardiovascular system. Good noted that, in the Iranian cultural context, the heart is seen as the seat of the emotions. He postulated that when a woman is experiencing emotional distress, her symptoms will reflect the cultural significance of the heart. *So, symptoms may have cultural as well as physiological meanings, and illness may serve as a metaphor for distress that cannot be spoken.*

I plunged into a study of these culturally shaped illnesses. In Latin America, people facing life stressors may suffer from *ataques de nervios,* an illness associated with dramatic symptoms that include uncontrollable crying or screaming, fainting, and chest pain. In Sudan, women may experience the *Zar* phenomenon, in which they fall into a trance-like state. These illnesses all have their origins in psychosocial distress, but manifest in the form of physical symptoms.

Wondering whether culturally shaped illnesses had been described in India, I spent a pleasant afternoon tucked up in a corner of the university library. I came across the work of an anthropologist named Mark Nichter, who wrote about "bodily idioms of distress," illnesses in which people express emotional distress through the physical body. Working in South India, Nichter noted that among the women facing significant social stresses, a particular constellation of symptoms was common: burning hands and feet, weakness, backache, and the complaint of leukorrhea (white vaginal discharge). He hypothesized that this condition was analogous to "semen loss" in men, a hypothesis that the Sri Lankan psychiatrist Gananath Obeyesekere had postulated years ago.

I read Nichter's article with a growing sense of excitement. Could it be that women suffering from "*safed panni*" in Garhwal were actually expressing emotional distress through their bodies? If "*safed panni*" were indeed a "bodily idiom of distress," this would explain the prevalence of the condition for women in this part of India face severe physical and mental stresses. It would also explain the lack of physical findings on examination of these women, and the puzzling way the condition would respond to treatment (a placebo effect?), then come back again. I gazed out of the library window, watching the snowflakes whirling through the air. *It's the only explanation that really makes sense*, I thought, fascinated by this new insight.

By the time I managed to tear myself away from the library, the storm had gathered momentum and the wind was howling wildly. When I drove up to the house, I could see Sonia and Raman standing at the living room window, their noses pressed against the glass.

"Come in quickly, Mama, or else you'll be blown away," Sonia shouted, excitedly.

An icy gust of wind propelled me into the house. The children took my hands and pulled me into the living room.

"We are going to eat our supper here, all cozied up under the blankets," said Sonia. Pradeep came out from the kitchen, wearing an apron, carrying a tray with a large cheese pizza on it.

"Mama, remember how much fun we had in Pauri? We used to lie in bed and sing songs and tell stories for hours and hours. Why don't we do that here in Canada?" asked Raman, snuggling up to me.

I shared an amused glance with Pradeep. We'd retreated to our bed to sing songs and tell stories on winter nights from sheer necessity—the power had flickered off and the house was freezing cold.

The following evening, Pradeep was hosting a meditation group at our house, and about fifteen people were expected. His passion for spiritual exploration and practice was fully alive again, and he'd become involved in two different meditation groups. Participants often came to our home to engage in intense spiritual dialogue with Pradeep.

That evening, I helped Pradeep greet the guests—a varied group of people of different ages and backgrounds, all with a passion for spiritual exploration. Usually, I didn't participate in the discussion, because I'd be on bedtime story duty with Sonia and Raman. But on this evening after the children had fallen asleep, I slipped back into the living room to listen to Pradeep explain a point of spiritual philosophy. He was leaning forward intently, gesturing with his hands, his eyes alight in his sensitive, mobile face. I noticed the tiny hairs on his arms standing on end, almost as if an electric energy was surging through his body. The people in the group were spellbound by his words.

I knew that Pradeep possessed a rare gift—an ability to translate abstract metaphysical concepts into ideas that anyone could understand. But that evening, I realized that his gift had much deeper dimensions. His passion for spiritual philosophy burned within him like a flame, kindling a fire within the hearts of his listeners. Looking at the faces of the people around the circle, I could see that his words held a mesmerizing power.

After the last guest had left, I slipped my arm around his waist and said teasingly, "Remember how Swami Krishnananda always wanted you to join the ashram as a swami-in-training? If you'd done that, by now I bet you would be well known as a guru. Just think—you might have disciples all around the world! Beautiful women throwing themselves at your feet!"

Pradeep replied seriously, "Having disciples is the last thing I want. Think of Osho, or Bhagwan Shree Rajneesh, as he used to be called. That chap was an amazing teacher—but he became corrupt. Do you know that he owned a hundred Rolls-Royces? And he was having sex with his female devotees, all in the name of spirituality."

"Why does that seem to happen so often?" I asked.

"Too much power comes with being a guru, and most people can't handle it. I would never want to be someone's guru. Forget about it."

"So does that mean you would never share the spiritual insights you've gained over all these years?" I asked.

"No, not at all," replied Pradeep. "I'd love to have the chance to share my ideas one day. But I know that my spiritual philosophy is not mature enough yet. And even when it is, I will never be a guru. Maybe I could be a guide to someone on a spiritual search. But ultimately everyone must find their own path. In fact, I would tell them—don't listen to me anymore! Go away!"

"Aha! So you'd be like Zarathustra, telling his disciples to get lost," I said, thinking of the character created by Friedrich Nietzche.

"Exactly," said Pradeep. "I think that was the best part of Nietzsche's philosophy—the way he insisted that each of us must find his own way."

We fell silent, lost in our own thoughts. *I thought that I was finding my way when we were working in* BMA*—it was so thrilling, so meaningful. But then all that chaos and disaster happened. Now I just don't know what to think. I love studying anthropology, but I'm not sure if it will help me find my way.*

I was still pondering this thorny problem the next day during my anthropology seminar in research methods. The professor was Dr. Richard Preston, a man who'd spent many years working with the Cree people of coastal James Bay in Northern Ontario. He was a wise and thoughtful man, and one day I stayed after class to seek his counsel.

"Sometimes, I feel more confused than ever," I said to him. "I don't think I am very well suited to health and development work in Garhwal, and I am not sure that my studies in anthropology are going to make it any easier when I go back. It's been fascinating to study all of this. But is anthropology going to give me the answers that I need?"

"Don't look to anthropology for definitive answers," replied Dr. Preston. "The great strength of anthropology is in raising questions, challenging us to look beyond the obvious."

"I wonder if we should even go back to Garhwal at all," I said. "Life in Canada seems so much less complex. We are happy here, and I know that even Pradeep would be able to create a meaningful life for himself here. Maybe we should just chuck our plans to return to India."

"That is just not possible," replied my professor, with calm conviction. "I have gotten to know you quite well, and it is clear to me that the story of Garhwal is not complete in your life. You can't leave this story unfinished."

I recognized the truth in his words at once. "Yes, I know you are right."

"Remember, it is not necessary or possible to find the right answers about health work in Garhwal. Just keep on asking questions, with care and thoughtfulness. That will be enough," he said, looking at me with compassion.

I left my professor's office feeling more settled in my mind. Intuitively, I knew that he was right. We had to return to India because the compelling story of Garhwal was not complete.

Spring was coming and I was considering my options for my master's thesis. When I thought about my experiences in BMA, I kept coming back to my work with the *dais*, who had taught me so much about women's health. Our short training program for *dais* had been based on a model developed by the WHO. These programs assume that the women being trained would understand the body in basically the same way as the trainers. But I now knew that the *dais*' views on health and disease were radically different. In a three-day program, trainers would be unlikely to change the basic way that the *dais* viewed the body. A focus on changing specific practices might be more appropriate.

I applied to the International Development Research Centre (IDRC) for a research grant to study the role of *dai* at the time of an obstetrical emergency in a Garhwali village. In the introduction to my proposal to the IDRC, I had described the problems of maternal mortality in places like Garhwal. Worldwide, about one woman every minute dies from causes associated with pregnancy and childbirth. Many other women suffer the long-term consequences of a complicated delivery.

The three leading causes of maternal death—obstetric hemorrhage, infection, and obstruction—can be reduced dramatically by rapid access to biomedical treatment. I already knew that the

Garhwali *dai* was a key figure in making decisions about seeking biomedical care at the time of an obstetrical emergency. Using anthropological methods, I planned to study the way that these women identify and interpret obstetrical complications. The knowledge I would gain about the *dai* and her practices could lead to a revision of the *dai* training program, making it more culturally appropriate and, hopefully, more effective.

Pradeep was enthusiastic about this idea. "When we return to India, you can begin your thesis research and we can both act as consultants to the NGO sector in Garhwal. We already have many links with local NGOs, and we know people in quite a few international agencies. I'm sure we can make it work," he said.

I was thrilled to receive a package in the mail that contained a letter informing me that my grant application was successful, and an invitation to an awards ceremony. A few weeks later, Pradeep and I left the children with my parents and drove to the IDRC headquarters in Ottawa, located in a highrise building on Kent St. Pradeep and I were ushered into an elegantly appointed conference room, filled with staff members as well as about twenty people who had received awards. A senior IDRC official took the podium to speak about the purpose of these grants.

"Canadians have a great deal to offer worldwide—our expertise in development initiatives, our commitment to excellence in research." He continued in a similar vein, extolling the virtues of Canadians abroad. I could feel Pradeep shifting in his chair and noticed him tapping one foot restlessly. I recognized the ominous signs portending an explosion, and groaned inwardly. The speaker finally finished talking and asked for questions. Pradeep leapt to his feet, and said, "I am from India. It seems to me that Canadians have a lot to teach people like me. I am glad of that! But tell me—have you ever considered what we Indians could teach Canadians?"

The speaker looked startled. "Well, yes, of course," he replied, awkwardly. "We at IDRC have always been committed to partnerships. It is never a one-way street."

The moderator of the discussion rose quickly, thanked Pradeep for his comment, and then said, smoothly, "Well, if there are no more questions, let's move on to the reception. Congratulations to all the award winners!"

As we walked out of the room, I hissed to Pradeep, "Why do you always have to rock the boat?"

Pradeep shook his head crossly. "What rubbish they talk! It is so irritating!"

At the reception, I tried to steer Pradeep carefully around the room. *Damage control,* I thought, keeping him well away from the IDRC speaker. Fortunately, one of the other people who'd received a grant came up to talk to us, and he and Pradeep were soon involved in an intense discussion about how development initiatives in India could be made more relevant. Soon after this conversation ended, I piloted Pradeep out of the room, into the elevator, and out of the building.

On the drive home, I said nothing to Pradeep about the episode at IDRC. We'd had this argument so many times before—I always wanted to be polite and politically correct, and Pradeep always wanted to be challenging and politically incorrect. *No point in going there again—he'll never see my point,* I thought. So, instead, I turned the conversation to our plans for moving back to India.

Rather than living in rural Garhwal, we'd decided to live in Dehradun, a midsized city at the edge of the foothills. We knew that Dehradun had excellent educational facilities, a priority for us now that Sonia and Raman were both in school full-time. We felt cautiously optimistic about the move. Though we would no longer be working for BMA, I would be doing my field research at the various subcentres where I had conducted *dai* training programs. Cyril had offered his full support for the project and had suggested that Leela could be my research assistant. I was thrilled at the prospect of seeing all the women we had worked with, and had hopes we might be able to contribute to BMA's health program in our new roles.

I knew that, this time, Dhanesh Balodi would not be troubling us, because we had heard that the murderer of BMA's founder was dead. As Pradeep had predicted, Dhanesh had been released from jail within a few months, and had again been threatening the ashram. This time, he had also begun stirring up trouble in nearby villages, angering many people around Anjanisain. The story ended at last in January 1994, when a group of village men surrounded him and stoned him to death.

We were stunned to hear this, as stoning is virtually unknown in Garhwal. A shroud of mystery veiled the circumstances of his death. The BMA worker who'd informed us either knew no details or was not willing to share them. We could only assume the village people had finally decided to take the law into their own hands, frustrated by the totally ineffective criminal justice system.

Our last few weeks in Canada flew by in a whirlwind of packing, preparation, and goodbye parties. My friend and mentor John Last had been invited to speak at McMaster University in the month of June, and we invited him and his wife, Wendy, to come and stay with us for a few days. One of the highlights of that delightful visit with John and Wendy was the annual Dundas Kite Festival that was held in a conservation area nearby. Ever the enthusiast, Pradeep had brought a selection of delicate paper kites from India to fly at this event. All around us, people were launching kites of many sizes and shapes, creating a splendid kaleidoscope of colour that shimmered and danced in the air. The children raced after Pradeep as he launched his elegant paper kite. As I gazed upward, I felt a sense of buoyancy and hope for our future. We would soon be back in Garhwal, where we were meant to be.

CHAPTER SEVENTEEN:

New Horizons

"Look, Mama, we can see the mountains from up here!" Sonia tugged at my hand and pointed, excitedly.

From our vantage point on the flat roof of our new house, we could observe the outlines of the foothills, draped in monsoon clouds. On the high slopes of the hill directly before us lay the town of Mussoorie. Our house was in the valley below, in the city of Dehradun. We'd arrived back in India in the sticky monsoon heat of July.

A few fat drops of rain splashed against our cheeks. Above us, a dark cloud loomed.

Hand in hand, we walked down the stairs to the main floor of the house, Sonia chatting happily about the prospect of meeting two of her cousins again. Pradeep's mother and father had arrived at our home the day before, and now his sister and her husband with their two children were expected. We'd be celebrating the festival of *Raksha Bandan* together, a special occasion for brothers and sisters.

A delicious aroma wafted toward us from the kitchen. Teeka Ram emerged, wiping his hands on an apron. Soon after we'd returned to India, Teeka had joined us again. Within a few weeks, Girish had arrived from his mountain village. We were thrilled that they still felt that close sense of connection to our family, and had welcomed them back to the household.

Raman came rushing up to us, saying, "There's a car outside our gate! Come and see!"

Having delivered his message, he shouted for Sonia and then dashed off to greet his cousins. Papaji and Mummyji were already walking out to greet the arriving family members, and Pradeep and I joined the welcoming party.

Anil, my brother-in-law, was unloading the car with quick, efficient movements. Nimmi, Pradeep's sister, stepped out of the front seat and gave a tiny tug to her sari, which settled into elegant folds. Mummyji enfolded her in a warm hug. The two boys hopped out of the back seat, calling out excited greetings to Sonia and Raman. I felt thrilled to welcome my sister-in-law's family to our new home, especially for a special occasion like *Raksha Bandan.*

I showed Nimmi around the rooms of the house, while Pradeep took Anil to the roof to admire the view of the valley and the mountains beyond. After that, we gathered at the dining room table to share a meal.

I filled *katoris* with steaming *dal,* and passed around plates of vegetable dishes: potato and cauliflower fried lightly with flavourful spices, summer squash, and *muttar paneer*—cottage cheese with peas. Teeka brought in a plate piled high with delicately scented *basmati* rice, and a bowl of *raita,* made with yoghurt and cucumber. Meanwhile, a seemingly endless supply of hot *rotis* poured from the kitchen, provided by Girish, whose *roti*-making skills were unparalleled.

The conversation initially centred around family matters, with Mummyji telling us the latest news about births, marriages, and deaths in the vast extended family. Then the talk turned to current affairs. Anil spoke highly of the current prime minister, P. V.

Narasimha Rao, who had taken over leadership of the Congress party after the assassination of Rajiv Gandhi three years previously. Prime Minister Rao, a quiet and unassuming man, was proving to be an astute political leader.

"His finance minister is Dr. Manmohan Singh. They are planning to reform the economy—make it more of a free market," said Anil. "You'll see—within a few years, India will be taking giant steps forward."

Papaji nodded. "I think it will happen. We Indians have been too content to follow old patterns. Now we must stand on our own feet, and compete in the world market."

I asked Papaji to tell us more about the work he was doing. Some years before, he'd retired from the Indian Civil Service and was pursuing a long-held dream, working with recently retired people, encouraging them to become involved with social service.

"Retirement shouldn't be a time for people to put their feet up and relax," he told us. "Older people have so much to offer in Indian society, and the need is great."

Papaji always had a serene demeanour, yet as I listened to him speak, I could feel the passionate intensity he felt for his work. Pradeep shared many of his characteristics—the thoughtful eyes, strong nose, and graceful, expressive hands. They both shared a fluid eloquence of speech, which could capture an audience within minutes. Pradeep's passion was directed toward his spiritual search, whereas for Papaji it was social service.

The next day, we prepared for the *Raksha Bandan* ceremony, symbolizing the bond between brother and sister. The sister ties a brightly coloured thread called a *rakhi* onto her brother's wrist, and he vows to protect and love her throughout his life. I knew this ceremony was especially important for Nimmi, since it had been two years since Pradeep had tied a *rakhi* onto her wrist.

We rolled out rattan mats on the floor, where we placed the large *thalis* laden with the materials we'd need for the ceremony.

The brightly coloured *rakhis* were quite elaborate, some braided or twisted, others decorated with feathers or beads. Beside the *rakhis* were the materials used in so many Hindu ceremonies—a little heap of red powder called *sindoor,* a small container of holy water, rice, and sweets.

The children gathered around eagerly. Sonia was particularly excited, as she knew she would be an important player in this ceremony.

"What does it mean when I tie that *rakhi* onto Raman's wrist?" she asked curiously, examining each of the threads on the *thali* in front of her.

"It means that Raman is making a promise to take care of you throughout your life," replied Pradeep, trying to suppress a smile.

"WHAT? Him? Take care of me?" Sonia replied, indignantly, her voice dripping with scorn.

Pradeep mollified her by saying that nowadays in many families of modern India, both boys *and* girls tie *rakhis* on each other's wrists so that everyone can protect each other.

"And don't forget that after you tie the *rakhi*, Raman has to give you money and sweets," he added.

The adults arrived and settled onto the rattan mats. We all watched as Nimmi selected a *rakhi* from the pile, and tied it onto Pradeep's wrist. She then dipped her finger into the water and then the *sindoor* powder, and gently touched the middle of Pradeep's forehead to make a red streak.

Sonia then tied *rakhis* on the wrists of all three boys, making the same red *sindoor* mark on their foreheads. She was rewarded with sweets and money from the boys, and her doubts about the symbolic meaning of the ceremony seemed to vanish rapidly.

The next morning, we said goodbye to Nimmi's family and, in the evening, Papaji and Mummyji left for Ghaziabad by train. Sonia and Raman felt bereft after their cousins left—they'd enjoyed the lively atmosphere of a house full of family members.

Soon after the family visit, Pradeep and I began to plan a trip to Anjanisain. My thesis research would be done at the BMA sites where we'd conducted *dai* training programs. We needed to meet with Cyril and discuss the plans for this work. The second goal of our trip was to pick up our beloved dog, Jimmy, who'd been living at BMA while we were in Canada.

We reached Anjanisain when it was already dark. As we negotiated the last twist of the road before reaching the ashram, I felt a heaviness in my limbs and an aching pressure in my chest. I glanced over at Pradeep. He was staring out the window, saying nothing, but every muscle of his body was taut. *He feels it, too....*

When we reached the ashram, flickering points of light pierced the darkness and distant voices broke the silence. The peculiar feeling of menace that I'd been experiencing began to dissipate, like mist burning off as the sun rose. We heard a shout of welcome from high above us, and saw some figures hurrying down the path to greet us. Two teenaged boys appeared to help with our luggage, and to lead us up the twisting path to the guesthouse. Sonia and Raman stumbled sleepily up the path, peering into the darkness and calling for their beloved dog.

"Jimmy will find you tomorrow, don't worry!" called a familiar voice. Cyril was striding down the path to greet us, a broad smile on his face. As usual, he was wearing a spotless white *kurta pyjama*, with a woollen shawl tossed over one shoulder. He looked handsome and confident, his voice resonant and filled with warmth. He hugged Sonia and then slung Raman up on his shoulders. The children giggled with delight.

After the children had been tucked into bed, Pradeep and I went out to sit on the verandah. We gazed at the valley below, which was lit with a faint glow from the moon.

A young boy appeared with tea in steel tumblers. Cyril joined us, settling himself comfortably beside us on the verandah and lighting a cigarette.

"Well, welcome back home! We've missed you!" he exclaimed.

Pradeep said nothing, and there was a brief, awkward silence. I quickly filled the gap, chatting about the time we'd spent in Canada and what Pradeep and I had been studying. I'd written to him some months before to ask if I could do my thesis research at BMA, and now he questioned me in more detail about my plans. He offered his full support, and suggested that Leela become my research assistant and accompany me on trips to remote parts of Garhwal.

He paused for a moment to light another cigarette, giving me a rueful smile. "I know, I know, you're going to tell me to stop chain smoking. But it's my only vice—surely you'll allow me that?"

He gave me a conspiratorial wink, and I responded with a sympathetic smile.

"And, now that you'll be going to the field sites, it would be wonderful if you could have a look at the health program," he said. "Tell me how it's going, and whether you have suggestions for improvement."

Pradeep stiffened. "You know we are not working for BMA anymore," he said, warily. "We are going to live in Dehradun and work as consultants to NGOs. We can't go back to that kind of field work."

"No, no, of course not," replied Cyril, smoothly. "But just act as a consultant to BMA—you know, on a contract basis, since Karen is going to the field sites anyway. You'll find much has changed. Those dark days are over now and it's time to move forward with new ideas and new plans."

He began to describe his vision for BMA in this next phase of the organization's life. Cyril spoke fluent English, but he had an elliptical manner of speaking that concealed rather than clarified his meaning. He seldom spoke in concrete detail—rather, he sketched outlines of an imagined future using compelling images and phrases.

"Karen, these women who work for us—just imagine their lives when they fully are able to access their own power. Think of Leela's leadership potential and what she could do for this organization. Think of Savitri's tremendous dedication—I can imagine her inspiring thousands of young women to further their education. Think of Champa, the young widow who joined us a year ago. She could be a role model for so many women who have lost their husbands. . . ."

Cyril leaned forward, his deep brown eyes shining.

"You see, Karen, I believe we must think beyond the boundaries of traditional development notions. Far beyond! Development is not just about providing a job for someone who is poor, or providing medications when someone is sick. We must truly tap into the heart and soul of these Garhwali women and find their gifts, their talents. It is they who must inspire us and lead us forward in our quest."

I gazed at him, mesmerized by his words.

What is it about him that always captivates me? His voice—it's like melted dark chocolate, so smooth and seductive. And his dedication! He's been working here for so many years. He really cares about women in Garhwal."

As Cyril continued to speak about the future of BMA, I found myself irresistibly drawn into the conversation.

Later that night as we were getting ready for bed, Pradeep said, angrily, "Don't you see what's happening? He is hooking you back into the whole mess! We agreed not to get involved again."

I replied, in a conciliatory tone, "No, don't worry. I am going to focus on my *dai* research. It's just that when I am in the field sites anyway, I can certainly check up on the health program, maybe write up a little report and give some suggestions. . . ."

An uneasy silence fell. I disappeared into the bathroom to brush my teeth, wondering if I'd triggered a new round of conflict between us. I crawled into bed beside him, and we lay quietly, listening to the soft breathing of the children in the other bed. Finally, I dropped off to sleep.

The next morning, we were woken by shrill cries of delight from Sonia and Raman. They were standing on the bed peering out the window.

"It's Jimmy! She came to find us!" shouted Raman joyously. Flinging open the door, we saw Jimmy lying in the sun just outside our guesthouse. A joyous reunion ensued!

Later that day, Pradeep and I walked to Leela's little house not far from the BMA headquarters. She and her husband Anil were delighted to see us, and they served us a lovely South Indian meal of paper-thin *dosas* and spicy *sambar*. The situation in BMA seemed much calmer, although it was clear that organizational and administrative problems continued. Leela and I were soon deep in conversation about the research project.

"I think that we should learn more about the role of the *dai* when some sort of problem happens during labour," I said. "Maybe we can understand how decisions are made about getting to a hospital. Without getting emergency care, some of these women die."

"I have seen it myself," Leela replied. "It is so sad when a young woman dies in childbirth."

We discussed the training program we had developed for the *dais,* and examined the folder that contained our training materials.

"What we need to do now is meet and talk to some of those women," I said. "We'll try to find out whether our training program actually changed the way they think about health, and whether they changed some of their practices."

Leela and I planned to make a series of visits to the sites where we'd conducted training programs. Health workers at the various field sites would contact the women who had been trained and invite them to workshops at the subcentres, where we'd study more about their knowledge and practices. Once we had evaluated our training program, we could make appropriate changes.

In late September, I set off on my first trip to begin the research on how Garhwali *dais* interpret obstetrical complications. My destination was the town of Gairsain, at the eastern border of Garhwal in District Chamoli. One of BMA's subcentres is located near this town, in a fertile valley of extraordinary beauty. I'd been there on several occasions, sometimes for medical camps, and at other times to conduct training programs for our health workers and *dais*.

I met Leela and Unita in the town of Srinagar, midway between Dehradun and Gairsain. From Srinagar, the road begins to climb steadily toward Rudraprayag, the little town at the confluence of the Alaknanda and the Mandakini rivers. A small stone temple perches on a stony outcrop overlooking the rushing torrents. Narrow stone steps lead down to the water, where devotees go to make offerings to the sacred river.

A few days earlier, a light rainfall had washed the air free of dust, and each leaf on the trees seemed to sparkle and dance. On the terraced fields above us, men using ox-drawn wooden plows were preparing the land for planting the winter crop of wheat.

The town of Karnaprayag lies about thirty-five kilometres beyond Rudraprayag. The word *prayag* means the confluence of two rivers, and in Karnaprayag, the Pindar River flowing from the east joins the Mandakini from the north. In the centre of the town stands a huge peepal tree surrounded by a circular stone bench. Tourist buses, private cars, and taxis crowd the town, horns blaring. With difficulty, we negotiated our way to a spot where the Jeep could park by the side of the road. It was well past noon and we were feeling hungry. We inspected the steaming cauldrons at the entrance to a nearby roadside *dhaba*, where we enjoyed a meal of spicy *dal*, rice, potato, and yoghurt—a typical Garhwali lunch.

"Look!" whispered Leela, with a giggle. "People are very curious. They are wondering why a white *memsahib* like you is enjoying a meal with the two of us."

Unita and I glanced around the little *dhaba*, following Leela's gaze. The young man flipping *rotis* on the enormous frying pan was staring at us with unabashed curiosity. Two old men sitting at the table opposite us were also gazing silently at the three of us.

"I have come all the way from Canada just to taste your excellent *rotis*," I said in Hindi, to the young cook. A comical look of disbelief crossed his face, followed by a blush of embarrassment. Unita and Leela dissolved into fits of giggles.

Our route from Karnaprayag took us along a road that ascends steeply, following the course of the Pindar River. A few kilometres beyond the town is Kaliasour, an area where the mountain slope is steep and bare of trees. Each rainy season, landslides block this part of the road, making travel impossible. On this occasion, the road was in fairly good condition, and was being reinforced and widened at certain key points by Indian army road crews.

Two hours later, we turned off the main road at Simli Bazar and headed toward Gairsain. This secondary road is much narrower, clinging to the curves of the hills and valleys. The stark grey, rock-strewn slopes of the Kaliasour area were gone, and we entered a gentler landscape, with forest on our left and a rushing stream and fields on our right. With each bend of the road, fresh vistas of beauty were revealed. We passed the temple complex of Adi Badri, a group of sixteen stone temples that were built in the eighth and ninth centuries. Because of the remoteness of the location, invaders never reached this place and the temples remained undisturbed over the centuries.

An hour later, we reached the BMA subcentre, a cluster of small concrete buildings on the outskirts of the town of Gairsain. As soon as we pulled up outside the main building, several young people rushed out to greet us. Savitri had been recently posted to the Gairsain subcentre and she was the first to reach us, her eyes sparkling with their characteristic enthusiasm. Before long, we were sitting in the sunshine catching up on the news. Leela, Unita, and I talked about the meeting we were planning for the following day. Savitri had spread the word about the gathering, and about eighteen local *dais* who had previously taken our training program were intending to come.

We decided to begin with a general discussion exploring the cultural context of their practice in more depth. Then we would invite the *dais* to share stories about women who had experienced complications during childbirth, encouraging them to explain how they understood the problem and how they would decide on the best course of action. Later in the day, Leela, Unita, and I would work individually with small groups of women, going over each part of the training program to assess its effectiveness.

By nine o'clock the following morning, women were arriving at the centre, laughing and chatting with each other. Most were over fifty, their faces weatherbeaten and lined by years of exposure to wind and sun. Some wore enormous silver nose rings up to fifteen centimetres in diameter, and many pairs of heavy silver earrings pierced through the upper borders of their ears.

It had been nearly two years since I had met these women, so we began an elaborate round of introductions. Each woman described her family, weaving a tapestry of relationships. Some of them contained dark threads: stories of husbands who had died young, sons and daughters who had moved far away, and tragic tales of grandchildren who had died in infancy. Many of these women were widows, yet they were able to find meaning in the rich patterns of their lives. The Indian widow is often portrayed as a tragic figure wearing a white sari, devoid of jewellery, someone whose identity has been lost at the moment of her husband's death. By contrast, these women were confident and self-assured, their work with childbearing women giving them a valued place in village society.

"Now you must tell us about your family. Where are you from, what is your husband's name and where do you live?" asked one of the *dais*.

"I am originally from Canada, a country on the other side of the world," I said. "But many years ago, I came to Garhwal, and as soon as I saw these hills, I felt at home. Perhaps in a previous lifetime, I was from this place." I paused, enjoying the buzz of conversation that immediately began. Years earlier, a village woman had offered me this explanation of my presence in Garhwal. Since that time, I'd enjoyed sharing this little tale, as intriguing as it was satisfying.

"You found your way back over so many oceans and mountains to our Garhwal," said the woman sitting opposite me, reaching over to pat my hand. "Now tell me about your husband, what is his name?"

"His name is Pradeep Kumar," I replied. A faint flicker of disappointment crossed the face of the woman who had posed the question. Pradeep has dropped his caste name, keeping only the common middle name Kumar. This makes it impossible for anyone to tell his caste. Knowing someone's caste is still very important in these village societies, and I suspected this woman was feeling thwarted. I maintained an innocent silence. After a few moments, she resumed her questioning, asking me if I have a son.

"Yes, and a daughter, too," I replied.

"Excellent, very nice," she replied.

When all of these preliminaries were over, I gradually turned the conversation to the topic of women's health. We began to share stories about childbearing in the villages.

"I was hoping to learn more about the way you cope with problems that come up at the time of delivery," I said.

"Here is the woman you must ask. Her name is Baisaki Devi," said one of the women, patting the knee of the woman beside her. The others nodded, telling me that Baisaki Devi was the woman they would call upon during difficult deliveries. I had met many of these "specialist" *dais* during our training programs, women whose reputation had been built on their intelligence and experience. Baisaki Devi was a good-looking woman with a lined face and strong features. I recognized her slightly—she had attended one of our early training programs. She was clearly held in awe by the other women.

"What do you think would help to make mothers healthier and safer at the time of delivery, in Garhwali villages?" I asked her.

Baisaki Devi replied promptly, "It would be good if we *dais* could meet and talk to the lady doctors at the government hospital. Sometimes, we go with the mother who has a problem, but the doctors never want to talk to us. They just say, 'It's another case messed up by the village *dai*.' I feel upset when they say that! I would like to see one of them in her fancy sari and high heels here in our village. What would she do?" She gave a hearty laugh, imagining an elegant city obstetrician climbing the narrow, twisting trail up the mountain to her village and then picking her way across the dung-strewn path to her house.

Then she said, more seriously, "But we people are also at fault. I never went to school and I can't do any book learning about deliveries. So whatever I know, I know, and whatever I don't know, I don't know."

I asked her why she was so famous in the area. She told me that she had learned much from her mother-in-law, who had been the *dai* of the village for many years. She said, "But also, the *devis* and *devtas* of this place can enter my body, and through them, I know what is the problem."

"Can you tell me about a time when this happened?" I asked curiously.

Baisaki Devi pursed her lips and shook her head abruptly. "This is something you can't understand," she muttered.

One of the other women said, "When the *devta* comes upon her, he speaks with a deep and harsh voice. He tells what has gone wrong in the labour. Perhaps the woman has not followed the proper customs; perhaps she has offended the *devta* in some way. . . ."

We all fell silent for a few moments. Baisaki Devi suddenly said, "Nowadays, many young women like to think that they are modern. They don't listen to what their mothers-in-law tell them about proper diet. They eat anything in pregnancy—even meat or eggs! They don't do the proper rituals. Of course the *devta* will be angry!"

That evening, I updated my journal with notes about our workshop and plans for subsequent visits to centres where we had conducted *dai* training programs. The work we'd done that day had revealed interesting insights on how the *dai* understands obstetrical complications. I realized that they use a variety of ways to understand problems that arise in labour and delivery that show influences of Ayurvedic, folk, and biomedical models. Their perception of danger arises out of the model they use to understand the problem, and their strategies are based on the meanings they have ascribed to the condition. Their ideas about danger in childbirth are often widely divergent from biomedical understandings.

I'd described a situation in which a woman had developed fever several days after delivery. She could be suffering from puerperal sepsis, a serious complication that requires immediate antibiotic treatment. Most *dais* interpreted this case vignette as a hot/cold imbalance, requiring adjustments to the diet rather than urgent referral.

The *dais* also described and interpreted various conditions of the newborn. Fever at this time was often considered a result of maternal overheating during pregnancy. The *dais* give dietary advice to the mother and prepare herbal remedies for the baby. Neonatal tetanus, which can present with muscle spasms and sei-zures, is usually interpreted as spirit possession, and is treated by ritual practitioners.

When choosing a form of therapy, the *dai* first aims to remedy the problem as she sees it. If that chosen therapy is not effective, she will subsequently try another form of therapy. She is prag-matic in her approach and will use biomedicine as an option in a serious obstetrical or neonatal complication. However, biomedi-cine is seldom the strategy of first choice, particularly when the problem is believed to have a supernatural cause.

The following morning, Leela, Unita, and I compared notes about our interviews with the *dais*.

"Did you notice that the *dais* didn't change the advice they give women about diet during pregnancy?" I said.

Leela giggled. "You're right about that, Madam! In fact, the women I talked to were worried that we didn't know some really important things about the body."

"Their ideas about diet are so linked to the way they think about the body. They believe that pregnancy is a condition of overheat, and that cooling foods must be taken throughout preg-nancy," I said.

"We were telling them that it was all right to eat eggs, nuts, and even meat in pregnancy. Not a single one took that advice!" Leela commented.

"So what do you think we should do about that?" I asked.

"Maybe we could go through our lists of hot and cold foods, and try to make a balanced diet out of foods acceptable to them," Leela suggested.

"Sounds like a good idea," I replied, jotting down ideas in my field notebook.

I asked Leela and Unita, "What about those little birthing kits that are distributed at the end of each training session? Did the *dais* you spoke to actually use them or not?"

"They did! At this subcentre, our health workers made an arrangement to supply the *dais* with fresh kits whenever they needed them. And do you know what? Even in villages far away from the subcentres where the kits were not available, the *dais* were still washing their hands with soap and purchasing new razor blades to cut the cord."

"I found the same thing with the *dais* I interviewed," I responded. "That's very interesting. I doubt the *dais* really believed what we said about the causes of neonatal tetanus. But they seemed willing to change their practice anyway."

"Another good thing I found out is this: the *dais* were encouraging pregnant women to come to the subcentre. So many of them are getting tetanus shots and prenatal care," Unita said. "And definitely they are more willing to get our nurses involved if problems come up during labour."

The previous evening, the three of us had spent some time with small groups of the *dais*, assessing the effectiveness of teaching methods we had used. We soon realized that traditional teaching tools such as diagrams and charts were poorly understood. Because the *dais* had no formal schooling, they lacked the skill needed to interpret them. Much more effective were interactive methods of teaching such as role play, songs, and stories. We also found that when our training program was endorsed by one of the specialist *dais*, the other women were more willing to make changes in their practice. Involving these specialist *dais* as members of the training team could be an important way to improve the program.

Just then, we were interrupted by the cheerful voice of the boy who worked in the kitchen of the subcentre. Breakfast was ready! Unita and Leela went off to join the other BMA staff members in the dining hall, but I wanted time alone to reflect on the morning's conversation. I carried the plate of hot *parathas* and potato outside, where I settled myself under a tree. Pulling out my field journal, I wrote:

> *The* dai *is a key figure in the drama of the obstetrical complication in a Garhwali village. She is the one who negotiates the illness experience with the woman, making sense out of the events as they unfold. She is also the mediator between the woman and her family, an influential member of the group who decides what type of treatment should be selected. When referral to hospital is considered, the* dai *provides important input into decision-making.*
>
> *Effective training programs must be built on a foundation of mutual respect in which the trainers acknowledge the central role the* dais *play in maternal care in the villages. In such an atmosphere, the* dais *will be open to new ideas.*

As I thought about all the women who'd participated so willingly in our programs, I remembered Baisaki Devi's words: "I never went to school and I can't do any book learning about deliveries. But of course I want to learn more! I am the one who is there with that woman giving birth, right by her side. I am the one who can help her the most."

CHAPTER EIGHTEEN:

Distant Thunder

After the *dai* workshop was over, I had one more burning priority: to assess the state of the health program. I'd heard worrisome rumours about problems all through BMA's health services. The nurse posted at Gairsain had left suddenly a few months previously, and Savitri had recently taken over her position. She'd help me understand what was happening.

We had our morning tea together, wrapped in shawls to protect us from the winter cold. I cradled the steel tumbler in both hands, enjoying its welcome warmth.

"So tell me how things are going, Savitri?" I asked, studying her face closely. She had matured since I'd last seen her, and the enthusiastic girl I remembered was now a competent young woman.

"Well, Madam, I think you know there are problems," replied Savitri, soberly. "You won't be very happy, I'm afraid."

She seemed reluctant to talk more about the health program, so I decided to wait until we visited the clinic before questioning her further. She asked me about Sonia and Raman, and I described some of the childrens' adventures in Canada. I also outlined the plans Pradeep and I had made to serve as consultants to the NGO sector in Dehradun.

"So you'll still be working with us in BMA?" asked Savitri, a sudden note of eagerness in her voice.

"Well, no, not exactly. But I'm hoping to come from time to time and help in some way."

A young boy called us to breakfast, and we joined the other BMA workers in the dining hall. After we'd eaten, Savitri and I walked over to the clinic, which adjoined the main subcentre buildings. The room was furnished with a heavy wooden table on which were jars with thermometers and tongue depressors, as well as a blood pressure machine and stethoscope. Facing the table were several folding metal chairs for patients. A tall, steel *almirah* that held medications and health education supplies stood against one wall, beside a fridge for the vaccinations and perishable medications. The clinic was neat and organized, but there was something undefinably different. The posters on the wall advertising child health looked faded and, on closer inspection, I saw that they had been patched. I picked up the heavy record book sitting on the desk, and flipped through the pages. A worrisome trend was immediately evident—there had been a steady decline in patient visits over the past six months. In the few weeks since Savitri's arrival, attendance had picked up a little.

Concerned, I asked Savitri to unlock the steel *almirah* where the medications and supplies were kept. Bottles of pills were neatly arrayed on the upper shelves; below were the stocks of bandages, slings, disinfectant, iodine. On the bottom shelves were stacks of health education materials—posters, flipcharts, and picture books.

I could see that many essential medications were missing.

"Savitri, you've run out of Septron, and Mebex, and even Vitamin A. And look at the wound supplies—there are not enough bandages."

To my dismay, I could see tears in her eyes.

"Madam, there are many problems. We have not been getting the medications, even though we ordered them weeks ago. And the fridge is not working, so we haven't been able to keep any immunizations."

"But, Savitri, how can this be happening? What has gone wrong? Hasn't Dr. Sachin been here?"

"He was here a few weeks ago. He's a good doctor and a very nice person. But he told us that there have been a lot of cutbacks in the funding for BMA. I am trying to keep things going, but it is hard."

Savitri's face, usually so animated, looked drained of energy. Small lines of worry etched her forehead and I noticed a slight droop in her shoulders. Deeply troubled, I sat down at the table and opened the record book again, hoping to find answers to a thousand questions whirling in my mind.

I'd sensed something different about the clinic as soon as I'd walked in. It was almost as if some essential spirit had just vanished. . . .

Trying to shake off my sense of unease, I said, "Well, let's make an inventory of what we have and what is needed."

We worked steadily for a couple of hours, tabulating the essential medications and supplies that were missing or in short supply. I would include this list in my report to Cyril.

"Savitri, I'd really like to go to a village and talk to some women—it would help me understand what's happening with the health program."

"There's a *Mahila Mangal Dal* meeting tonight in a village just a few kilometres away," Savitri replied. "If we leave soon, we'll get there well before dark."

Galvanized into action, we packed a bag with medical supplies and locked the clinic. Savitri pointed out the trail leading up to the village. Far away, we could see tiny figures of women carrying loads of wood emerging from the forest. If we left immediately, we'd meet them when they reached the trail.

Savitri and I followed a path that traced the curve of the Gairsain valley and then gradually wound upward. To our left, we could see a broad expanse of farmers' fields covered with the pale green of the winter wheat crop. The harsh cry of a bird announced the presence of a long-tailed drongo, which swooped down from a tree above us. Bulbuls chattered noisily in the bushes nearby. Despite my worries about the health program, my spirits began to lift.

After walking briskly for half an hour, we caught up with the women returning from the forest. They were ready to lay down their bundles and take a break. Although I'd never met these women, they seemed to know all about me. News travels fast in these villages! The conversation soon turned to medical matters. A woman of about thirty told me about her two-year-old son who'd fallen ill the previous week. The little boy had developed a high fever, and then a rash had broken out over his trunk, arms, and legs. After several days, he seemed to improve, but then suddenly took a turn for the worse, developing a hacking cough and shortness of breath. The fever returned, even higher than before.

From her description it sounded like the child was suffering from pneumonia following a bout of measles. I asked what they did.

"My father-in-law called the *chota* doctor who lives in the village over that hill. He came and gave my son injections, and a bottle of glucose. I think he's getting better, but can you have a look at him, Madam?"

The sun was high in the sky, and even though it was January, we could feel the heat beginning to build. The women got to their feet and heaved the huge bundles of sticks onto their backs. Savitri and I followed them along the path to the village, both lost in thought.

The barking of a dog roused me out of my reverie. Far away, I could see the terraced fields surrounding the village, covered with the delicate green of new growth. Soon, I could see the slate roofs of a cluster of village houses.

"We'll be there in just a few minutes, Madam," said Savitri, a note of enthusiasm returning to her voice.

As we neared the village, a band of laughing children came running to greet us. The women, bent double under their heavy loads, began to breathe a little easier as they approached their homes. Reena Devi, the mother of the sick child, led Savitri and me to her house. She lived in a traditional double-storied stone building, with the animals sheltered in pens on the ground floor and the extended family living above.

Reena invited us inside, and motioned for us to sit on a wooden bed covered with thick cotton quilts. An elderly woman entered the room, her head wrapped in a length of colourful cotton cloth. Reena introduced us to her mother-in-law, who sat down on a rickety wooden chair opposite us. While we chatted with the elderly woman, Reena slipped out of the room. She returned a few minutes later carrying a tray with steel tumblers of tea and a plate of biscuits—that essential ritual of hospitality in every Garhwali home.

After I'd finished my tea, Reena led me into the adjoining room where her son was resting. Once my eyes had become accustomed to the dim light, I could see the child lying curled up on a *charpoy*. I took out my stethoscope and listened to his chest. The typical crackling sounds of resolving pneumonia could still be heard at the lung bases, but the child was breathing easily and had no fever. I looked at his thin arms, and noted the spot where an IV line had been inserted.

"Looks like he had measles, and then after that pneumonia set in," I said to Reena. "He's still weak, but he is recovering pretty well. Just try to get his weight up over the next few weeks."

Leaving the little boy to sleep, we rejoined Reena's mother-in-law in the main room. I said, "You know, Reena, measles can be prevented by getting a shot done. And also pneumonia can be treated by liquid medicine if you catch it early. No need for intravenous, and all that expense."

Reena said, "Madam, when our children fall sick, we want strong medicine. My son was so sick that he needed injections every day for three days and a whole bottle of glucose."

I didn't have the heart to argue with her, especially when I knew the state of our subcentre's clinic. The *chota* doctor's treatment had worked, although IV treatment in a village can be fraught with complications.

Savitri and I rested at Reena's house for an hour, and then walked to the centre of the village where the meeting would be held. *Mahila Mangal Dal* committees had been established in many of the villages where BMA was working. At these meetings, village women could find a safe space to share ideas. On this occasion, about twenty women gathered in an open area in the centre of the village. Rough cotton *dhurries* were rolled out for them to sit on. As I studied the women, a surge of hope rose within me. *Perhaps we'll be able to collectively think of ways to improve the situation. Surely there are answers. . . .*

Savitri and I talked about the health program, describing how it had started and how we hoped it would evolve. Then Savitri explained that the funding for the program had been reduced, which was the reason why a number of services had been cut. The women listened attentively and a lively discussion ensued. We asked for their reflections about the changes in the health program, and I could see that they were feeling disappointed about the decline in services. But none of them was able to generate any suggestions for change.

After the meeting, Savitri and I said our goodbyes to the women and set off on our return journey, wanting to reach the subcentre before dark. We walked most of the way in silence. I was thinking of my studies in Canada, and the anthropologists who'd offered compelling critiques of international development, questioning both the assumptions underlying development initiatives as well as the methods used. Much of this critique could apply to the work we'd done in Garhwal. My studies in anthropology had given me many new insights, which were fascinating but also disturbing.

I tried to turn my thoughts away from critiques of development to focus on more immediate problems. I was worried not only about the decline in the health program, but also about the lack of ideas for its improvement. Savitri told me that Cyril was planning to hold a meeting the following month in Dehradun, where the current state of the program would be at the top of the agenda. I told Savitri that Pradeep and I would attend this meeting, and that we would help in whatever way we could.

Our conversation turned to lighter subjects, and Savitri entertained me with gossip from the various subcentres. Despite BMA's myriad problems, I still felt attached to it and hoped desperately that something could be done to turn the tide.

Just then, a gust of wind buffeted us. Dark clouds loomed above, and within minutes, rain began to splatter against my cheeks. Soon, a heavy downpour began, and we slipped and slid on the muddy path. We reached the subcentre in the gathering dusk, shivering and thoroughly drenched.

"*Aiye!* Come in!" called one of the workers, flinging open the door. We hurried into the welcoming warmth, our teeth chattering with cold. After we'd changed into dry clothes, we were served plates of vegetable, *dal,* and *roti,* much-needed sustenance after that long hike. When I'd finished my dinner, I excused myself and disappeared into the little room where I would sleep the night. I was longing to get into bed and warm up, and I also wanted time to write in my journal. Ever since the visit to the clinic earlier in the day, I'd had a queasy feeling in the pit of my stomach. Something serious had gone wrong in the health program, and Savitri was also aware of it.

The room I'd entered was crowded with furniture—two tall, steel *almirahs* whose shelves were stacked with bulging file folders; a bookshelf piled high with publications; a steel trunk containing extra winter bedding; and a wooden cot covered with a brightly patterned cotton quilt.

With a sigh of relief, I closed the door behind me and got into bed. I wrapped myself in the quilt, and took out my journal. I turned to a fresh page and wrote:

> *Meeting with village women in Gairsain, January 22, 1996: Today, Savitri and I went to a village to attend a Mahila Mangal Dal meeting. We met a woman whose child had developed measles followed by pneumonia. He'd never been immunized, and also had not received treatment at the subcentre's clinic. It seems that the village women have lost confidence in our health services.*
>
> *It's very clear to me that things are not going well. The women said that the services we're offering aren't as good as they were two years ago. But it's not just the cutbacks that are causing the problem. I now realize that there are deeper problems with this health program.*

I stopped writing, conscious of an uncomfortable tightening in my chest. I just could not analyze the health program's problems any further today. Closing my journal, I slipped it back into my travel bag. I was suddenly conscious of profound fatigue—the day had been physically exhausting as well as emotionally intense. Although my body was craving sleep, I felt too mentally stimulated to relax. I rummaged in my travel bag and pulled out a slim volume of Mary Oliver's poems, entitled *Dream Work*. Her poetry had always spoken to me, with its powerful use of nature imagery and beauty of her language. Opening the book at random, I began to read a poem called *Wild Geese*. My eyes lingered on the last few lines:

> *"Whoever you are, no matter how lonely,*
> *the world offers itself to your imagination,*
> *calls to you like the wild geese, harsh and exciting,*
> *over and over announcing your place*
> *in the family of things."*

One phrase seemed to glow with significance—*"The world offers itself to your imagination."* I whispered these words to myself, pondering their meaning. Was this a clue to the mysterious connection I'd always felt in Garhwal? For this land had never failed to offer itself to my imagination, its hills and valleys resonant with myth and legend, its mountains displaying beauty beyond compare. The poem spoke of a world of infinite enchantment, whose dimensions we can scarcely grasp.

What would it mean to be attuned to that mystery, to be able to hear the harsh and exciting call of the wild geese? Without any conscious thought, I realized that it was Pradeep, my beloved, who had always seen the world as a place of magic and mystery— a place where nothing is random, where meanings may be hidden but are never lost.

On the long ride back to Dehradun the next day, my mind was filled with thoughts of Pradeep. When I'd said goodbye to him the previous week, he'd been sitting in our little home office, the desk piled high with budgets, proposals, and correspondence. Our NGO consultancy initiative was going well, but I knew that this work was not Pradeep's calling, and never had been.

What would he do if he were not involved with NGO work? Devoting one's life to a spiritual search can be life-altering—many swamis I had met in Sivananda Ashram had left their jobs, wives, and children in order to pursue their spiritual quest. I knew that Pradeep was deeply committed to family life, so I wasn't worried that he'd do something as radical as that. But how could he get more space and time within his present life to pursue his spiritual quest?

Our vehicle was following the road beside the river, one of the prettiest parts of the drive. I recognized the terrain—we were near the temples of Adi Badri.

"Leela, let's stop at the temples! I've always wanted to see them," I said, with sudden enthusiasm. The driver edged the vehicle to the side of the road, and stopped the engine. As Leela and I clambered out of the Jeep, the driver pulled a *biri* out of a packet in his pocket. Stretching out on the front seat, he began to smoke contentedly.

The temple complex is set back from the road, surrounded by the protective embrace of towering trees. Intricate stone carvings decorate the exterior walls of each structure, and brightly coloured pennants flutter from their tops. A stunning black sculpture of Vishnu occupies the centre of the largest temple.

I wandered among the temples, trying to imagine the lives of the artists who had created them. In this sacred landscape of Garhwal, the ancient human urge to create something that speaks to the Divine becomes manifest. Temples mark sites of particular religious significance. Often, these are magnificent structures such as the one at Lakha Mandal in Uttarkashi District and at Tungnath in Chamoli District. This temple complex at Adi Badri is much smaller, but no less impressive.

Then there are more humble manifestations of the creative impulse—small, rock-hewn shrines marking the source of a spring or the start of a forest path. In some places, these shrines are no more than a stone or boulder crudely painted with a sacred symbol. All these human creations, from the rough-hewn stone to the splendid temple, make us aware that we are in sacred territory that must be explored with an attitude of reverence.

After our visit to the temples at Adi Badri, I felt a sense of peace filling my heart. My worries about BMA's health program eased, and I was able to relax and enjoy the rest of our journey.

We reached Dehradun just as the sun dipped below the horizon. Jimmy barked a joyous greeting, and the children charged out of the house to fling their arms around me. Pradeep followed, and beside him walked Ginny Srivastava, our dear friend from Udaipur. Ginny was a Canadian woman who'd married an Indian and had lived in Rajasthan for over thirty years. She was a woman of substance—both in her work, as well as in her physical appearance. A tireless champion of women's rights, she was ready to do battle with anyone who stood in her way. As always, she wore a cotton sari tied firmly around her ample girth, and her fair hair was pinned up in a bun.

"I've been in Dehradun the past few days for meetings," she said, enveloping me in a hug. "Just thought I'd check in on all of you."

Ginny stayed with us for two days, and during that time, we went for many long walks in the tea gardens. I talked to her about the current state of BMA's health program, and my worries that the whole thing was simply not sustainable. She asked me some penetrating questions about how the program had been organized.

"Do the village women feel that it is *their* program? What I mean is, are they invested in it personally?"

"Well, they are definitely using the health services and I think they appreciate them," I replied, hesitantly.

"That's not what I meant. The women themselves must be involved right from the planning stages of any development initiative—so that you are sure that the program is answering their needs."

I fell silent, recognizing the truth of Ginny's words. I suddenly realized that although the village people had always appreciated BMA's health services, they did not have a sense of ownership of the program. Could this be why we seemed unable to generate solutions collectively?

Ginny described some of the work she'd been doing with ASTHA, the NGO that she and her husband had founded in the state of Rajasthan. Her focus was on helping tribal women organize themselves to fight for their own rights. At present, these women were struggling to get fair wages for their agricultural work.

"In our work, we draw on the strength of the women themselves," she said. "They know what is causing their poverty. What we do is give them the tools to organize and use their collective power."

Late that night, I pulled out my journal and tried to write about the complex web of problems underlying the health program. The lack of participatory planning was clearly a serious flaw. Added to that, BMA itself had some fundamental problems in its organization and management. After a strong start in the villages around Anjanisain, BMA had received a large budget from Save the Children that resulted in an enormous expansion over a short period of time. The pressure to spend the yearly budget on time often resulted in inappropriate expenditure and stress on senior management who were responsible for accounting for the budget. The strain on the leadership in BMA was made worse by an influx of too many untrained workers. The geographically scattered subcentres added to the difficulties of coordination and communication.

"What are you writing about, with such a serious look on your face?" asked Pradeep, getting into bed beside me.

"It's BMA's health program. Things are not going well in the clinic at Gairsain, and I suspect similar problems are happening

at the other subcentres. Apparently, there have been funding cutbacks, and the morale of our health workers seems really low."

"Our health workers?" Pradeep asked, icily. "We are not part
of BMA anymore, and their problems are not our problems. Just
forget about it all!"

Wanting to avoid an argument, I murmured, "Of course you
are right, they are not our health workers anymore." But as I
drifted off to sleep, my last thoughts were of Savitri, with lines of
worry creasing her forehead.

CHAPTER NINETEEN:

Into The Fearful Deep

I awoke early and lay quietly in bed, listening to the world wake up around me. From the house next door, came the sweet voice of a woman, singing devotional *bhajans*. From the kitchen, came the faint clatter of pots, as Girish began to prepare morning tea. Though it was still early in February, the first signs of spring were already in evidence. I could hear the twittering of sparrows that nested on our roof, and the raucous cries of crows in the distance. Shafts of sunlight slanted across the floor and the air wafting through the window held a hint of warmth.

The meeting that day would be the pivot point for our health work in BMA. A chill of anxiety raced up my spine. We'd laid the foundation of the health program more than six years previously, with such a sense of optimism and excitement. Over the difficult years that followed, we'd struggled to build a program that would endure and evolve. But during the time Pradeep and I had been away in Canada, much had changed. Our recent evaluation of each health centre had revealed serious problems in every aspect of its running. I now wondered whether the situation was already beyond remedy. I stared up at the ceiling, my eyes following a crack in the plaster. *Surely, something can be done—we just can't let all that work go to waste.*

By early afternoon, the senior staff of BMA began to arrive at our home. Sachin Srivastava, the doctor who'd taken on our work when we'd been in Canada, was one of the first to appear. As usual, he had a smile on his face and a cheerful thought to share. Somehow, he'd managed to weather the turbulent climate of BMA without losing his equanimity. Accompanying him was a young woman I didn't recognize—Sachin told us that she had recently graduated as a general practitioner and was thinking of joining BMA.

As our guests arrived, Pradeep and I welcomed them and invited them to the dining room, where Girish and Teeka were laying out lunch. They'd prepared a delicious feast of *dal*, rice, *raita*, and several vegetable dishes—*aloo mattar, palak paneer, bindi bhaji*. One plate held a stack of hot *rotis*, which Girish replenished as rapidly as they disappeared.

I felt too tense to eat. I took a seat at the far end of the living room, and watched as the room gradually filled with people I knew so well. Several senior health workers were there, including Leela and Indu. Hem Gairola had come, though he looked remote and distant. Sachin sat between the young lady doctor and Pradeep, who was looking tense and preoccupied. Cyril was away in Delhi and couldn't attend this meeting, but he'd written out some thoughts and ideas for the health program and had sent these along with Leela.

After we'd finished our lunch, we began to discuss the current state of the health program. I summarized the problems facing the Gairsain clinic, and Sachin confirmed that a similar situation existed at the other sites. The group spent several hours debating what could be done to remedy the situation. I listened with a growing sense of unease as lofty ideas were raised and impractical plans suggested. Leela shared Cyril's thoughts about the health program. I'd sent him the results of my evaluation, but without acknowledging the serious problems raised in the report, he encouraged us to think of expansion. He suggested new funding agencies, larger budgets, more clinics, broader horizons. I felt a strange sense of *déjà vu*—I had heard this from Cyril so many times before.

Suddenly, it dawned on me that nothing was going to work. There were fundamental flaws in this health program, and pouring more money and human resources into it would not help. In a blinding moment of epiphany, my delicate glass castle of illusion about our work in BMA was shattered. I rushed out of the room, my eyes blinded by tears.

In the days that followed, I felt an acute sense of confusion. Over the years in Garhwal, Pradeep and I had had our share of both successes and failures; we'd suffered great hardships and delighted in great joys. Even at the most difficult times there was no sense of a break in the narrative of my life. But after this painful moment of disillusionment, I perceived that our whole approach to health work had been flawed, and at that point, the narrative of my life tore apart. All sense of meaning began to vanish.

Pradeep was worried about my anguish, and tried to reason with me. "I don't see why you are so upset about BMA's health program. After all, that was just one part of our work in Garhwal. There are lots of other things we've done—there's Sivananda Hospital, and our work with so many other NGOs, and with the Voluntary Health Association of India. Think of all the health workers and *dais* you've trained—that work won't be lost. And that literacy primer you wrote, which is now being picked up by many NGOs."

I was inconsolable. Somehow, my vague and romantic dreams about doing health work in the Himalayas had transformed into a specific dream about our health program in BMA. I wanted to create a model primary health-care program for Garhwal, something that would evolve and endure. Now I knew that would never happen.

What had it all been about, then? The whole thing—coming to India, marrying Pradeep, working in Garhwal? What was I really searching for?

I thought of the stories I was told as a child, the narratives that shaped my earliest understanding of identity. My mother told me about the mist-shrouded island off the coast of Norway where her forebears built sturdy fishing boats and went out to sea to gather the ocean's harvest. My father's mother told me about her family who also lived near the sea, on the west coast of England. These ancestors built elegant, three-masted schooners that travelled the oceans. The vessels of my ancestors sailed through my childhood imaginary world, and I dreamed of adventure, daring, and danger.

Perhaps I was drawn to India simply in pursuit of that adventure. Perhaps Pradeep was just part of that romantic fantasy. . . .

I began to study the journals I had written over the years I'd lived in India. As I leafed through the pages, stories and images from those early days came spilling out. A pressed leaf from an oak tree fluttered from the pages. On our honeymoon trip to Gangotri, Pradeep and I had climbed the tree and posed for an intimate photograph. My brother, Len, had captured our embrace on film, our faces framed by the rich green leaves of the oak.

I turned to the page where I had written about the day we'd reached Gaumukh. About our moments together at the glacier, I read, ". . . and here, at the edge of the icy stream flowing from the glacier, we made some special promises to each other. We vowed to live a life of exploration and inquiry. We vowed to search for spiritual truth that transcends the boundaries of religion. We vowed to love and care for each other, and to honour what is highest in the other. Above all, we committed ourselves to the relationship itself, placing it above any disagreements that might arise. . . ."

The narrative swept me back eleven years. I saw Pradeep and myself holding hands beside the glacial stream in Gaumukh, making those promises to each other. Now those words sounded impossibly romantic and hopelessly naïve. *What a fool I was,* I muttered aloud.

I had told myself a story about my journey to India, a story about wanting to cross the barriers of culture, class, and religion. I had told myself that I wanted to embrace a life of voluntary poverty and serve those who had so much less. I had created an image of myself as an idealistic and courageous young woman. Yet now I saw the shadow side of that image—a desire for adventure disguised as altruism; a thinly veiled egotism. *Yes, in this world of darkness, a deeper truth is emerging. A truth I never dared to face before.*

I awoke one night with a stabbing pain in the chest, so severe that I had to get out of bed and pace around the bedroom. A cool analytical medical voice in my mind interrogated my symptoms. *Onset of pain?* Sudden. *Location of the pain?* Left-sided, directly over the heart. *Radiation of the pain?* None. *Quality?* Sharp and stabbing. *Precipitated by exercise?* No. *Shortness of breath?* No. *Wheezing or cough?* No. *Previous history of similar pain?* No. *Risk factors for cardiac disease?* None. *Family history?* None.

The calm medical voice concluded: *This pain is highly unlikely to be either cardiac or pulmonary in nature.*

While I found this analysis reassuring, it did nothing to relieve the pain. I continued to pace around the room wondering what was wrong with me. After some time, a quiet medical anthropologist's voice offered an opinion: *This is the pain of heartbreak.*

Gradually over the next few weeks, my world began to shrink. I stopped working, and then I stopped meeting people. I retreated to the bedroom, where I kept the curtains drawn and the lights off. The bed became my cave, a place where I could hide from the world. Pradeep became increasingly concerned about my well-being, and he tried his best to draw me out of my isolation. Every evening, he encouraged me to go with him for a walk in the tea gardens near our house, a familiar ritual we'd enjoyed ever since we'd moved to Dehradun. I invariably refused, saying that I was too exhausted. He suggested going on a drive, visiting friends, or taking a holiday. All these ideas seemed impossible.

Eventually, he stopped suggesting anything, and would simply lie down beside me and hold my hand. We often lay for hours like this, in complete silence.

One day I said, "It's very strange—I can actually feel a sort of soothing energy coming out of your hand into mine."

"It's my *prana*," said Pradeep. "I am sending you all the healing energy that I can."

I lifted his hand and studied it closely. I knew that hand so well—the smooth, brown skin; the fine-boned, sensitive fingers; the square, neatly cut fingernails. I kissed his palm, and whispered, "I am so sorry about all of this."

"It's not your fault," he murmured.

I cuddled close to him, and eventually fell asleep. The next morning, Pradeep rose quietly, not wanting to disturb me, and went downstairs to help the children get dressed. Some time later, Raman came quietly into the bedroom and began to shake my shoulder, gently.

"Mama, please come outside," he pleaded. "You must see the garden—the flowers are smiling everywhere."

I allowed myself to be pulled to my feet and followed him down the stairs and out the front door. Walking outside, my senses were immediately assaulted by the searing heat and the blinding light. Raman pointed excitedly to the garden, where I could see that flowers had burst into bloom. But something strange had happened. The world around me was like a black-and-white photograph—the colour had disappeared, leaving nothing but shades of gray. This stark world of angles, planes, and lines, devoid of contour and depth, was profoundly disturbing.

"I must go back inside," I said abruptly. "There's something wrong."

I pulled away from the children and turned back to the house, stumbling on the verandah steps, desperate to get back to the safety of my cave.

Weeks passed, and I remained lost in my shadow world. Each time the first rays of light appeared in the morning, I hoped perhaps that day would be a little better. But nothing seemed to change. The long hours of daylight dragged on, until I was desperate for night to come.

One day, Pradeep came in and sat on the bed beside me. He took my hand in his, and said, "Listen, Kinny, you are really ill. You are suffering from a serious depression."

It seemed as if he was speaking from a great distance away. Finally, I said, "Do you think so?"

Pradeep nodded silently, and squeezed my hand.

I said, "So, it finally did happen to me. Depression. Just like all those family members of mine. . . ."

I closed my eyes and rolled over to face the wall. Pradeep sat quietly beside me, gently stroking my back. I lay for a long time in silence, turning the thought over in my mind. I'd always feared depression so much—that terrible cloud that hung over our family. *I thought it would be so painful, but really it isn't that bad. Mostly, I feel nothing, nothing at all.*

Pradeep was quiet for a long time. Finally, he said, "Do you remember how Swami Brahmananda said you were on a spiritual journey, but you just didn't recognize it? Maybe this depression is part of that same journey. Think of how much you've learned since those days in Rishikesh."

"Yes, I've learned a lot," I replied.

"So tell me something about that spiritual journey," said Pradeep.

"Well, it's only recently that I've finally begun to understand it all," I said, after a long pause. Suddenly, the stabbing pain in my chest began again, making me catch my breath.

After a few minutes, I continued. "I know now that the whole journey was meaningless. Completely meaningless. That's what I've learned."

Pradeep stared at me for a moment, and then got up abruptly and left the room. I recognized from the stiff set of his back that he was angry. *But why*, I wondered—*I was simply answering his question.*

I became increasingly preoccupied with thoughts of death. I could not bear the thought of my life stretching out ahead of me, years of this eerie shadow existence. Fantasies about death gave me a strange sense of comfort. Into my imaginary world sailed those vessels of my ancestors that had once brought me delight. But now I dreamed of a fishing boat far out at sea, lost in a heavy mist. I dreamed of a three-masted schooner foundering on jagged rocks. I imagined myself slipping into the ocean, the water closing over my head, my descent into oblivion.

Feeling increasingly concerned about my mental state, Pradeep took me to see a classmate from his medical college who was practicing psychiatry in the city of Dehradun. He diagnosed major depressive disorder, and prescribed antidepressants for me. I felt a strong sense of resistance to taking the medication. It seemed ludicrous to think that taking a pill could bring me out of the strange inner world in which I was lost.

Pradeep watched me take the medication every morning. After a few weeks, I noticed that the fog in my mind seemed a little less dense, and I was more able to focus on what others were saying. Whether it was the effect of the medication, or simply the natural course of the illness, I seemed to be taking the first tentative steps to recovery.

The leaden feeling in my legs eased slightly, and a little colour returned to the natural world. I started going on short walks. Outside, I noticed that the sharp world of angles, planes, and lines was gradually softening into more familiar shapes and contours. Some close Canadian friends of ours had come to India for an extended visit, and were living in a rented house not far from us. I began to go every day to meet them, finding comfort in their reassuring presence.

Although I was making some progress, I was still troubled by a pervasive sadness. I could not imagine starting work again. My castle of dreams had been shattered, and I knew that I could never build it again.

One afternoon, Pradeep reached for my hand and said, quietly, "We need to leave India. There is no future for us right now, in this country."

"What should we do then?" I asked dully.

"I think we must move to Canada. You'll feel better in your own country."

The idea of making such a move seemed impossibly complex. I struggled to organize my thoughts. Finally, I asked, "What would you do in Canada?"

"Don't worry about me," replied Pradeep. "I can be happy any-where I live. And you know that I am no more interested in NGO work. In fact, I am no more interested in the practice of medicine at all. It is time for me to take a new direction in life."

I nodded, slowly, realizing that Pradeep was longing to pursue his spiritual quest once more.

"I will study acupuncture," he said. "When we were in Canada, I found out that there's scope for someone with this kind of train-ing. And perhaps I will help others to learn about meditation. I'll be fine."

Pradeep patted my hand, and then went off to make us a cup of tea. After he'd left, my mind whirled in confusion. Trying to decide about even the simplest thing had become a tedious chore. How could I possibly sort through a decision as life-changing as a move back to Canada? As I sat pondering this problem, I suddenly thought of Bill and Susan, the first friends I had made in India. At difficult times in my life, I had often turned to them for advice. An urge to visit Sivananda Ashram rose within me.

Pradeep was delighted to hear this idea. "It's the first time you've wanted to do something for months and months," he said. "Go to the ashram and stay for a little while. I'm sure it will help."

A few days later, Pradeep, the children, and I set out for Rishikesh in a rented taxi. As we drove up the familiar road to the hospital, a faint flicker of excitement stirred within me—the first positive emotion I'd felt in months. We arrived in mid-afternoon, and we went straight to Sivananda Hospital to meet Dr. Kutty. As usual, the waiting room was packed with women who had come from far and wide for consultation. Dr. Kutty's face lit up with delight when she saw Pradeep, who'd always been like a son to her. She beckoned us into her consulting room, hugged the children, and then turned to greet me.

"But what is this? You are looking sick!" She frowned, and motioned for me to sit on the stool beside her consulting table. She took my wrist to check my pulse, and then pulled down my eyelid to check me for anemia. Then she shot Pradeep an accusing glance. "You are not taking proper care of her, are you?"

Nobody could face Dr. Kutty when she became angry. Pradeep stammered, "Well, she . . . she has been ill. I am trying. . . . I am not sure. . . ."

Dr. Kutty gave an irritated snort. With an impatient wave of her hand, she stopped the flow of patients and ordered tea and biscuits. Pradeep managed to turn the conversation away from my state of health by commenting on the positive changes in the hospital. Dr. Kutty told us proudly that a new floor was under construction, and that she'd invited several surgeons to use the operating room facilities. She also informed us that the two young doctors we had recruited before we left Sivananda Ashram were doing good work.

One of the compounders from the dispensary gave us a tour of the hospital with its new additions. After we'd left, we climbed the long flight of stairs into the central portion of the ashram. Wherever we went, we were greeted warmly by ashram residents. Lata Mataji and Ammaji were delighted to see Sonia, now a lively nine-year-old girl. Ammaji pulled Sonia onto her lap, and shared some stories about the little baby they'd cherished so much.

We had one more visit to make—to Vijaya Mataji, my first Hindi teacher. As I knocked at the door of her *kutir*, vivid memories of those Hindi lessons came to mind. I saw myself bending earnestly over my textbook, and then Vijaya Mataji sweeping the book away, saying *"Bolne se seek jayiegi!* You will learn by speaking!" I saw us laughing helplessly as we struggled to communicate. I saw her bringing delicious dishes out of her little kitchen at the end of every lesson.

Vijaya Mataji gave a cry of delight when she saw all four of us standing outside her door. But when she looked more closely at me, her expression changed to dismay. *"Beti, kya hogaya?* What happened to you? You are nothing but bones, just bones."

She pinched my upper arm, clucking disapprovingly. Then with a wave of her hand, she ushered us onto her tiny verandah, pulling a couple of stools from under the *charpoy* for Sonia and Raman to sit on. She bustled off to put a pot of water onto her little kerosene stove. Returning minutes later with cups of tea, biscuits, and *namkeen,* she began to pepper us with questions about our lives in Dehradun.

Her eyes danced with excitement when she listened to me speaking Hindi, saying, "*Arre*, I cannot believe how sweetly you can talk! I must have been a good teacher, *hai na?*"

After we'd left Vijaya Mataji's home, we made our way to the ashram dining hall where we ate a simple supper of *kitcheree, roti,* and yoghurt. Then we walked up the steep path to the highest level of the ashram, to the same building where we had lived so many years before. Several flats had been set aside for guests, each one identical in design to my first home in India. After Pradeep and the children had left for Dehradun, I sat on the balcony of the guest room and listened to the sounds of the evening. There were the thumps of the *langur* monkeys landing on the roof, and the harsh cries of the peacocks that nested behind the building. Voices singing the evening *kirtan* floated up from the *satsang* hall, and from across the river, came the faint clanging of temple bells. Lost in memories of our early days in India, I hardly noticed the hours slipping past. When darkness fell, I roused myself from my reverie and walked back inside the room, closing the balcony door quietly behind me. A tiny lizard scuttled across the wall and disappeared behind the tube light. I lay down on the cot, and fell into a deep and dreamless sleep.

Early the next morning, I walked down the steep path to Swami Brahmananda's *kutir*, just as I had done so many times before. I slipped off my *chappals* and walked quietly into the room. Ten years had passed since I had first attended one of Swamiji's morning sessions. His little room was exactly the same—the simple cot, the photograph of Swami Sivananda sitting on the metal bookshelf, and the clay vessel to hold his drinking water. Swami Brahmananda himself was looking more frail, but his serene presence was unchanged. Recognizing me at once, he offered me a gentle *Hari Om*. How much I have experienced since that first meeting with him, I thought wonderingly. After the session was over I stayed for a little while, absorbing the sense of peace that pervaded the room. Swamiji asked me about my spiritual journey, and I said that I had lost my way and that nothing made sense anymore.

Looking at me with compassion, he said, "In your Christian tradition, you have entered the 'dark night of the soul.' You must accept it, embrace it, for there are great spiritual gifts to be found in that darkness."

Later that morning, I wandered into the ashram library and studied the collection of Christian texts. One book contained short excerpts from the works of medieval Catholic saints. My eyes fell on something written by St. Francis de Sales, a sixteenth-century saint. The biography said that his had been the way of love as a devotional path. He wrote,

> "Be patient with everyone, but above all with yourself. Do not be disheartened by your imperfections, but always rise up with fresh courage. How are we to be patient in dealing with our neighbour's failings if we are not patient in dealing with our own? They who are fretted by their own failings will not correct them. All profitable correction comes from a calm and peaceful mind."

It seemed as if that gentle saint had reached across the centuries to console me. I looked up from the book and gazed at the large photograph of Swami Sivananda on the wall, whose calm countenance seemed to embrace all the pain and the joy of life. How extraordinary that I should be comforted by the words of a Catholic saint while sitting in the library of a Hindu ashram.

I replaced the book on its shelf and quietly left the library. I walked down a short flight of stairs, passing the building where Swami Nadabrahmananda had lived. Though he'd died several years previously, his memory was fresh in my mind—I recalled him showing us photos of himself with his Canadian devotees in

Banff, and then unwrapping the moon rock from its silk coverings. His eyes had radiated joy in life, even though his body was ravaged by old age and infirmity.

Below this building was a garden that bloomed with flowers—yellow dahlias nodding in the breeze, red roses flaming near the rock border. Beside the garden was Om Kutir, the building where Bill had lived for more than twenty-five years, in a simple room on the ground floor. I knocked on the door, and a familiar voice called out, "*Hari Om!* Come in!"

Pushing open the door, I stepped into the dim interior. Bill came forward to greet me. His lean body was beginning to stoop a little with age, and his face bore deeper lines. But something more significant had changed—he was now wearing the orange clothes of the Hindu renunciant.

"So you did it—you took *sannyasa*," I breathed. Bill had always worn white clothing, symbolizing his commitment to a spiritual path. But now he had taken full vows and had been initiated as a swami.

"Yes, my name is now Swami Atmaswaroopananda," replied Bill, with a smile. "And Susan has also taken her vows—she'll be here any minute. Come in, come in."

I followed him into the room, and took my accustomed seat on one side of the tiny dining table. The room looked the same as ever. A framed photograph of Bill with Swami Chidananda, taken many years ago during one of Swamiji's early visits to Canada, sat on the desk. Photos of Bill's family in Canada hung on the walls.

Susan arrived. Her head was close-shaven, and she, too, was wearing the orange clothes of the swami. I congratulated her on her decision to take *sannyasa*, and she told me her new name—Swami Amritaswaroopananda. She described the ceremony in which their guru, Swami Chidananda, had presented them with their robes and given them their spiritual names.

Bill busied himself with carefully measuring out water and milk for tea, then putting the pot to heat on his small two-burner stove. The familiar ritual set me at ease, and I felt myself relaxing into the moment. At the most difficult times of my journey in India, I could always count on Bill and Susan's love and guidance.

Bill brought out the tea and Susan produced a plate of biscuits. She took a seat opposite me, and Bill settled himself on his cot, his long legs stretched out in front of him.

They asked about the children, and I shared some of their latest escapades. Susan and Raman had been great friends—he used to enjoy sitting on her lap, pinching her cheeks and then bursting into mischievous laughter. I told them about Sonia's current passion for writing poetry, and then I talked a bit about Pradeep, telling them how much he was longing to return to his spiritual quest.

"So now tell us how *you* are," said Bill, quietly. He always seemed to know when I was in distress. I began to relate the story of the decline of BMA's health program, slowly at first, and then with increasing passion, describing that shattering moment when I'd concluded that I was on the wrong path altogether.

Bill was silent for some time and then said, thoughtfully, "Do you remember that conversation we had so many years ago? We talked about how you were imagining your life with Pradeep, a life that was filled with expectations about him. When he turned out to be different from what you expected, you felt disappointed. You suffered. I think that's happened again, in your health work with BMA. Am I right?"

"Yes, I suppose so," I admitted slowly.

"Perhaps you built up an imaginary future, an idealized idea of what your health program might be like?"

"Well, yes, that was my dream. But surely that is a natural thing for humans to do—I can't imagine living a life without dreams. And with those dreams come expectations. Isn't that inevitable?"

"No, it is not inevitable. Remember the truth of the *Bhagavad Gita*—you must work with all your heart, but leave the results to God. The problem remains that you feel yourself to be the central actor in your life, and thus you are not willing to be led by God."

"The central actor—what do you mean by that?"

"You see, you are attached to the idea of 'I as the doer.' You need to pray to understand the movement of Divine will in your life. Once you acknowledge your own weakness and spiritual need, you'll be able to move forward with the grace of true humility."

Later, we went for a long walk by the bank of the Ganga. Both Susan and Bill thought that our decision to go to Canada seemed wise.

"I'm sure you'll be back again one day," said Susan, reassuringly. "This land has become part of who you are—you can never leave it completely."

I hugged Bill and Susan, feeling a deep sense of gratitude to both of them. They turned and began to walk up the long flight of stairs back into the ashram. As I watched them go, I thought about the friendship we'd shared ever since my arrival at Sivananda Ashram. There was something so quintessentially Canadian about them, although they'd lived in India for over twenty years. Perhaps it was this bond we shared that made me feel so relaxed with them, able to let my guard down completely. I thought about their decision to leave Canada and commit themselves to this austere path of spirituality. *I wonder if they've found their true path in life, or do they ever have doubts?*

Still turning this question over in my mind, I began to wander along the row of stalls lining the bank of the river. Before returning to Dehradun, I wanted to buy a sculpture of Shiva Nataraj, the Divine being whose dance symbolizes the cosmic cycles of creation and destruction. In a little shop close to the bridge, I found just what I was looking for—a bronze sculpture of the dancing Shiva, his left foot raised and his right foot crushing a demon. His four arms extend in the cardinal directions, the upper-left hand holding a flame that symbolizes awareness while the lower-right hand points downward in a gesture that symbolizes fearlessness. The image of the dancing Shiva balances the dynamism of action with the stillness of contemplation.

I settled myself on the steps of one of the bathing *ghats* leading down to the river to wait for the evening worship. At sunset in this sacred place, devotees sing the *Jai Jagdish Aarti*, one of the most beloved hymns of the Hindu faith. I listened to the voices rising and falling in graceful cadence, relaxing into the moment.

I thought about Bill's words: "The problem with you is that you are still attached to the idea of 'I as the doer.' You need to pray to understand the movement of Divine will in your life. In that moment of surrender, you will find the peace your heart is seeking."

"God, pray, Divine will, surrender"—these are all words that arise in a faith tradition in which the Divine is perceived in the most intimate terms, in an "I-thou" relationship. To Hindus, Christians, Jews, and Muslims, these words have a profound meaning. The seeker acknowledges her own ignorance and frailty, and inclines her heart and soul toward a Divine Being both dimly perceived and at the same time intimately known.

Yet what do these words mean for a Buddhist, a Daoist or for an agnostic? What do these words mean for someone like me, who has so many questions? I gazed down at the sculpture of the dancing Shiva in my lap. If we think about the universe as a dynamic dance, can we transcend the need for words like God and Divine will? The dance of the universe is revealed in the richness of the world, in the myriad names and forms that surround us. Suppose the seeker strives to attune herself to that cosmic dance, to move in its rhythm—will she then find the peace her heart is seeking?

The *Jai Jagdish Aarti* was coming to a close. I watched as the devotees knelt beside the river to launch hundreds of tiny leaf boats. The lighted candles in these fragile vessels created sparkling pinpoints of light that danced on the rippled surface of the river. The last colours of sunset faded into the evening sky. I breathed deeply into the moment, and I felt the tight knot in my chest begin to loosen. A feeling of tranquility washed over me, bringing a delicate promise of peace.

Garhwali Woman

Savitri and Leela

Karen at the Dai Workshop

Aarti Devi

Sonia and Raman with their beloved dog Jimmy

The woman on the pilgrimage

CHAPTER TWENTY:

The Cloud Messenger

Pradeep and I began the final tasks of packing and organizing for our move to Canada. One day, I heard a knock at our door and, to my surprise, Savitri was standing there. Since I'd withdrawn from contact with BMA months before, I hadn't seen any of the health workers. But there she was, her engaging smile lighting up her face. I felt a great rush of affection for her, a powerful emotion flowing through my body like a life-giving stream.

"Savitri! *Aiye! Aiye*! Come in!" I said, waving her into the house.

Pradeep walked into the room, his arms loaded with bundles of files that we had been sorting out. Seeing Savitri, he dropped the files onto the dining table and greeted her with a welcoming smile. We shared a cup of tea, the way we'd done so many times in the past. Trying to keep the conversation light, Pradeep asked about some of the people we knew in the villages. Savitri shared a juicy tidbit of the latest gossip, something to do with a love affair involving a young relative of Aarti Devi, the old *dai* in Anjanisain.

But then she turned to me, and asked, "Madam, I heard that you are leaving India. I hope this is not really true?"

"Yes, it is," I replied, quietly. "We stopped working with BMA quite a few months ago, you know, and after that. . ." My voice trailed off.

Pradeep had been watching my face closely, and he said, "Why don't you and Savitri go for a walk in the tea gardens?"

I stood up. "Yes, let's do that."

Savitri and I walked in silence for several minutes. When we reached the tea gardens, we followed a path that took us far away from the houses. In that soothing quiet, I felt myself relax a little.

Finally, I said, "You see, Savitri, we just felt that we couldn't go on working with BMA. There were so many problems. I just gave up hope. I am so sorry."

"I know there were a lot of problems with BMA, and that you were really unhappy. But Madam, please don't think that your work is over in India. There must be so many other things you could do."

I sighed. "Well, we thought about doing something else, but just couldn't think of anything we really wanted to do. I think we need to make this big change in our lives."

Savitri was silent for a few moments. Then in a rush of emotion she said, "Madam, please don't give up your ideas about health work in Garhwal. I have an idea."

"What is that?"

"Why don't you start up your own NGO? I could help. I would work for nothing; you don't need to pay me at all. But I know we could do something together—something really useful for the women of Garhwal."

My eyes filled with sudden tears. I clasped her hand and said, "You would be the best partner I could imagine, Savitri. But I just can't go on right now. I just can't."

We walked silently together for some time. Finally, I said, "You've become a really good nurse, Savitri. No matter where you work in Garhwal, I know you'll do a great job."

Savitri replied, "It's because of you, Madam. You always believed in me, and so I started to believe in myself."

Her words were like balm to my wounded soul.

"Thank you for saying that," I said. "It means a lot to me."

Savitri had to catch a bus later that afternoon. As we prepared to say goodbye, she said, impulsively, "Don't worry! We'll get a chance to work together again one day. I just know it."

As she walked away, images of her crowded into my mind. I remembered the nervous young girl meeting me in Pauri, who transformed into a keen student absorbing medical knowledge, who then became a compassionate nurse treating patients in the village. She had courage and tenacity, as well as a kind heart. I hoped she was right, and that one day our paths would cross again.

As the time for us to leave India drew near, I felt a great urge to go on a journey to say farewell to this land that I loved so much. My plan was to go on a pilgrimage to the place where Pradeep and I had first conceived the idea of working in Garhwal, on our trip to the mountain town of Kausani in 1981. I remember the moment when Pradeep confided to me that he wanted to settle somewhere in these hills and provide medical services to the mountain people. Nobody had ever encouraged these dreams, as they were wildly impractical from a worldly point of view. But I, another impractical dreamer, was instantly seized by his vision. I felt an unusual sense of connection to this part of the world, and perhaps this is why Pradeep's dream caught fire within me, too.

The spark kindled in Kausani did not die after I returned to Canada—the glowing embers of that little fire kept me warm for the four years we were separated, and then burst into a bright flame after I married Pradeep and moved to Rishikesh in 1985. Pursuing that dream had led us on our eventful journey through Garhwal over the next eleven years.

Now, to honour those years, I wished to make a pilgrimage—a journey guided by the compass points of my heart and soul. For many months, I'd been living behind a dark veil of sadness, and now I longed to find a way to draw aside that veil and search for a light for my inner world.

The perfect opportunity for my solitary journey arose in June of 1996, when I was invited to Kausani to attend an NGO conference. I stayed in the Gandhi ashram, just opposite the hotel where Pradeep and I had spent our first night together. On the day of my pilgrimage, I rose just before sunrise and went out to sit on the same stone wall where we had sat, fifteen years ago. The sun rose over the Himalayan peaks, scattering shafts of golden light across the mountains. The sky became suffused with a rosy glow, gradually brightening into the promise of a beautiful day.

I left the ashram quietly, feeling that my pilgrimage must begin without the chatter of goodbyes and well-meaning advice. I planned to follow a winding trail down through the forest and into the Garur valley far below. I would then follow the river along to reach my destination, the ancient stone temple of Baijnath.

I had walked for about half an hour when I met several little girls on their way to school. They were about seven years old, their hair neatly tied up in braids, bright red ribbons holding them in place. We stopped to chat, the girls giggling in delight at the funny sight of the *videshi* woman who could speak Hindi. Then they said their *Namastes* and ran off up the path, darting sparkling backward glances at me as they ran.

Far below me stood an old traditional stone house of Kumaon, with the family living in upper storey and the lower storey used for housing the animals. I admired its sturdy construction, guessing it was about a hundred years old. Just beside the house a magnificent jacaranda tree was bursting into purple blossom. A young woman emerged from an upper door and walked down the stairs to the yard, where she began the morning chore of feeding and watering her cattle.

From my vantage point, I could see a glorious panorama of Himalayan mountains. Most splendid is Trishul, whose three peaks are said to resemble Lord Shiva's trident. Below me lay the Garur Valley, clothed with the rich green of the Himalayan forest. Neatly terraced fields patterned the valley floor, watered by a river that curled like a silver ribbon beside the fields. I sat down on a sun-warmed rock to contemplate this scene. *I can perceive beauty again, after so many weeks of darkness. I'll treasure this memory, keep it in my heart forever.*

I began to follow the trail again, which took a steep downward turn and led into the forest below. To my right was a stand of walnut trees, laden with nuts encased in green, leathery husks. As I walked deeper into the forest, majestic oak and horse chestnut trees formed a canopy overhead. A flock of bulbuls swooped suddenly down from the topmost branches of an oak tree, their raucous cries shattering the serenity of the forest. Several smaller birds fluttered away in alarm as the flock swept through the trees.

After nearly two hours of steady descent, I emerged from the forest onto a trail bounded on both sides by farmers' fields. The summer crops had been harvested and fields were being made ready for the monsoon planting. I exchanged a few words with the women working in the fields, but kept up my pace, not wanting to disturb my tranquil state of mind. The trail took a sharp curve to the left and re-entered the forest. A woman carrying a large wicker basket on her head approached me. These baskets are used in this part of the hills for carrying manure from the barn to the fields. The woman greeted me and took the basket off her head, easing it to the ground and sitting down on the grassy verge of the path. I sat down beside her and we exchanged the usual pleasantries.

"Is your home far from here?" she asked me.

I replied, "My parents' home is very far away, but I feel in my heart that my home is in these hills."

She looked at me with a sudden penetrating glance and said, "You have lived here for many years, then? But now perhaps you are leaving this place. . . . Am I right?"

I felt a rush of astonishment at her perception. Was I so easy to see through?

I replied, "Yes, you are quite right. I am going back to the country I came from and I feel sad to leave these hills."

She impulsively put her hand over mine and said, "The hills will always be with you in your heart. And I am sure that one day you will return to us."

My eyes filled with tears at this point and I couldn't say anything more.

We sat silently for a while and then she said, "Ah, well, I must go now." She picked up the basket beside her, stood up, and settled it on her head.

After bidding farewell to the woman, I wondered if perhaps she had been one of those mystical guides who appear to pilgrims in need of assistance. Her perception about my imminent departure from the hills had been remarkable. Her kindly words of consolation and her assurance that I would return one day gave me comfort.

It was well past noon by then and I was hungry. Reaching the crest of a hill, I saw a teashop ahead of me, those ubiquitous places of comfort for travellers all over these mountains. Two older men were sitting on rickety wooden benches sipping tea. A younger man, clearly the proprietor, was sitting behind the smoky *chulha*, a stove made out of clay. Wood smoke wafted through the air, its smell mingling with the pungent aroma of *dal*. I ordered tea and an *aloo paratha* from the young man. One of the old men asked me where I was going. When I told him that I was headed to the Baijnath temple, he nodded approvingly. He told me that the Baijnath temple was very ancient, built on the foundations of an even more ancient one.

Refreshed by the light meal, I bade farewell to the men in the teashop and began to walk along a trail that skirted farmers' fields. The farms looked quite prosperous, considerably more so than in Garhwal. Far away, I could see the spreading branches of an enormous *peepul* tree. The sun had become uncomfortably hot, and the tree looked more and more inviting as I trudged along. A stone bench had been built around its great girth, inviting wayfarers to sit in its shade. I gratefully laid down my pack and sat on the cool stone, enjoying the breeze blowing up from the valley. The leaves of the *peepul* tree are heart-shaped and suspended in such a way that when the wind blows through them they make a faint clacking noise. Listening to the sound, I gazed out over the valley with quiet contentment.

I began to walk the trail again, which continued to wind slowly downward through farmland. The splendid silence of the forest was over. I heard the shouts of children, the lowing of cattle, and then a sudden burst of women's laughter. Five women dressed in colourful red saris appeared around a curve of the trail, carrying on an animated conversation with each other. They came to an abrupt halt when they saw me, their faces registering surprise. We chatted for a little while, and I told them that I was making my way to the Baijnath temple. They nodded their approval.

"You have not far to go," one of them replied. "Soon you will see the river. Take a right turn and keep following the river. After a while, you'll begin to see many other people. All will be going towards the temple."

"They come by bus and by car from all over, sometimes from far away," added another woman.

"You'll get many blessings from your visit to our Baijnath temple," said the oldest woman of the group, smiling at me in a kindly way.

After saying their "*Namastes*" to me, the women set off along the trail. Watching them walk away, I realized that over all the eventful years in Garhwal, these moments of connection with village women have given me the greatest joy. Perhaps by this pilgrimage to Kausani, I was beginning to unveil the subtle dimensions of my eleven-year quest in the Himalayas. I had come to Garhwal filled with naïve enthusiasm and had created impossible expectations for myself about building a medical program with specific outcomes and goals. The failure of those expectations had perhaps been inevitable. My outer journey in Garhwal had been filled with tough challenges and unexpected gifts. At dark times, I had also faced conflict and confusion.

Yet my outer life had always been intimately related to an inner movement of mysterious dimensions. That inner journey had led me to ever-deepening layers of understanding: how people of a different culture live and work, how they experience their bodies in health and illness, how they create meaning within their lives. At another level, I had explored the meaning of love—for Pradeep and my Indian family, for my children, and for the people of Garhwal.

At the most profound level, I'd experienced precious moments of attunement in which I'd felt a sense of unity or oneness with the natural world. I also recalled moments of connection with others that were so deep that all boundaries between us seemed to dissolve. My spirituality lay in this mystery of pattern, within nature and within human lives.

I thought of my conversation years ago with Swami Brahmananda, when I told him earnestly that I was not on a spiritual journey, but that I had come to Garhwal to do medical work. Speaking with both amusement and compassion, he had answered: "You have come to the holy heart of India and yet you do not think you are on a spiritual journey. That is indeed God's *leela!*"

Perhaps when we focus only on the outer movement of our lives, we risk becoming lost in an impenetrable thicket of expectations, goals, and outcomes. The answer may be to look for the sense of play—the *leela*—underlying life's movement. Following these delicate patterns of our lives, we may discover hidden meanings and spiritual insight.

The sharp hollow tapping of a woodpecker on a tree nearby woke me out of my reverie. I was standing on the same spot on the trail where the woman had left me, completely oblivious to the passage of time. I picked up my backpack and began to walk along the trail once more, enjoying a delicious sense of lightness of being.

I reached the river not long afterward, and from this point I could see the cluster of temples that made up the Baijnath complex. Cars and buses jockeyed for space in the small parking lot beside the road. The blasting of horns mingled with the excited voices of the pilgrims, who spilled out of the vehicles in colourful streams.

The Baijnath temple complex comprises one major temple with several smaller ones clustered together, all magnificent examples of early medieval North Indian temple architecture. I wandered through the temple grounds, admiring a striking carved image of Nandi the bull, the vehicle of Lord Shiva, which stands outside the main temple in a little pillared shrine. Some of the most well-preserved sculptures were those set into niches in the outer walls of the buildings. The most remarkable was a sacred image of the six-headed god, Kartikeya, who is the second son of Lord Shiva and the goddess Parvati. He is the purifier of human ills, fighting off the demons of anger, ignorance, and greed. Although Kartikeya is a warrior, his carved stone face expressed great tranquillity.

Evening was drawing closer, and my pilgrimage was coming to an end. Before leaving the temple, I offered a prayer to remember the attitude of the true pilgrim—to be open, aware, humble, and mindful. I paused for a few moments on the stone steps in front of the temple, watching a village woman offering worship before

Nandi, the bull. She lit an incense stick and scattered some rose petals, then bowed in prayer.

The afternoon was beginning to fade into evening. Leaving the temple grounds, I caught a local bus that took me back to the Gandhi ashram in Kausani. I ended my pilgrimage where it had begun, sitting on the stone wall overlooking the Garur valley. The first monsoon clouds were beginning to form on the horizon, darkening the sky with the blessed promise of rain. A warm evening breeze sprang up, ruffling my hair.

One of the clouds was shaped like a swallow, with one wing dipping toward the valley below and another one stretching into the sky. The breeze was delicately sculpting the cloud, creating the impression of a mythical bird sweeping across the sky.

It's the Cloud Messenger, I thought, remembering the poem by Kalidasa. In one of Pradeep's first letters to me, he'd recounted the tale of the lonely lover who had begged a monsoon cloud to be the messenger of his devotion. Closing my eyes, I imagined the faces of those I loved so much in the hills of Garhwal: Teeka, Leela, Savitri, Girish, Unita, Indu. . . .

"You will always be in my heart, and I will come back one day," I whispered.

The cloud swirled into splendid colours of pink and mauve as the sun dropped below the horizon. I felt myself relax into that timeless moment of peace.

Epilogue

The lay of the land was so familiar, yet so much had changed. The Gandhi ashram was still there, commanding a view of the Garur valley far below. But now a modern hotel occupied the hilltop beside the ashram, its gardens awash with flowers.

"Could this have been the place?" I asked Pradeep. We walked slowly into the lobby of the hotel, where we were greeted by the hotel manager.

"Was there once a small hotel here, just five rooms, overlooking the valley?" asked Pradeep.

"Yes, there was," replied the manager. "But that was torn down years ago to build this hotel."

Pradeep and I exchanged a glance. So this was indeed the place where it had all begun. We wandered outside into the beautiful gardens, and found a spot to sit and gaze over the valley.

We'd just celebrated our twenty-fifth wedding anniversary in Ghaziabad, with many members of Pradeep's extended family. After that grand party, we retraced that memorable journey we'd taken in 1981. We began in Lucknow, and now we were in Kausani, the Himalayan town where we'd first talked about working in these hills. How far we had travelled in our life's journey since that day!

We could both sense that idealistic young pair beside us, weaving a gossamer fabric of dreams about an unusual life of adventure and discovery. Following those dreams, we had lived the truth of the "pairs of opposites" that the Hindu sages of old had described. Our joyful experiences of love and connection contrasted with the ugly realities of revenge and murder. The delight of challenges and accomplishment were later mirrored by confusion and disillusionment. But we've learned to live the human journey, accepting the pairs of opposites and celebrating it all.

A delicate wisp of cloud floated across the sky, casting dancing shadows on the valley below. I thought of Pradeep as a medical student sending his message of devotion across the world through the Cloud Messenger, and smiled at the memory. In the India of today, people don't have to rely on Cloud Messengers to communicate—everyone has a cellphone! In Canada, I often pick up the phone to hear a familiar Garhwali voice. It could be Girish or Teeka calling from Garhwal, or perhaps Leela from Kerala. Not long ago, Savitri called from her home in Pauri, where she works as a nurse.

I began to see our lives as a great spiral, beginning from this very point in Kausani, moving through those eventful years in Garhwal, and then Canada. Now once again we've begun to plan a return to the Himalayas. We've purchased a small piece of land in Dehradun, near the home of Piyush and Suchitra, and we've had a multi-purpose building constructed. *Samagra* is the name of our new home, where Suchitra coordinates a women's employment program focusing on handicrafts, and an after-school tutoring program for children from slum communities. The house is filled with the whirr of sewing machines, the chatter of women, and the laughter of children. I watch my sister-in-law with admiration, as she skilfully coordinates all these programs.

Pradeep is filled with the same passionate energy he's always had. Over the past twenty five years, he's continued his spiritual search, learning from sages and scholars from East and West, but ever guided by his own inner light. He's developed a philosophy called Naturality, which blends a theoretical foundation with meditation practice. He teaches in many parts of the world, but his primary base is in Rishikesh, where we began our life together.

And I? I know my work will relate to the health of Garhwali women in some way. But this time, I won't do so much earnest planning—instead, I'll wait to see what doors open before me.

I'll come to Garhwal with a light heart.

Acknowledgments

Thanks are due to Anne Bokma, Donna Kirk, Valerie Nielsen, MG Vassanji and Diane Zsepecsky for comments on early drafts of the book.

Also to Swami Atmaswaroopananda (Bill Eilers) and Swami Amritaswaroopananda (Susan Eilers) for their suggestions and encouragement throughout the writing process.

Special thanks to my daughter Sonia Kumar, whose detailed comments on each draft of the manuscript were tremendously valuable.

To Robert Nielsen, whose wise advice of "Don't lose the story!" helped to make the book a more personal narrative.

To Marilyn Craven, who always believed in this book.

To Mojdeh Rostami for her beautiful cover illustration and for drawing the maps of India and Garhwal.

To John Last, my great friend and mentor, who read and commented on numerous drafts of the manuscript. Without his unfailing encouragement, practical advice and editing suggestions, I would have never managed to complete this book.

And finally to my beloved, Pradeep Kumar (Jivasu), whose commitment and love began the whole journey, a journey that becomes more fascinating with each passing year.

Notes about the book

This is a memoir in the style of creative non-fiction. All the events described in the book are true, but some details and timelines have been changed to make the narrative flow more smoothly. The principal characters of the book have been represented as faithfully as possible. Many of the episodes involving the village midwives were excerpted from field notes that I kept during the years I spent in Garhwal. In those notes, I identified these women only by their initials. In Cloud Messenger, I have given them fictional names.

Garhwal has changed in many ways since we worked there. In the year 2000, a people's movement to form a separate hill state composed of the districts of Garhwal and Kumaon was successful. Carved out of the vast state of Uttar Pradesh, Uttarakhand now has a governing structure that can better focus on the needs of mountain dwellers. Nevertheless, Uttarakhand faces many challenges, and remains one of the poorest states in India.

Perhaps the biggest social change in Garhwal is the advent of cell phones, which has vastly improved communication. A woman with an obstetrical emergency in a remote village can now call for help, and an emergency vehicle can be despatched to pick her up by the road. Deforestation continues to be a serious environmental problem, although national reforestation programs have improved forest cover in some parts of Garhwal. In June 2013, glacial meltwater and unusually heavy rains led to a devastating flood that claimed the lives of thousands of Garhwalis. Environmental scientists believe a combination of global warming and deforestation may have been factors in this disaster.

Population growth has slowed significantly and literacy rates have risen. However, as educational levels rise, young people continue to migrate out of Uttarakhand in search of better job opportunities in the cities.

But some aspects of Garhwal never change. Whenever I visit, the village people still welcome me with the same warm hospitality as ever. Pilgrims still walk the trails to the sources of the holy Ganga high in the mountains. In Rishikesh, people still float little leaf boats down the river during the evening worship, the flickering lights of candles reflecting off the surface of the water. And standing guard over all of Garhwal are the Himalayas, magnificent and mysterious.

About the Author

Karen Trollope-Kumar studied medicine at Dalhousie University in Nova Scotia. In her fourth year of medical studies she met her future husband, Pradeep, on a student visit to Lucknow. After graduation, she worked as a family physician in Thunder Bay before moving to India to marry the man she loved. They have two adult children, Sonia and Raman, who spent their early childhood in India.

After returning to Canada in 1996, Karen completed a PhD in medical anthropology, the study of health in its social and environmental context. She worked as a family physician in Hamilton and also became actively involved in medical education at McMaster University. She currently works as a family physician at the Grand River Community Health Centre in Brantford, Ontario. She and Pradeep spend part of every year in Dehradun, India, where they lived and worked early in their married life.

CPSIA information can be obtained
at www.ICGtesting.com
Printed in the USA
LVOW12*0021070917
547827LV00002B/7/P